Tax Systems and Tax Reforms in New EU Members

T0330637

The past decade has seen countries that were formerly part of the Eastern European Communist area undergo a fundamental transition, moving from centrally planned economic systems to becoming market economies. Those countries that have most successfully implemented this transition tended to instigate comprehensive tax reforms as part of a common objective to enter the EU.

Tax Systems and Tax Reforms in New EU Members focuses on five national cases: the Czech Republic, Estonia, Hungary, Poland and Slovenia. Through analyzing budgetary as well as political constraints and discussing the determinants of the current structure of the individual tax systems and the prospects for reform, this book identifies and analyzes the common aspects of taxation, the broad issues of the countries' tax policies and the importance of building an efficient tax administration.

Tax Systems and Tax Reforms in New EU Members will prove to be invaluable to students studying international economics as well as those working in the field.

Luigi Bernardi is Professor of Public Finance at the University of Pavia (Italy), **Mark W. S. Chandler** is an Assistant Professor at the Stockholm School of Economics in Riga, **Luca Gandullia** is Professor of Public Finance at the University of Genoa.

Routledge studies in the modern world economy

Tax Systems and Tax Reforms in New EU Members

Edited by Luigi Bernardi,
Mark W. S. Chandler and
Luca Gandullia

Foreword by V. Tanzi

Routledge
Taylor & Francis Group
LONDON AND NEW YORK

First published 2005 by Routledge

First issued in paperback 2012

Published 2017 by Routledge
2 Park Square, Milton Park, Abingdon, Oxon OX14 4RN
52 Vanderbilt Avenue, New York, NY 10017

Routledge is an imprint of the Taylor & Francis Group, an informa business

Typeset in Times by Wearset Ltd, Boldon, Tyne and Wear

British Library Cataloguing in Publication Data
A catalogue record for this book is available from the British Library

Library of Congress Cataloging in Publication Data
A catalog record for this book has been requested

Publisher's Note
The publisher has gone to great lengths to ensure the quality of this reprint
but points out that some imperfections in the original may be apparent.

ISBN 13: 978-0-415-65433-3 (pbk)
ISBN 13: 978-0-415-34988-8 (hbk)

Contents

Figures

Tables

Contributors

Evelin Ahermaa, Researcher, Estonian Institute of Economic Research, Rävala 6, 19080 Tallinn, Estonia.

Luigi Bernardi, Professor of Public Finance, University of Pavia, Dipartimento di Economia Pubblica e Territoriale, Università di Pavia, Strada Nuova 65, 27100 Pavia, Italy.

Mark W. S. Chandler, Assistant Professor, Stockholm School of Economics in Riga, Strelnieku iela 4a, LV 1010 Riga, Latvia.

Fedele de Novellis, Senior Economist, Ref-Research on Economics and Finance, Via-Gioberti 5, 20123 Milano, Italy.

Matteo Maria Galizzi, Research Assistant, University of Insubria and Marie Curie Fellow, Universitat Autonoma de Barcelona, Dipartimento di Economia, Università dell'Insubria, Via Ravasi 2, 21100 Varese, Italy.

Luca Gandullia, Associate Professor of Public Finance, University of Genoa, Dipartimento di Scienze Economiche e Finanziarie-DISEFIN, Largo Zecca 8-14, 16124 Genova, Italy.

Jeffrey Owens, Head of the OECD Centre for Tax Policy and Administration, OECD, 2, rue André Pascal, 75775, Paris, CEDEX 16, France.

Salvatore Parlato, Senior Economist, Ref-Research on Economics and Finance, Via Gioberti 5, 20123 Milano, Italy.

Simone Pellegrino, PhD student, University of Pavia and University of York, Dipartimento di Economia Pubblica e Territoriale, Università di Pavia, Strada Nuova 65, 27100 Pavia, Italy.

Paola Profeta, Assistant Professor of Public Economics and Lecturer of Economics. Università di Pavia and Università Bocconi. Dipartimento di Economia Pubblica e Territoriale, Università di Pavia, Strada Nuova 65, 27100 Pavia, Italy.

Francesca Sala, PhD student, University of Pavia, Economist, Ref-Research on Economics and Finance, Via Gioberti 5, 20123 Milano, Italy.

Simona Scabrosetti, PhD student, University of Pavia, Dipartimento di Economia Pubblica e Territoriale, Università di Pavia, Strada Nuova 65, 27100 Pavia, Italy.

Vito Tanzi, Senior consultant Inter-American Development Bank, 5912 Walhonding Road, Bethesda, MD 20816, USA.

Viktor Trasberg, PhD, Lecturer at the Department of Economics and Business Administration, University of Tartu, Lossi 3, Room 321, 51003 Tartu, Estonia.

Lucia Vergano, PhD student, University of Pavia and University College of London, Dipartimento di Economia Pubblica e Territoriale, Università di Pavia, Strada Nuova 65, 27100 Pavia, Italy.

Francesca Zantomio, PhD student, University of Pavia and University of York, Dipartimento di Economia Pubblica e Territoriale, Università di Pavia, Strada Nuova 65, 27100 Pavia, Italy.

Foreword

Tax systems and tax reforms in transition economies

Vito Tanzi

This book deals with tax reform in New EU countries. It describes the changes that have occurred in the tax systems of a group of countries that underwent a transformation, or a transition, from being centrally planned to becoming market economies. This has been a remarkable journey that has required enormous and difficult reforms. There was no road map for these countries to follow, because it was a journey on uncharted territory. No group of countries had ever traveled this territory before. However, there was the advantage of knowing where to go, if not how to get there. The destination was the creation of tax systems and tax administrations not too different from those of the EU countries.

In theory, one could assume that all that these countries had to do was to make copies of the tax laws of some EU country and make them their own. This, however, would be missing completely what tax reform is and how tax systems must be nested in the economy of a country. They must reflect the structural characteristics of a country's economy if they are to be successful. The economies of the countries discussed in this book have been undergoing fundamental changes. Some of theses changes are still taking place. Thus, in some ways, their tax systems have been adapting themselves to moving targets. It is to be expected that this process will continue for a few more years until the economies of these countries become fully market oriented, with characteristics, structures, and institutions similar to those of the other European countries. That this is not yet the case can be seen, in part, from the levels of their per capita incomes that are still much lower than those of the group of countries that they are joining.

When the journey started, much of the wealth of these New EU countries was owned by the state. The citizens were not expected to save and accumulate assets because the state, often through the public enterprises in which most citizens worked, would take care of them in old age or in illness. They did not need to save as a precaution for being unemployed, because there was no official unemployment. The state enterprises were required to absorb any citizen who wanted a job. A large part of the income received by the workers was in kind. The part received in cash was only a small fraction of the income produced by a worker and there were a lot of constraints, imposed by scarcity, on how this cash could be used. Thus, to a great extent, the state determined both the *level* and the *pattern* of the consumption by individuals. Individual decisions had little influence on the allocation of resources. This was done through state planning and reflected the views of the planners.

In some ways classical central planning was an effective and esthetically attractive social instrument that fascinated many western social scientists. Unfortunately, by limiting individual liberties and by killing individual incentives, it carried an enormous cost in terms of economic efficiency and political liberty. This cost became progressively higher with the passing of years when the revolutionary enthusiasm, which might have existed in the earlier years, faded and cynicism and corruption rose. As time passed, the centrally planned economies became increasingly inefficient and unable to satisfy the consumption needs of their populations.

In that central-planning environment, the role of the tax system was limited and there was hardly any need for a western-style tax administration. Taxes on labor income were collected directly from the state enterprises, by simply adjusting the cash transfers that they received from the central bank to pay the wage bill. There was no objective definition of enterprise income to determine precisely the taxes on profits. The payment from an enterprise to the state was negotiated; it was not based on the actual profits. The depreciation allowances for the use of capital assets bore little or no relation to the useful life of the real assets used. There were no laws that defined the turnover taxes. These were determined arbitrarily in the plan and reflected both social considerations that favored particular items (children's clothes, art books, etc), as well as supply and demand conditions. When there was excessive inventory of an item, the turnover tax was reduced to induce citizens to buy more of this item. Therefore, the turnover taxes could be in the thousands and changed frequently.[1]

A decade ago, in an introductory chapter to a book on *Transition to Market* (1993) that I edited, I wrote that 'this was an almost idyllic situation from a tax administration's perspective. The confrontational situation that exists in the West between taxpayers and tax administrators was largely absent.' I cited the director of taxation of one of these countries in transition who had told me, somewhat nostalgically, that 'the life of a tax administrator was easy (during central planning). He often had to deal with just one enterprise. Much revenue came from an occasional telephone call. Now you have to work for every cent' (Tanzi 1993, p. 7). Thus, one thing that these countries had to learn was how to collect taxes from taxpayers that would rather evade paying them.

The reforms introduced by the New EU countries had to cope with economies in which prices and wages are free to fluctuate, private sector activities become important, there are no controls on the output of enterprises, so that their incomes are not known and payments can be made in various forms and no longer through just one 'monobank'. This new situation would demand both new tax systems and new tax administrations. Furthermore, these had to be adjusted over the years to conform with the changes in the structure of the economy. It would not be imprudent to say that the tax systems of these countries have come a long way and that from now on they will need more fine tuning than radical surgery.

When we look at the current situation of the countries discussed in this book, we are surprised by some aspects. The first surprise is the closeness of their current tax burdens. In fact these tax burdens are all close to 40 percent of GDP, having come down from higher levels. A tax burden of 40 percent of GDP may be close to, or even lower than, the European average but it is very high considering these countries' still low per capita incomes. From an international statistical perspective, the tax burden of these countries could be expected to be somewhat lower. Thus, a question that needs to be raised is whether the current tax levels are sustainable over time.

It would be reasonable to speculate that they are likely to fall as the transformation of these economies continues. This fall would require a reduction in public spending.

The second surprise is that, in spite of their high tax levels, all of these countries, with the exception of Estonia, have developed high budgetary deficits, which have been growing in recent years. This implies that these countries have not succeeded yet in reducing the role of the state to a level that can be financed through ordinary tax revenue. The state is still expected to do too much despite various reforms aimed at reducing its role and responsibilities. This aspect could become a problem that would extend beyond the need to meet the Maastricht criteria. The fiscal gap must be closed by reducing public spending rather than by increasing the high level of taxation.

The third surprise is the extent to which labor income is taxed. This is partly due to the large payments for social security contributions, which in some of these countries, such as the Czech Republic, are among the highest in the world. This heavy burden on labor income must be reduced if the development of growing underground activities is to be prevented. This growth of underground economic activities is already under way in several of these countries and is likely to accelerate with the passing of time.

The fourth surprise is the almost uniform move towards fiscal decentralization. Undoubtedly this is a political reaction against the powerful central governments of the past. Once the communist regimes were replaced, the citizens of these countries were anxious to have more 'voice' and more control over decisions that affected their lives. However, regardless of its political merit, this process of decentralization is likely to constrain future tax reform and to affect negatively future macroeconomic developments. Experience from around the world indicates that it is often more difficult to reduce fiscal deficits in a fiscally decentralized environment.

A fifth and pleasant surprise is the growing use of environmental taxes in these countries. The centrally planned past had left these countries with major environmental problems that affected health and life expectancies. Many in these countries have low life expectancy, perhaps due to the quality of the environment. Thus, the attempt to reduce this problem through the use of tax instruments is one that deserves praise.

After labor income, consumption is the other tax base that carries much of the tax burden. All these countries have introduced value added taxes, which with some adjustments will conform with the requirements of the European Union. However, there are still too many excises and other small taxes. Some of these will have to disappear in future years. Property taxes are still playing a marginal role. This is not surprising since, until a few years ago, there was no or little private property. However, in future years, it would be preferable to give a growing importance to this tax base, especially for financing the local governments, while reducing the reliance on revenue sharing arrangements that transfer to the local governments parts of the revenue from personal income taxes and corporate income taxes.

Let me add a few comments on the income taxes. It is surprising the extent to which incomes from capital sources are lightly taxed. This is an element that will contribute to the faster growth of these countries' economies but at the cost of lower tax revenue and a less progressive tax incidence. If not-taxing capital requires overtaxing labor and, thus, giving a strong incentive to the shadow economy, then over the long run the stimulative effect of low capital taxation on the economy will be much reduced. There is also evidence that Gini coefficients have been growing in several of these countries so that equity issues might become more important in determining tax reforms in future years. The income tax rates on labor income, per se, are not unusually high but when they are combined with high social security taxes they tend to overburden labor income.

There is some evidence of tax experimentation in some of these countries. For example, Estonia has introduced a linear (i.e. flat rate) tax on labor income. The tax rate is 26 percent. Thus, it has given up the idea of using the income tax for redistributive purposes. This tax combined with the exemption from taxation of much capital income makes it almost a twin of the value added tax in its effects. The result is that consumption is taxed much more than saving. This probably promotes more saving, but at the cost of increasing income inequality over time. Another interesting innovation in the tax system of Estonia is that, for enterprises, only distributed profits are taxed (also at 26 percent) while retained profits are tax free. Since I made a proposal along this line three decades ago, I was happy to see my proposal implemented (Tanzi 1975). This feature is a strong incentive to reinvest the earnings of enterprises. Thus, it promotes investment.

This brings me to the question of tax incentives. In spite of attempts at reducing the scope of tax incentives, there is still the propensity, on the part of the policy-makers of these countries – certainly stimulated by their past experience with central planning – to try to direct or influence the economic decisions of enterprises or even of individuals with incentives. This of course reflects a lack of trust in the ability of a market economy to make the right choices. It is an indication that the period of transition is not yet complete. In future years the road chosen by Estonia – i.e. a simpler tax system with fewer or no tax incentives – should be the favored one.

Note

1 For a description of the tax systems under central planning, see Tanzi (1994). For a discussion of the difficulties in creating effective tax administrations in transition economies, see Tanzi (2001).

References

Tanzi, V. (1975) 'Should we tax corporations?', in Bird, R. and Oldman, O. (eds) *Readings on Taxation in Developing Countries*, third edition, Baltimore: Johns Hopkins Press.

Tanzi, V. (1993) 'Financial markets and public finance in the transformation process', in Tanzi, V. (ed.) *Transition to Market: Studies in Fiscal Reform*, Washington, DC: IMF.

Tanzi, V. (1994) 'Reforming public finances in economies in transition', *International Tax and Public Finance*, 1: 2.

Tanzi, V. (2001) 'Creating effective tax administrations: the experience of Russia and Georgia', in Kornai, J., Haggard, S. and Kaufman, R. R. (eds) *Reforming the State: Fiscal and Welfare Reform in Post-Socialist Countries*, Cambridge: Cambridge University Press.

Preface

The manuscript of this book was delivered at the beginning of May, 2004, when ten New Members were entering the European Union. This enlargement was a great historic event for the EU. The enlargement is the largest since the European Community was created in 1957 by the six original members. Moreover almost all New Members were part of the Eastern European communist area. Their shift towards a market economy required the building of a suitable tax system, as one of the main reforms. Actually, the last decade of these tax reforms has provided a remarkable laboratory in tax policy design and practice. This is particularly true for those countries that quite early introduced comprehensive market-oriented tax reforms, while at the same time preserving their revenue raising capacity under the pressures of the existing levels of social security and welfare expenditure.

At the moment, it is not at all easy to find a comprehensive picture of what happened, is happening and will happen in the tax systems of the New Members of the EU. Thus, it is difficult to have a clear and updated idea of the present state of the New Members' fiscal systems, presented in a user-friendly format. The first aim of this book is to fill such a gap. In order to do so, we have collected a large set of data, institutional features and indicators of fiscal burden from different sources. The book focuses on five national cases (Czech Republic, Estonia and the other Baltic states, Hungary, Poland and Slovenia). These cases have been selected to include the main countries and give a proper sample of the variegated realities of the New Members. The book is an ideal companion to *Tax Systems and Tax Reforms in Europe*, edited by L. Bernardi and P. Profeta and published by Routledge in 2004.

As a starting point, Tanzi's Foreword reminds us that the New Members' journey from being centrally planned to becoming market economies has been a remarkable one, that has required enormous and difficult reforms. For these countries there was no road map to follow. However, the final destination was the creation of tax systems and tax administrations not too different from those of the EU countries. When the journey started, the role of the tax system in these New EU countries

was limited and there was hardly any need for a western-style tax administration. Taxes on labor income were collected directly from state enterprises. The tax payment from an enterprise to the state was negotiated; it
was not based on actual profits. There were no laws defining the turnover
taxes. As Tanzi underlines, when one looks at the current situation of the
countries covered by this book, there are some surprising aspects that
deserve attention – first of all, the closeness of their current tax burdens to
about 40 percent of GDP, having come down from higher levels. It would
be reasonable to speculate that these burdens are likely to fall as the transformation of these economies continues. Hence a reduction in public
spending will be required. As a second surprising element, it turns out that
many of these countries, in spite of their high tax levels, have developed
high budgetary deficits which have been growing in recent years. The third
surprise is the extent to which labor income is taxed. This is partly due to
the large payments for social security contributions. The fourth surprise is
the almost uniform move towards fiscal decentralization. Undoubtedly this
is a political reaction against the powerful central governments of the past.
A fifth and pleasant surprise is the growing use of environmental taxes.
Coming to specific taxes, Tanzi notices that all these countries have successfully introduced value added taxes. However, there are still too many
excises and other small taxes. Some of these will have to disappear in the
near future. Property taxes are still playing a marginal role. As to income
tax, it is surprising the extent to which incomes from capital sources are
lightly taxed. This is an element that will contribute to the faster growth
but at the cost of lower tax revenue and a less progressive tax incidence.
An interesting innovation in the tax system of Estonia is that only distributed profits are taxed while retained profits are tax free. This feature is a
strong incentive to reinvest the earnings of enterprises and promote
investment.

An overview of tax systems in New Member countries is given in the
Gandullia's chapter (Chapter 1). This chapter presents evidence about tax
systems' structure and evolution; their common current features are then
illustrated, together with quantitative indicators, aimed at evaluating their
main equity and efficiency profiles. New Members can be considered as
successful examples of tax reform implementation. Unlike other transition
economies, they have been able to avoid fiscal crises and have shown a
capacity of tax revenue collection close to the EU levels. At present, they
show models of taxation similar to those in the EU, but in some key
aspects there are wide discrepancies. The mix between direct and indirect
taxes is different, with New Members relying much more than EU countries on indirect taxes; at the same time they show levels of implicit tax
rates on consumption much lower than the European average: this is a
symptom of tax bases being far from comprehensive. In the field of personal income taxation, the degree of statutory progressivity appears lower
than in most EU countries. This is the result of both the frequent adoption

of linear tax models and the exclusion of most capital income from the tax base. In the field of corporate taxation, New Members apply very low (compared with international standards) statutory tax rates with narrow tax bases. On average, these countries show levels of effective taxation on investment lower than the European benchmarks. Finally, the tax burden on labor continues to be high. The tax wedges are close to the European average for many New Members; however, in some countries the tax wedge on lower-pay labor appears to be much higher than the European average.

The chapter of Bernardi and Chandler (Chapter 2) discusses some broad issues of New Members' fiscal systems. The authors firstly remind us that the main purpose of taxation is to finance public spending. On this account, it has often been argued that governments in New Members are still too big. Bernardi and Chandler observe that, in fact, the particular situation of New Members may call for a relevant public intervention in the welfare area. However, in some New Members there has been a move towards partially funded private pension schemes and itemized social insurance funds targeted to single risks. Some scaling down of public expenditure is anyway called for: to redirect and better target social programs; to make a more efficient use of resources in education, health and public administration; and finally as a consequence of strengthening budgetary procedures. According to authoritative opinions, total fiscal pressure would also be still too high in most New Members and should decrease by a relevant amount. Bernardi and Chandler's tentative answer is that total fiscal pressure may go down, even if less than the just quoted normative prescription. According to the structure of taxation by economic function and to implicit rates, the trade-off between efficiency and equity in taxation is definitely present, and moreover appears particularly binding. In these circumstances, it is quite difficult to strike a welfare maximizing balance between efficiency and equity. This chapter also examines separately the four main categories of taxation in the New EU Members. The first is the personal income tax. Although some countries have clearly attempted to implement a uniform taxation of income, they represent a minority. To increase the progressivity of income taxation is a debated issue, and the solutions adopted by single New Members vary considerably. The taxation of corporate income has also been imaginative in the New Members. Dynamic efficiency requires that mild taxation of corporations should be maintained. However, corporation tax should not vanish, especially not to allow a further diffusion of avoidance activities. The – painfully increasing – harmonization of excises to EU standards is mandatory. The VAT structure hence becomes the only degree of freedom that can be exploited to lighten consumption taxation. Regarding the comparative efficacy of VAT and personal income tax, the authors find that in the region the VAT tax base is at least 80 percent larger than that of personal income. In several New EU member states, radical changes to the social security system have left the population somewhat more exposed to the instability of the financial markets. However, it is interesting to observe that the nations that are commonly held to be the most capitalism savvy, namely the Czech Republic and Slovenia, have retained the collective pooling of risks, which is common in the rest of the EU.

Profeta's chapter (Chapter 3) analyzes several issues in taxation and tax reforms in New EU Members from a political economy perspective, focusing both on the positive and the normative aspects thereof. Major problems in the development of a new tax policy in these countries are addressed, such as how to raise revenues, the definition of the role of government, the relations among different government tiers, the establishment of new fiscal institutions, tax administration and the taxation of small enterprises. All these aspects have a political determinant, in the sense that actual policies and institutions being put in place strongly depend on the political process and on the political will of policy-makers, which is in turn based on the political support they can enjoy. Profeta argues that, in transition countries, this support is often based on economically and politically powerful interest groups, rather than on the majority of voters. These interest groups, together with other political constraints faced by policy-makers, have a strong impact on tax reforms in New EU Members.

In their chapter (Chapter 4) de Novellis and Parlato warn us that the analysis of the fiscal policy framework that will prevail in an enlarged Europe must definitely take into account the macroeconomic and public finance characteristics of accession countries – their first best strategy in managing both the transition towards the Union and the weak points of fiscal rule design at present governing the EU 12 eurozone. Accession countries are generally small and open economies, so that most of the shortcomings of financial and market liberalization apply to them, i.e. a critical exposure to financial and currency crises. Hence an optimal policy should at first glance avoid a prolonged transition before the adoption of the euro. A non-secondary aspect in defining a fiscal rule concerns the public finance features of these countries, which are generally characterized by low debt, high deficit and high capital expenditure. As a consequence, the softer is the budget constraint in the transition, the higher will be the risk of weak sustainability in the long run. More broadly speaking, the fiscal rule should be coherent with the general macroeconomic strategy that will be adopted in managing the enlargement. If the enlargement is to be conducted with a strategy of long transition, then fiscal rules must be soft-constraining, i.e. fiscal rules based on debt should prevail. Conversely, with a no-transition strategy, almost by definition there is no need of rules softening the transitional period. Thus, a nominal ceiling to the deficit-to-GDP ratio could be maintained. However, given that in 2004 half of the EU countries are expected to violate the 3 percent ceiling, the debate on the rewriting of the Stability and Growth Pact (SGP) cannot be deferred any longer. Furthermore, the persistence of low GDP growth in

Europe has given more strength to the argument about the consistency of the SGP with growth enhancing policies. It follows that the choice of a fiscal rule for accession countries is intertwined with the reform of the SGP. Put in these terms, de Novellis and Parlato's proposal is to internally revisit the SGP, by adopting a multiple target approach, which is consistent with the spirit of Maastricht accession criteria. Specifically, the rule of 3 percent should be maintained, but weighted by the level of debt-to-GDP ratio and, where available, by the cyclical adjusted primary balance. Moreover, the new SGP should be addressed towards a golden rule conditional on the debt-to-GDP ratio, in order to promote public investments without putting into risk the long run fiscal sustainability.

Tax reforms require an efficient tax administration, which should be especially aimed at fighting against the hidden economy, which is particularly widespread in New Members. In Chapter 5, Trasberg addresses these issues and starts by explaining the theoretical concept of tax gap and the reasons why it can serve as an analytical cornerstone for analyzing tax administration developments in the transition countries. The tax gap is linked to the inadequateness of tax administration and the extent of the shadow economy. Both those aspects lead to tax avoidance or tax erosion, which in turn reduce budget revenues. In fact, attempts to balance the budget by increasing statutory tax rates induced businesses to further evade taxes and leave the official economy sector. Tax administration developments in New Members during the years of transition are then focused. Gaps of tax revenues were also due to inefficient administrative arrangements and the outburst of the shadow economy. In most of the transition countries, competent and capable tax-administrating institutions were missing or were still in the build-up phase. Tax laws and regulations often changed, while law enforcement was remarkably weak. Not surprisingly, such circumstances were followed by large-scale tax erosion and other shadow economy activities. Different studies show the significant increase of the unofficial economy during the early years of market reforms. The size of the shadow economy seems to be due to the high tax burden, in combination with government bureaucracy's inefficiency and corruption. Tax erosion was also related to the absence of tax culture in transition societies. The lack of tax ethics and a tradition for voluntary compliance increases tax evasion and ultimately the tax gap. Nevertheless, in all EU New Members, advancements of economic reforms and the strengthening of the tax administration have indeed decreased the extent of shadow economy activities and the tax gap itself.

Finally, the chapter by Owens (Chapter 6) deals with competition for foreign direct investment (FDI) and the role of taxation. It is particularly concerned with the case of South Eastern European (SEE) countries, but this experience is easy to generalize to New Members. The chapter starts by showing how the tax systems can influence the location decisions of FDI, considering different types of FDI. Then it illustrates the experience of SEE countries, where until recently a number of tax impediments to FDI have been present, such as unstable and non-transparent tax policies, progressive corporate tax structures, and double or possibly multiple taxation of distributed profits. At the same time these countries have made and make wide use of tax incentives in the form of tax holidays, reinvestment allowances, accelerated depreciation, investment tax credits and allowances. A key finding of the chapter is the coexistence in SEE countries of generous but largely inefficient tax incentives for domestic and foreign direct investment. It is shown that perhaps the most effective investment 'incentive' is realized addressing impediments in the basic tax system (i.e. simplifying tax calculations, lowering statutory tax rates on business where possible, using a single rather than multiple corporate tax structure, streamlining complex capital cost allowance systems). More generally, to provide a stable regime which is applied in a transparent and non-arbitrary fashion is essential to attract and retain investment.

The journey of this book stops here. The journey of New Members has still a long way to go. We make some suggestions for the improvement of their tax systems. Public spending and fiscal pressure should be fairly reduced to improved efficiency, but without dismantling the welfare state. The tax mix must be changed, by increasing direct taxes and reducing both indirect taxes and social contributions. We warn that interest groups, together with other political constraints faced by policy-makers, have a strong impact on tax reforms. We suggest some suitable fiscal policy rules to manage the enlargement of the EU, which imply a deep revision of the Stability and Growth Pact. We notice that New Members have still to build an efficient tax administration. Most of all, these European countries should be aware that from the *Magna Carta* era, in the 13th century, a tax system is a foundation of any free democracy.

Luigi Bernardi, Mark Chandler and Luca Gandullia

Acknowledgments

This book is part of research into taxation in different international areas, carried out at the Department of Public and Environmental Economics, University of Pavia, Italy, under the direction of L. Bernardi. Financing from the Fondazione Cassa di Risparmio delle Provincie Lombarde is gratefully acknowledged.

The Editors are grateful to S. Scabrosetti, who, in addition to her own chapter, provided excellent research assistance during the whole project. They also thank C. Bronchi, M. Galizzi, L. Pench and R. Puglisi for information, comments and suggestions in a number of areas. Country chapters were all revised by national experts, who are listed in the relevant chapters. Thanks also to them.

Part I

A general picture of tax systems and tax reforms in New EU Members

1 An overview of taxation

Luca Gandullia[1]

1.1 Introduction and main conclusions

It is commonly recognized that the last decade of tax reforms in countries that are in transition from the previous centrally planned economies has provided a remarkable laboratory in tax policy design and practice. This is particularly true for those countries (such as Hungary, Czech Republic, Poland, Slovenia and the Baltic states) that moved rapidly and early into transition to introduce comprehensive tax reforms, a common objective being their accession to the EU. At the beginning of transition these countries had to create new fiscal institutions and new market-oriented tax systems, simultaneously preserving their revenue-raising capacity under the pressure of the existing levels of social security and welfare expenditures.

Compared with the other transition countries, the EU's New Members can be considered as successful examples of tax reform implementation. Through early transition they have been able to avoid the fiscal crisis encountered by other transition economies. In New Members, the increase in income inequality has been generally lower than in the other transition countries. Moreover, they have shown a capacity in collecting tax revenues that is higher than in the slow transition reformer countries and close to the EU levels.

In all the ex-transition, now EU member, countries, the process of tax reform has been significantly influenced by their histories. Instead of making copies of Western-type tax systems, they followed a more evolutionary process that has led to the design of tax systems reflecting the structural characteristics of their economies.

At present, the New Members show models of taxation that are reasonably close to those in the EU, but in some key aspects there are wide differences. The following seem the most relevant. First of all, the tax mix is different and the distance from the EU benchmark has increased during the last decade; while the incidence of total taxes and social contributions is close to the European average, the tax mix between direct and indirect taxes is considerably different, with the New Members relying much more on indirect taxes and less on direct taxes.

Second, the degree of progressivity of personal income tax is lower than in most EU countries. The group of Baltic states applies a flat rate taxation; a linear system of personal income taxation has recently been introduced (2004) in the Slovak Republic. In Poland, the effective structure of the personal income tax (PIT) is almost linear. It should also be noted that the real progressivity of the PIT is even lower as the tax bases are narrow due to the exclusion of most capital income.

In the field of corporate taxation, New Members apply very low (compared with international standards) statutory tax rates with narrow tax bases. The most emblematic case is given by Estonia where the corporation tax on retained earnings has been completely abolished. In recent years, the tax bases have been partially broadened, but the reduction in tax rates has been considerable. On average, these countries show levels of effective taxation on investment much lower than the European benchmarks. The gap increases considerably if the effects of tax incentives are considered. More generally, in the presence of low statutory tax rates, the distortions on investment decisions induced by the corporation tax appear lower than in the EU. Many countries give strong tax preference to retained earnings over distributed profits. This result, together with the low taxation of capital income, shows the efforts to promote savings and investment.

In the field of indirect taxation, as noted above, New Member countries rely heavily (and more than the EU countries) on consumption-based taxes, but at the same time they show levels of implicit tax rates on consumption much lower than the European average, meaning that the tax bases are far from being comprehensive.

Finally, the tax burden on labor continues to be as high as it was in the early stages of transition. The tax wedges are close to the European average for many New Members. However, in some countries the tax wedge appears to be much higher than the European average for lower-paid labor.

This chapter is organized as follows. Section 1.2 illustrates the starting point of tax systems and reforms at the beginning of the transition process. Section 1.3 presents some indicators of the macro structure and evolution of the tax systems over the last decade, focusing on tax ratios by legal categories and on the allocation of revenues across sectors of government. Section 1.4 gives a comparative analysis of direct and indirect taxation in the selected countries, while section 1.5 presents some indicators to measure and compare their main equity and efficiency profiles.

1.2 Tax systems and reforms during transition

The tax systems in force during the socialist command economy were not comparable to the Western-style ones, their role being deeply different and more limited (Tanzi 1992; Tanzi and Tsibouris 2000). Most tax revenue was obtained from three major sources (enterprise tax, turnover tax and payroll tax), while taxes on personal income accounted for a very small share of total revenue (Dabrowski and Tomczynska 2001; Martinez-Vazquez and McNab 1997). Tax rates were numerous and non-parametric, tax structures were complex and tax liabilities were discretionary and negotiable. The earnings of state-owned enterprises were the main source of financing government spending. Not-basic consumer goods were subject to highly differentiated turnover taxes. Payroll taxes were collected by enterprises on behalf of employees. The enterprise taxes, the most important source of revenue, were used to centralize and regulate enterprise incomes.

In centrally planned economies, taxes were not collected on the basis of codified tax laws and rules for the determination of taxable bases and applicable tax rates. They were collected mostly on the basis of negotiations between government and enterprises. Thus, there was little need for a tax administration because of the presence of few taxpayers (mainly large enterprises) and the role of a mono-bank in processing payments.

The impact of transition on the public finance system was radical. The process raised the fundamental need to create (together with economic reforms) necessary and well-working fiscal institutions (Tanzi and Tsibouris 2000). The old tax systems could not simply be reformed at the margin, but completely new tax systems were needed. The basic choice was between the adoption of a modern market-oriented tax system with a 'shock therapy' approach and the adoption of new tax systems following a more evolutionary approach (OECD 1991; Tanzi 1992).

At that time, important economic and institutional constraints were present. The path of tax reform during the transition period was largely determined by the legacy of the past systems (Martinez-Vazquez and McNab 1997; Stepanyan 2003): an interventionist tradition; taxes were frequently negotiated; the tax systems lacked transparency and there was no experience with voluntary compliance; the previous tax systems were not designed to pursue efficiency and equity objectives; finally, the tax administration was underdeveloped. Given these constraints, there was a general consensus between foreign experts on the desirability of a more evolutionary and country-specific approach to tax reforms. Emphasis was placed on the need to modernize tax administration and to adopt taxes that could be enforced, with a stable revenue raising capacity.

Progress in tax reform has varied across individual countries in transition. The main EU accession countries (Hungary, Czech Republic, Poland, Slovenia and the Baltic states) rapidly moved early into transition to introduce comprehensive tax reform, a common objective being their accession to the EU. This is the main reason why, in these countries, tax reforms generally moved faster than in other transition countries (Martinez-Vazquez and McNab 2000). Compared with the other countries of the former Soviet Union the specific group of Baltic states can be considered as successful examples of tax reform implementation

(Stepanyan 2003; Dabrowski and Tomczynska 2001). These countries managed to adopt, in a relatively short period, new tax systems consistent with the best international standards and to recover the tax revenue levels prevailing before transition (see also Chapter 8).

For most transition countries, the early stages of this process led to a substantial decline in the traditional tax bases and to a consequent fall in tax revenues. However, between transition countries, those (such as the Czech and Slovak Republics, Poland, Hungary and Slovenia) that made the most progress in terms of market-based reforms have seen their revenue share in GDP maintained or sometimes increased (Tanzi and Tsibouris 2000; Dobrinsky 2002). For instance, in Poland, the tax system performed well during the 1990s, particularly in its revenue raising capacity on a continuous basis (Lenain and Bartoszuk 2000); as a consequence, Poland has been able to avoid the fiscal crisis encountered by other transition economies. The same countries were among the transition countries in which the increase in income inequality has been generally lower (according to the data reported by Tanzi and Tsibouris 2000).

In all the accession countries, the process of tax reform has been significantly influenced by their history and their state at the starting point of the process. In the design of the tax systems, countries continued to favor an interventionist stand providing special tax treatments and incentives, which in turn have led to tax erosion, economic distortions, compliance costs and equity problems. This heritage from past experience with central planning reflected, as noted by Tanzi in the foreword, a lack of trust in the ability of a market economy to make the right choices. Only in the second half of the 1990s has this trend been partially reversed.

During the 1990s, in most transition countries tax policy reforms were generally more advanced than reforms in tax administration (Martinez-Vazquez and McNab 2000; see also Chapter 5). The experience of transition economies has shown the interrelation between tax policies and tax administration (Stepanyan 2003), with the reform of tax administration playing a crucial role in successful tax policy implementation. Even in this field the leading transition countries (like most New Members) have shown a capacity far collecting revenue from the main taxes (corporate tax, VAT and social contributions) that is higher than that of the slow transition reformer countries and close to the EU benchmarks (Schaffer and Turley 2001).

1.3 Tax systems: structure and developments

The data made available by the EU Commission (2000) for the period 1992–98 allow for comparisons over time and cross-sectionally to be made between New EU Members and existing EU members countries. Looking at the ratio of taxes to GDP as a signal of the country's preference for the size of the public sector, in the period 1992–98 (see Table 1.1) tax ratios

Table 1.1 Structure and development of fiscal revenue in New Members and EU 15 as a percentage of GDP, 1992–98

	1992								1998							
	CZ	EE	HU	PL	SI	NM	EU	NM–EU	CZ	EE	HU	PL	SI	NM	EU	NM–EU
Direct taxes, of which	10.9	13.3	10.1	12.2	7.4	10.8	13.5	–2.7	9.0	11.1	8.7	11.2	7.8	9.6	13.7	–4.1
Personal income	3.8	8.5	7.5	7.6	6.8	6.8	9.6	–2.8	5.2	8.5	6.5	8.3	6.6	7.0	9.3	–2.3
Corporation income	7.1	4.8	2.6	4.6	0.6	3.9	2.3	1.6	3.7	2.6	2.2	2.9	1.2	2.5	3.0	–0.5
Indirect taxes, of which	15.4	12.3	17.9	14.6	14.5	14.9	13.4	1.5	12.4	14.3	16.3	14.4	18.9	15.3	13.9	1.4
VAT	7.6	9.2	6.0	0.0	6.8	5.9	6.7	–0.8	6.6	8.8	7.9	7.9	9.1	8.1	7.0	1.1
Excise duties	4.0	1.9	6.2	0.0	3.6	3.1	3.4	–0.3	3.7	3.8	4.2	3.9	4.4	4.0	3.5	0.5
Others	3.9	1.2	5.8	14.6	4.1	5.9	3.3	2.6	2.1	1.8	4.2	2.7	5.5	3.3	3.5	–0.2
Total tax revenue	26.3	25.6	28	26.8	21.9	25.7	26.9	–1.2	21.4	25.4	25.0	25.6	26.7	24.8	27.6	–2.8
Social contributions	16.5	12.1	18	11.3	18.6	15.3	14.5	0.8	16.9	12.1	13.9	12.2	13.8	13.8	15.0	–1.2
Employers	10.2	11.9	14	4.1	7.6	9.6	8.1	1.5	11.0	11.9	11.6	4.4	4.4	8.7	8.2	0.5
Employees	3.8	0.0	3.3	4.2	10.1	4.3	4.8	–0.5	3.9	0.0	2.1	4.5	8.5	3.8	5.0	–1.2
Self employed	2.5	0.2	0.7	3.1	0.9	1.5	1.6	–0.1	2.0	0.2	0.3	3.3	0.9	1.3	1.9	–0.6
Total fiscal revenue	42.8	37.7	46.0	38.1	40.5	41.0	41.4	–0.4	38.3	37.5	38.9	37.8	40.5	38.6	42.6	–4.0
Administrative level																
Central government	33.2	16.6	24.9	24.1	18.6	23.5	22.8	0.7	28.0	20.1	21.5	22.3	23.6	23.1	22.9	0.2
Local government	3.9	9.0	3.1	2.8	3.3	4.4	3.0	1.4	4.6	5.3	3.5	3.4	3.1	4.0	4.0	0.0
Social Security	5.8	12.1	18.0	11.3	18.6	13.2	14.5	–1.3	5.7	12.1	13.9	12.2	13.8	11.5	14.9	–3.4

Sources: EU Commission (2000) for New Members (unweighted average); Eurostat (2000) for EU 15 (1997 unweighted average).

Notes
Czech data start from 1993 and social security is only health.

increased on average within the EU (going from 41.4 to 42.6 percent), while the same figures for the New Members show an opposite trend, with the average ratios decreasing from 41.0 to 38.6 percent.

This results from the different pattern of two groups of countries: in some of the New Members (Estonia, Poland and Slovenia) the ratio has remained stable, while for those countries (Czech Republic and Hungary) where at the beginning the ratios where higher than the average (and higher than the EU average) the reduction has been significant (from 42.8 to 38.3 percent in the Czech Republic and from 46.0 to 38.9 percent in Hungary).

At the end of the period (1998) the difference between the highest ratio (40.5 percent in Slovenia) and the lowest (37.5 percent in Estonia) is less than at the beginning of the 1990s, indicating a process of convergence among the New Members, while the distance from the EU countries has increased by about 3.6 percentage points. On average, the tax pressure in the New Members (0.4 points lower than the European average in 1992) becomes 4.0 percentage points lower than in the EU at the end of the period (1998).

The lower tax burden is due to the lower incidence of both tax revenues (2.8 percentage points) and social security contributions (1.2 percentage points). Within tax revenues, the incidence of direct taxes is much lower than in the EU (4.1 percentage points), while the share of indirect taxes is higher (1.4 percentage points).

Among the accession countries the share of individual taxes in GDP shows large differences. The difference between the highest and the lowest figure is about 2.2 percentage points for direct taxes, 6.5 points for indirect taxes and 4.8 points for social security contributions. Similar differences are not found in EU member countries (Gandullia 2004).

More updated comparable figures are available but only for the OECD member countries (Czech Republic, Hungary, Poland and Slovak Republic; OECD 2003a). In the years after 1998 (1999–2002, provisional data) the tax-to-GDP ratio has decreased for all these countries, excluding the Czech Republic, where the ratio increased from 38.9 to 39.2 percent. The ratio decreased from 39.1 to 37.7 percent in Hungary, from 35.0 to 34.3 percent in Poland and from 34.4 to 33.8 percent in the Slovak Republic. Even if the data from the EU Commission and those from the OECD are not directly comparable (in addition the coverage of countries is different), it can be argued that during the decade 1992–2002 a general process of reduction in tax pressure has taken place in most of the accession countries.

The tax structure by legal categories, measured as the distribution of tax revenue among major taxes (direct taxes, indirect taxes and social security contributions) has changed over time (see Table 1.2), while in the same period the tax mix has remained quite stable within the EU members.

Table 1.2 Tax mix in New Members and EU 15 as a percentage of total taxation, 1992–98

	1992								1998							
	CZ	EE	HU	PL	SI	NM	EU	NM–EU	CZ	EE	HU	PL	SI	NM	EU	NM–EU
Direct taxes, of which	25.5	35.3	22.0	32.0	18.3	26.6	32.6	-6.0	23.5	29.6	22.4	29.6	19.3	24.9	32.2	-7.3
Personal income	8.9	22.5	16.3	19.9	16.8	16.9	23.2	-6.3	13.6	22.7	16.7	22.0	16.3	18.2	21.8	-3.6
Corporation income	16.6	12.7	5.7	12.1	1.5	9.7	5.6	4.2	9.7	6.9	5.7	7.7	3.0	6.6	7.0	-0.5
Indirect taxes, of which	36.0	32.6	38.9	38.3	35.8	36.3	32.4	4.0	32.4	38.1	41.9	38.1	46.7	39.4	32.6	6.8
VAT	17.8	24.4	13.0	0.0	16.8	14.4	16.2	-1.8	17.2	23.5	20.3	20.9	22.5	20.9	16.4	4.4
Excise duties	9.3	5.0	13.5	0.0	8.9	7.4	8.2	-0.9	9.7	10.1	10.8	10.3	10.9	10.4	8.2	2.1
Others	9.1	3.2	12.6	38.3	10.1	14.7	8.0	6.7	5.5	4.8	10.8	7.1	13.6	8.4	8.2	0.1
Total tax revenue	61.4	67.9	60.9	70.3	54.1	62.9	65.0	-2.0	55.9	67.7	64.3	67.7	65.9	64.3	64.8	-0.5
Social contributions	38.6	32.1	39.1	29.7	45.9	37.1	35.0	2.0	44.1	32.3	35.7	32.3	34.1	35.7	35.2	0.5
Employers	23.8	31.6	30.4	10.8	18.8	23.1	19.6	3.5	28.7	31.7	29.8	11.6	10.9	22.6	19.2	3.3
Employees	8.9	0.0	7.2	11.0	24.9	10.4	11.6	-1.2	10.2	0.0	5.4	11.9	21.0	9.7	11.7	-2.0
Self employed	5.8	0.5	1.5	8.1	2.2	3.7	3.9	-0.2	5.2	0.5	0.8	8.7	2.2	3.5	4.5	-1.0
Total fiscal revenue	100.0	100.0	100.0	100.0	100.0	100.0	100.0	0.0	100.0	100.0	100.0	100.0	100.0	100.0	100.0	0.0
Administrative level																
Central government	77.6	44.0	54.1	63.3	45.9	57.0	55.1	1.9	73.1	53.6	55.3	59.0	58.3	59.8	53.8	6.1
Local government	9.1	23.9	6.7	7.3	8.1	11.0	7.2	3.8	12.0	14.1	9.0	9.0	7.7	10.4	9.4	1.0
Social Security	13.6	32.1	39.1	29.7	45.9	32.1	35.0	-3.0	14.9	32.3	35.7	32.3	34.1	29.8	35.0	-5.1

Sources: see Table 1.1.

At the beginning of the 1990s, the broad fiscal structure of New Members comprised social security contributions (37.1 percent), indirect taxes (36.3 percent) and direct taxes (26.6 percent). Compared with the EU figures, it was higher (by 2.0 percent) than the share of social security contributions and lower than the incidence of tax revenues. Among taxes, in the New Members the share of direct taxes was lower (6.0 percent) and the share of indirect taxes higher (4.0 percent). It should be noted that the higher incidence of indirect taxes was mainly due to the presence of 'other' taxes, different from VAT and excise duties. Within social contributions, the incidence of employers' contributions was higher (3.5 percent).

Among individual New Member countries, the tax structure was considerably different. On one hand some countries (Estonia and Poland) had tax structures based about two-thirds on taxes and the remaining third on social contributions, which was in line with the EU average. On the other hand, in Slovenia the share of tax revenues was very low (54.1 percent), while the share of social contributions was high (45.9 percent).

At the end of the period (1998), the tax mix changed as the result of the reduction in direct taxes (1.7 percent) and social security contributions (1.4 percent), and was compensated for by an increase in the share of indirect taxes (3.1 percent). The decrease in direct taxes was due to the large reduction in corporate income taxes (3.1 percent), partly offset by an increase in personal income taxes (1.3 percent). In the field of indirect taxation, as an effect of the process of convergence to the European standards, the main change is represented by the large fall of 'other taxes' (6.3 percent), almost exactly offset by the increase in the VAT revenue.

The comparison with the EU average shows that, at the end of the period, the tax structure of New Members is even more different than at the beginning of the 1990s. More specifically, in 1998 the tax mix between taxes and social contributions was almost equal for EU members and New Members. But the tax mix has changed between direct and indirect taxes. The difference in share of direct taxes in the comparison between New Members and EU countries has increased from 6.0 to 7.3 percent, while the same difference regarding indirect taxes has increased from 4.0 to 6.8 percent.

The variation in the share of individual taxes between New Members countries has continued to be considerable. For instance, in 1998 the share of direct taxes ranged from 19.3 percent in Slovenia, 22.4 percent in Hungary to 29.6 percent in Estonia and Poland. The share of personal income tax ranged from 13.6 percent in the Czech Republic to 22.7 percent in Estonia. The share of the corporate income tax ranged from the low 3.0 percent in Slovenia to the 9.7 percent in the Czech Republic.

Selected New Members also differ in the way they provide arrangements between the central and the sub-national levels of government. Table 1.2 shows the attribution of tax revenues to the three sub-sectors of general government (central, local and social security sectors). In 1992, only Hungary showed a tax structure by level of government not very different from the EU average. The share of central government receipts in the other New Members varied from 77.6 percent in the Czech Republic to 45.9 percent in Slovenia and 44.0 percent in Estonia. The share of local government ranged from 7.3 percent in Poland to the high 23.9 percent in Estonia. Finally, the share of social contributions varied from 13.6 percent in the Czech Republic to 45.9 percent in Slovenia.

During the 1990s, the tax structure changed on average, with the decrease in the shares of local government and social security offset by the increase in the share of the central government. The Czech Republic and Estonia appear the most (tax) decentralized countries among New Members, while the other countries show similar tax structures, in line with the EU average.[2]

1.4 Institutional features of current tax systems

Personal income tax

Modern personal income taxes have been introduced in recent years (Hungary in 1988, Poland in 1991, the Czech Republic in 1993). After the reforms, New Member countries adopted neither a full comprehensive income tax model nor (as recommended by foreign experts – like McLure 1992 – in order to encourage private savings) an expenditure tax model, but rather a hybrid tax base. Before reforms, countries were used to applying separate schedules to different sources of income; generally the systems were not progressive.

Today (see Table 1.3) the personal income tax (PIT) rates are progressive in some of the accession countries, but many of them (the Baltic states) apply a flat rate taxation; a linear system of personal income taxation also exists in the Slovak Republic after the 2004 tax reform. In Poland, the recent tax reform proposal (still not enacted) moves in the same direction. The flat rate is 26 percent in Estonia, 25 percent in Latvia, 33 percent in Lithuania and 19 percent in the Slovak Republic. However, even in these countries PIT is made partially progressive by basic relief (Estonia) or the exemption of a minimum amount of the personal employment income (Lithuania).

The maximum number of tax brackets is six (Slovenia). The lowest marginal tax rate applied to the first bracket is in the Czech Republic (15 percent); the highest level is applied in Lithuania (33 percent). Top marginal tax rates range from 19 percent in the Slovak Republic to 50 percent in Slovenia. Until recently, in the Slovak Republic, the tax schedule was progressive with five tax brackets and marginal rates ranging from 10 to 38 percent. A comprehensive tax reform has been launched, effective from January 2004. The core of the reform consists of a flat marginal tax rate of 19 percent on all personal (and corporate) income and the increase of

Table 1.3 Structure of the personal income tax in New Members

Country	Tax unit	Number of brackets	Minimum tax rate	Maximum tax rate	Highest rate applies from (euro)	Tax base	Reliefs
Czech Republic	Individual	4	15	32	10,400	Most capital income taxed separately (15–25%)	Basic relief. Marital status relief. Child relief.
Estonia	Individual	1	26	26	n.a.	Most capital income exempt.	Basic relief. Child relief.
Hungary	Individual	3	18	38	5300	Capital income taxed separately at a flat rate	Tax credits for wage income, social security contributions and private pension contributions.
Poland	Individual. Option for joint taxation (splitting system)	3	19	40	9600	Most capital income taxed separately (15–20%)	Basic relief (tax credit) and relief for wage income and social security contributions.
Slovak Republic (before 2004 reform)	Individual	5	10	38	13,600	Most capital income taxed separately (15–25%)	Basic relief. Marital status relief. Child relief.
Slovak Republic (after 2004 reform)	Individual	1	19	19	n.a.	Interest income is taxed separately. Dividends are tax exempt.	Basic personal allowance. Marital status allowance.
Slovenia	Individual	6	17	50	33,200	Comprehensive	Basic relief. Family allowances.

Sources: Countries' chapters; OECD (2003b); Martinez-Serrano and Patterson (2003).

basic relief for low income earners (OECD 2004). The reform introduces a flat rate tax, where progressivity is obtained through a basic personal allowance (19.2 times the minimum subsistence amount), which is doubled in the presence of a dependent spouse. Among the accession countries, the degree of progressivity of the personal income tax appears higher in Slovenia, also as a result of the basic personal tax relief (Čok 2003; see also Chapter 11).

In all countries the tax unit is the individual; only in Poland may married couples opt to be taxed on their joint income; in this case a splitting system is applied where the tax bill is twice the income tax due on half of the joint income, provided the joint income does not include capital income taxed at the flat 20 percent rate (OECD 2003b).

Standard relief is implemented in most countries through tax allowances in the form of fixed deductions from the PIT base. Apart from the Polish optional splitting system, marital status tax relief and child relief can be found in the Czech Republic, Slovak Republic and Slovenia. In Hungary, a non-standard tax relief is applicable in the form of employee tax credits, which decrease with the level of wage income.

Tax bases are far from being comprehensive. In most countries (with the exception of Slovenia) capital incomes are taxed outside the PIT under separate (preferential) schedules or are tax exempt. The only non standard system of taxing capital income can be found in Hungary, where dividends are taxed separately at the 20 percent tax rate, increased to 35 percent for 'excess dividends', that is dividends paid in excess of a specified rate of return on equity (actually double the prime national discount rate).

In Poland, the erosion of the tax base determined by tax relief and special tax regimes has, until recently, been relevant (IMF 1999b). Moreover, the PIT expenditure programs, introduced in 1992 and intended to compensate lower-income taxpayers for the withdrawal of price subsidies, were extremely regressive (Cavalcanti and Li 2000). The classic tax-cuts-cum-broadening-tax-base reform model proposed in 1999 has still not been enacted (IMF 2003). It should also be noted that since 2002 most capital income has been taxed under a separate schedule (20 percent on interest and capital gains, 15 percent on dividends).

The present systems are the result of fundamental tax reforms implemented during the transition and during the 1990s. For instance, when the PIT was introduced in Hungary (1988) there were 11 tax brackets (60 percent was the top marginal tax rate); marginal tax rates and brackets changed almost on a yearly basis; the 1999 tax reform reduced from six to three the number of tax brackets and the corresponding tax rates in order to reduce the burden of taxation on labor (IMF 1999a); following reductions, the top marginal tax rate reached the level of 38 percent.

In the Czech Republic, the number of brackets and level of top rates have been reduced since the introduction of the PIT in 1993 (Bronchi and

Burns 2000); the last reduction took place in 1999 with the number of brackets reduced from five to four in 1999 and the top marginal tax rate from 40 to 32 percent, because very few taxpayers were taxed at the highest bracket.

In Poland, despite the presence of three tax brackets most taxpayers (94.9 percent) fall into the first bracket whose upper limit is about €9600 (see Chapter 10). This explains the tax reform proposal of a linear income taxation (the proposal has still not been enacted mainly for revenue reasons; see Lenain and Bartoszuk 2000).[3] The effective structure of the Polish income tax system is close to the flat tax model, realized through basic relief (standard fixed tax credit) and a first tax bracket which includes almost all income.

Finally, in all New Members, PITs are the exclusive competence of central government; however, in the Czech Republic, Estonia, Slovak Republic, Poland and Hungary, the tax revenues are also allocated to subnational government.

Corporate income tax

The two largest accession countries, Hungary and Poland, were the first to reform their Soviet-inspired *enterprise profit tax* (Martinez-Vazquez and McNab 2000). Poland introduced a uniform enterprise profit tax in 1989, then replaced it with a modern corporate income tax in 1992. In Estonia, CIT was adopted in 1993 (as in the Czech Republic) and reformed in 1999 and 2000; in Latvia, the CIT replaced the profit tax in 1995 (Brekis and Revina 2003).

Present corporate taxes in New Members are linear and central. In the Czech Republic, the tax revenues are allocated between the central and local governments. Only Hungary applies a local levy on corporate taxpayers on a tax base similar to the value added.

As illustrated in Table 1.4, statutory CIT rates in accession countries are currently moderate and generally lower than those in EU countries. Apart from the Estonian case, where retained earnings are untaxed, the lowest tax rate can be found in Hungary (18 percent), the highest in the Czech Republic (31 percent).[4]

Similarly to EU countries, the reduction of corporate tax rates has been particularly relevant during the second half of the 1990s. In Poland, the tax rate was lowered from 40 percent (in the period 1989–96) to 27 percent (2003).[5] In Hungary, the tax rate was halved in 1995 (from 36 percent to 18 percent), but at the same time a 'supplementary tax' levied at 23 percent was imposed on distributed profits (replaced in 1997 by a classical withholding tax on dividends at 20 percent, or at the reduced applicable treaty tax rate). In Latvia, where the CIT is relatively recent, the tax rate was 25 percent in 2001, and was then reduced to respectively 22, 19 and 15 percent in the following three years. In the Slovak Republic the tax rate

Table 1.4 Structure of the corporate income tax in New Members

Country	Statutory tax rate	Integration with PIT for dividends	Depreciation		Inventories	Carry forward of losses (number of years)	Main tax incentives
			Buildings	Machinery			
Czech Republic	31	Final withholding tax (15%) and relief at corporate level	Declining-balance (25 years)	Declining-balance (6 years)	Weighted average	7	Investment tax incentives. Tax holiday (10 years for new firms and 5 years for expansion).
Estonia	26	Exemption	Financial accounting (IFRS)	Financial accounting (IFRS)	Financial accounting (IFRS)	Not applicable	–
Hungary	18	Classic (final withholding tax 20%)	Straight-line (25 years)	Straight-line (14.5%)	LIFO	5 (unlimited for start-ups)	Investment reserve of 25%. R&D (deduction of 200% costs). Investment tax incentives.
Poland	27	Classic (final withholding tax 15%)	Straight-line (40 years)	Declining-balance (14%)	LIFO	5 (only 50% of the loss deductible in each year)	Accelerated depreciation of 30% in the first year. Special Economic Zones.
Slovak Republic	19	Exemption	Declining-balance (30 years)	Declining-balance (6 years)	Weighted average	5	Tax holiday (10 years for new firms or expansion).
Slovenia	25	Partial (40%) exemption	Straight-line (20 years)	Straight-line (4 years)	LIFO	5	10% investment reserve. 20% tax relief for investment in fixed assets.

Sources: Countries' chapters; Jacobs *et al.* (2003); Martinez-Serrano and Patterson (2003).

has been cut from 40 percent (1999) to 29 percent (2000), 25 percent (2002) and 19 percent (after the 2004 tax reform).

At the time of transition, the applicable tax rates were very high compared with international standards (55 percent in the Czech Republic, 50 percent in Hungary and up to 75 percent in Poland). Now, on average the statutory tax rate in selected accession countries is 24.33 percent (it is 23.6 percent considering all the accession countries; see Jacobs *et al.* 2003), which is considerably lower than the current average tax rate of EU member states (31.68 percent) or the OECD average (30.79 percent).

The main non-standard CIT is represented by the Estonian experiment (Raju 2003) where, after the 1999 reform, the tax is no longer levied on any retained earnings, but only on distributed profits and capital gains; the tax rate is set at 26/74 of the net distribution (26 percent of the gross distribution). This levy is not a withholding tax and is consequently not reduced under tax treaties.

The experiment (in line with a proposal made by Tanzi 1975) has been based on different characteristics (Raju 2003): the argument that the ability to pay can be evaluated only at personal level (not at the level of legal persons); the tax base is not the enterprise's profits (actually the tax code does not define 'profits' for tax purposes), but their use (dividends and other specific kinds of income distribution); the timing of taxation of corporate income, which is deferred until their distribution; and finally, the argument that not taxing corporate profits assures more neutrality, through the elimination of the distortions caused otherwise by the tax system.

The selected countries apply different systems of integration with the personal income tax: some of them (Hungary and Poland) apply a 'classic' system, even if dividends are taxed with a final withholding tax, at rates generally lower than marginal PIT tax rates. Some countries apply a system of exemption, full (Slovak Republic) or partial (40 percent in Slovenia); in Estonia, dividends are taxed only at corporate level. Finally, the Czech Republic combines a final withholding tax with partial tax relief at corporate level.

More specifically, Hungary and Poland apply a classic system of corporate taxation, even if dividends are taxed through final withholding taxes. In Hungary, corporate earnings distributed as dividends are effectively taxed at a rate of 34.4 percent (increased to 46.7 percent for 'excess distributions'). Distributions higher than normal are penalized through the application of an higher tax rate, which increases the incentives for companies to reinvest profits (where the effective tax rate is 18 percent) rather than distribute them (IMF 1999a). Thus, Hungary, together with Estonia (and Lithuania), provides a substantial preference for retained earnings, as opposed to distributed profits.

In the Czech Republic, the double taxation of corporate (distributed) earnings is alleviated both at personal and corporate levels. On dividends, a final withholding tax is levied at a rate (15 percent) equal to the lowest marginal PIT rate; moreover, the company may credit 50 percent of the withholding tax against its corporation income tax liability, reducing in these instances the effective corporate income tax on distributed earnings to 36.17 percent. Slovenia applies a system of partial exemption (only 60 percent of dividends are taxed under PIT). After the 2004 tax reform, the Slovak Republic has replaced the classic system with a system of dividends exemption.

Corporate tax bases appear lower than their potential because of extensive exemptions and tax incentives. In the Baltic states, the degree of tax erosion caused by preferred tax treatments is still considerable (Brekis and Revina 2003).

In the earliest stages of transition, foreign investors were given special tax privileges in the form of tax holidays and reduced CIT rates. In the early 1990s, Hungary removed various tax exemptions and incentives, but this trend was reversed in the second half of the 1990s when the range of activities qualified for tax incentives was expanded (IMF 1999a). The same trend can be found in Poland, which during the mid 1990s re-introduced extensive tax exemptions, targeted at foreign investors, as instruments to compete with Hungary and the Czech Republic in attracting foreign direct investments (Martinez-Vazquez and McNab 2000; Schratzenstaller 2003). In 1997, the Czech Republic introduced more investor-friendly policies and tax holidays targeted at large investments. The Slovak Republic was the last to enter the competition for foreign direct investment starting from 1998.

In addition, in Poland, corporate tax liabilities have traditionally been reduced by tax incentives for investments in certain sectors or made by certain firms, for instance export-oriented firms and start-ups (Lenain and Bartoszuk 2000). Preferential tax regimes have been granted in Special Economic Zones, even if they will be repealed after the entry of Poland in the EU (see Chapter 10). In this field, the 2000 tax reform (partly enacted) achieved substantial progress on tax policy (IMF 2003), broadening the corporate tax base through the elimination of many previous investment allowances, the revision of the structure and rate of depreciation deductions and the closure of loopholes in the legislation. However, the role of tax-related investment incentives still appears substantial (Schratzenstaller 2003; Appel 2003).

As in Hungary and Poland, the Czech Republic (see Bronchi and Burns 2000) soon after the transition introduced a number of corporate tax incentives (mainly in the form of tax holidays) in order to promote new investment, innovation and entrepreneurial activity. However, these schemes failed to achieve their aims (OECD 1995) and were abolished at the time of the introduction of the modern CIT (1993). The growing pressure of international competition induced the authorities to re-introduce a range of investment incentives at the end of the 1990s.

Also in the Slovak Republic, but more recently (2004), a comprehensive tax reform has been introduced. The core of the reform consists of a flat marginal rate (19 percent) applied to all corporate incomes, financed by the elimination of almost all tax incentives and exemptions (OECD 2004; Miklos 2004).

As reported in Table 1.4, in taxing corporate profits a number of approaches can be observed, especially in the determination of taxable income. As already illustrated, in Estonia the tax base is not linked to profits, with retained earnings untaxed. Distributed earnings are assessed according to the International Financial Reporting Standards (IFRS), without adjustments for tax purposes.

In the calculation of the tax base, buildings may be depreciated in all New Members. The declining-balance method is in use in the Czech and Slovak Republics, the straight-line system is compulsory in the remaining countries. The useful life ranges from 20 (Slovenia) to 40 years (Poland). For tangible fixed assets (plant and machinery) the Czech Republic, Poland and Slovak Republic apply the declining-balance method. The Czech Republic also recognizes a first-year deduction of 10 percent in addition to the annual depreciation for the acquisition of new machinery. Hungary and Slovenia restrict depreciation to the straight-line method. In the evaluation of inventories, two main methods are applied. Hungary, Poland and Slovenia permit the last-in, first-out (LIFO) method, while the Czech and Slovak Republics allow the option for the weighted-average cost method. None of the New Members allows a carry-back of losses; the carry-forward is allowed in all countries, subjected to restrictions. Losses can be carried forward only for five years in most countries (seven years in the Czech Republic). In Poland, the amount of loss to be set off from taxable income in each year is limited to 50 percent of the loss. The carry-forward is unrestricted in Hungary for start-ups.

Finally, the selected countries make large use of specific tax instruments targeted to increase domestic and foreign investment (see for details Jacobs *et al.* 2003). Tax holidays can be found in both the Czech and Slovak Republics for new firms or expansion of existing firms. In Hungary and Slovenia, companies may utilize a tax-free reserve of profits, to be used to finance new investment. More generally, tax incentives targeted at new investment are frequent in almost all the selected countries.

The desirability of many existing preferential tax schemes has been questioned as an instrument to promote domestic and foreign investment (OECD 1995; Owens Chapter 6, this book), for example their compatibility with European law (Meussen 2003).

Consumption-based taxes

As illustrated earlier (Table 1.2) countries rely heavily on indirect taxes that account (in 1998) for about 39.4 percent (against 32.6 percent in EU countries) of total tax revenue and 15.3 percent (against 13.9 percent in the EU) in terms of GDP. VAT revenue covers the main share (20.9 percent of total tax revenue and 8.1 percent in terms of GDP). In addition the excise revenues show figures higher than the EU average (10.4 against 8.2 percent in terms of total tax revenue and 4.0 against 3.5 percent in terms of GDP).

In the early stages of transition, one of the most immediate tax policy objectives in the area of indirect taxation was to replace the complex and inefficient turnover taxes (Martinez-Vazquez and McNab 2000). In Poland for instance, the turnover tax had been applied with more than 100 different tax rates (see Chapter 10). An even more complex sales taxation was in force in the Czech Republic (Bronchi and Burns 2000). The basic choice was between a single stage retain sales tax or a traditional value added tax (Cnossen 1998). The desire to join the EU induced almost all the central and eastern European countries to adopt the basic EU value added tax model. Hungary was the first country to introduce VAT (1988), followed by Poland (1993), while Slovenia was the last country (1999).

The value added tax systems applied in most new member countries are very close to the European model. These countries have recently carried out reform in the field of VAT in order to comply with the provisions of the EU Directives. Some of them have requested transitional measures.

The VAT structure is predominantly dual – or (more frequently) multiple – rate (see Table 1.5). Only the Slovak Republic shows a single-rate structure, as a result of the recent flat tax reform. The standard VAT rate ranges from 25 percent in Hungary to 18 percent in Estonia. It should be noted that the Hungarian rate is equal to the highest applied in the EU (specifically in Denmark and Sweden; see Cnossen 2002). Most countries apply one or two reduced rates, ranging between 3 (Poland) and 15 percent (Hungary). Many countries apply a 0 percent rate on some basic products and services.

The presence of multiple-rate structures in the selected countries (with the exception of the Slovak Republic) can be explained, other than through the heritage of the past multiple-rate turnover taxes, by the attempt to mitigate the regressive burden distribution of the VAT measured against income. However, the rate differentiation still appears to be an ineffective and ill-targeted instrument.

Currently, the standard rate applied on average in the selected New Members (21 percent) is higher than the EU (un-weighted) average (19.4 percent).

For many countries, bringing the agricultural sector into the tax net has been one of the most important EU accession requirements in the field of indirect taxation. Until 2000 in Poland, the entire sector was *de facto* zero-rated (Lenain and Bartoszuk 2000), while currently a reduced rate (3 percent) is applied on most non-processed agricultural products.

The range of activities exempted from VAT or subject to reduced tax

Table 1.5 Tax rates for selected consumption-based taxes in New Members

Country	VAT		Excises		
	Standard rate (%)	Reduced rate (%)	Cigarettes (euro/1.000 pieces)	Unleaded gasoline	Diesel fuel
Czech Republic	22	5	18.71 or 21.62	325.3	244.6
Estonia	18	0–5	11.1 (+23% of the main retail price)	224.4	163.7
Hungary	25	5–15	13.99 or 27.99 or 41.98	368	317.3
Poland	22	0–3–7	23.78 or 16.02 or 20.37	387.8/363	288.6/259.5
Slovak Republic	19	0	11.89 or 21.41	269.9	256.2
Slovenia	20	8.5	45%	363.9	318.4
EU minimum	–	–	60	287	245

Sources: Countries' chapters; Martinez-Serrano and Patterson (2003).

rates still appears to be wide. A good example is given by the Czech Republic, which combines a high statutory standard tax rate (22 percent) with a wide range of items subject to reduced taxation; the effect is that the VAT productivity is very low by international comparison (Bronchi and Burns 2000). As for the personal and corporate income taxes, VAT is central, but in the Czech Republic the revenues are also allocated to regions and municipalities.

The accession to the EU will have more impacts in the field of excise taxation. Accession countries show wide differences in the way they levy excises on alcoholic beverages, tobacco and on hydrocarbon fuels. In this field during the 1990s some common trends can be identified: the move toward the conversion of *ad valorem* rates into specific rates; the increase in effective tax rates (even if they are still below international levels); the gradual equalization of rates applied to domestic and imported products; the convergence of tax rates among neighboring countries. The advantages of a specific excise regime over *ad valorem* taxation in terms of revenue raising capacity, reduction of consumption and in terms of contrast to trade diversion have been recommended to the accession countries by international observers (see for instance, Cnossen 2001 in the field of tobacco taxation).

For some excises (for instance those on wine and on spirits) accession will have few effects in terms of an increase of tax rates, which are already in line with the EU minimum requirements. On the contrary (see Table 1.5) most countries will have to increase significantly the tobacco duties and, some of them, the rates on hydrocarbon fuels (Martinez-Serrano and Patterson 2003; see also Chapter 2).

1.5 Equity and efficiency profiles of current tax systems

Looking at the structure and evolution of the New Members tax systems, Table 1.6 shows the economic structure measured as the share of individual taxes in GDP and in total taxation by economic category (consumption, labor and capital). It should be noted that the economic tax mix, indicating a country's preference for one tax over another, shows some differences from the EU standard. While, in EU countries, taxes on labor contribute more than half total tax revenue, taxes on consumption less than 30 percent and taxes on capital more than 20 percent, in the New Members the contribution of taxes on labor and of taxes on consumption is higher (respectively, 2.2 and 6.3 percentage points); the contribution of taxes on capital is much lower (9.5 percentage points) mainly as a result of the shadow economy's wide evasion and the low taxation of income from financial capital.

The distance from the EU standard increased during the 1990s; this means that the tax structure of New Members in the early 1990s was much closer to the EU structure than in more recent years. Within the New

Table 1.6 Structure of taxation by economic function and implicit tax rates in New Members and EU 15

	Early 1990s								Late 1990s							
	CZ	EE	HU	PL	SI	NM	EU	NM–EU	CZ	EE	HU	PL	SI	NM	EU	NM–EU
Structure according to the economic function as a percentage of GDP																
Consumption	13.2	11.4	14.9	9.7	13.9	12.6	12.3	0.3	11.1	13.5	14.1	13.0	16.0	13.5	12.6	0.9
Labor	20.8	19.9	23.7	18.8	24.9	21.6	20.7	0.9	21.4	19.8	19.2	19.1	21.4	20.2	20.6	–0.4
Capital	8.9	6.1	8.0	8.6	1.6	6.6	7.7	–1.1	5.7	4.1	5.3	4.2	1.3	4.1	9.1	–5.0
Structure according to the economic function as a percentage of total taxation																
Consumption	30.7	30.4	32.0	26.2	34.2	30.7	28.1	2.6	29.1	33.8	36.7	34.3	39.5	34.7	28.4	6.3
Labor	48.6	52.9	50.8	50.6	61.5	52.9	52.9	0.0	55.9	53.1	49.7	50.4	52.6	52.3	50.1	2.2
Capital	20.7	16.2	17.2	23.1	4.0	16.2	19.0	–2.8	14.9	12.5	13.7	11.1	7.6	12.0	21.5	–9.5
Implicit tax rates																
Consumption	18.4	14.4	18.5	11.9	18.4	16.3	22.7	–6.4	15.6	15.9	19.2	16.3	21.0	17.6	23.6	–6.0
Labor employed	37.0	37.5	40.8	37.3	36.9	37.9	36.9	1.0	38.6	37.1	39.6	32.2	38.4	37.2	37.4	–0.2
Capital and business	n.a	29.4	n.a	n.a	29.7	n.a	16.2	n.a	n.a	20.2	n.a	n.a	31.2	n.a	21.0	n.a

Sources: EU Commission (2000) for New Members (unweighted average); Eurostat (2003).

Members, the tax preferences appear not very different, with the main exception of Slovenia, where the contribution of consumption taxes is much higher than the average and the contribution of taxes on capital much lower.

A full picture of the distribution of the macro-tax burden is given by the *implicit tax rates*, measured as individual tax revenues expressed as a percentage of their respective tax base.[6] Even if the contribution of taxes on consumption to the total tax revenue is higher in New Members than in the EU countries (as a result of the higher propensity to consume in New Members), the implicit tax rate is considerably lower (17.6 percent against 23.6 percent). The distance from the EU average has slightly decreased over the period. The reason is that most countries (with the exception of the Czech Republic) have increased the effective taxation on consumption; in Poland and in Slovenia for instance, the implicit tax rate on consumption increased by, respectively, 4.4 and 2.6 percentage points.

As in EU countries, the effective taxation of labor appears higher than that on consumption and, for Estonia and Slovenia, on capital. However, the evolution over time of the implicit tax rate on labor has been different in EU members and New Members countries. In the EU, the tax rate has risen from 36.9 to 37.4 percent, while in the New Members the tax rate has decreased from 37.9 to 37.2 percent. However, it should be noted that in two countries (the Czech Republic and Slovenia) the implicit tax rate on labor has increased, while a large fall has taken place in Poland and, to a less extent, in Hungary.

Other than at macro-level by economic function, the distribution of the tax burden can be observed at micro-level and compared for some New EU countries, OECD members. Table 1.7 illustrates specific measures of horizontal tax equity, where both the personal income tax and social security contributions are taken into account. The table (based on OECD 2003b) compares the average effective tax rates of two different categories of tax payers: a single individual without children and a one-earner married couple with two children, both earning the same income level (100 percent APW). In each country, differences in the effective tax rates represent how the tax system treats the different economic positions of taxpayers. Looking only at the personal income tax, horizontal equity seems to be pursued effectively in all the selected countries. For instance, in the Czech Republic, Hungary and the Slovak Republic, the average effective tax rate is halved for the one-earner couple with children. In all the countries, social security contributions are flat, thus not directed at horizontal tax equity purposes.

A more comprehensive picture can be obtained from the last column of the table, where average effective tax rates are determined taking into account both the tax system (personal income tax and social security contributions) and the benefit system (cash transfers). The Czech and Slovak Republics and Hungary appear as those countries that give more emphasis

Table 1.7 Measures of horizontal tax equity in selected New Members

Country	Average effective tax rate (income tax)		SSC		Average effective tax rate (income tax + SSC − cash transfers)	
	Single individual without children (APW)	One-earner married couple with two children (APW)	Single individual without children (APW)	One-earner married couple with two children(APW)	Single individual without children (APW)	One-earner married couple with two children (APW)
Czech Republic	11.2	5.3	12.5	12.5	23.7	3.7
Hungary	16.6	7.6	12.5	12.5	29.1	7.8
Poland	6.0	4.0	25.0	25.0	31.0	25.0
Slovak Republic	6.5	3.2	12.8	12.8	19.3	3.1

Source: OECD (2003b).

to horizontal tax (and benefit) equity. More generally, this result is confirmed when all the effects of the different fiscal treatments of families are considered (see OECD 2003b).

With reference to *vertical equity*, Table 1.8 reports measures of statutory tax progressivity, constructed by comparing the share of income paid in tax by taxpayers at different income levels (van den Noord and Heady 2001). Table 1.8 (based on OECD 2003b data) presents measures of statutory tax progressivity for low-wage (67 percent of the APW) and high-wage (167 percent of APW) people, taking into account only the personal income tax or the social security contributions. Personal income taxes are progressive in all selected countries, but (with the exception of Hungary) at degrees generally lower than those existing in the EU countries (see Gandullia 2004). Hungary shows a pronounced tax structure across different income levels, while the progressivity is more concentrated at above-average income levels in the Slovak Republic. Poland appears as the country with the lowest progressivity across different income levels; in this country, until very recently, the progressivity was even lower due to the regressive effects of the tax expenditure programs (Cavalcanti and Li 2000). Finally, in all the selected countries, statutory social security contributions are neutral or progressive.

In the field of labor taxation it is well known that the tax burden in New Members has been historically high, mainly due to the need to finance the high level of social security and welfare expenditures; as a consequence, countries have not been able to deter effectively the underground economy and to relieve unemployment (Tanzi 1993b; see also the foreword).

Table 1.9 reports the total tax wedge on labor in the selected countries (100 percent APW) and its evolution during recent years (where homogeneous data are available). The tax burden has decreased in Hungary, Poland and the Slovak Republic, while it has increased in the Czech Republic. Currently, labor is still most heavily taxed in Hungary, even if in the last seven years the reduction in the tax wedge has been larger than in the other selected New Members. It should be noted that given the average tax wedge on labor in the most important EU countries

Table 1.8 Statutory tax progressivity in selected New Members

Country	Low-wage progressivity		High-wage progressivity	
	Income tax	*Total*	*Income tax*	*Total*
Czech Republic	2.48	3.01	3.62	4.24
Hungary	6.71	8.01	15.51	18.81
Poland	1.60	2.27	1.40	1.96
Slovak Republic	1.71	1.88	5.06	5.97

Source: Own calculations based on OECD (2003b) data.

Table 1.9 Tax wedges on labor (as a percentage of labor costs) in selected New Members

Country	1996	1997	1998	1999	2000	2001	2002
Czech Republic	42.6	42.9	42.8	42.7	43.1	43.1	43.5
Hungary	52.0	52.0	51.6	50.7	49.6	49.0	46.3
Poland	44.7	43.9	43.2	43.0	43.0	42.7	42.7
Slovak Republic	n.a	n.a	n.a	n.a	41.9	42.1	41.4

Source: OECD (2003b).

(43.5 percent; see Gandullia 2004) labor appears to be less taxed in Poland and the Slovak Republic and much more than the average in Hungary.

The taxation of labor appears to be most relevant for lower-paid labor. As in most EU countries, some measures have been introduced in the selected New Members to reduce effective tax wedges on low-paid workers. All four countries apply lower tax wedges on low-income (67 percent APW; OECD 2003b). However, according to the last available data (2002), the tax wedges on lower-paid labor in the New Members are still much higher than the European average. Compared with the European average (34.11 percent), the tax wedge is always above 40 percent in the selected countries (ranging from 40.3 percent in the Slovak Republic to 42 percent in Hungary).

With reference to the effective taxation of (corporate) capital, some studies report estimations for specific countries (see for instance, Holeckova *et al.* 2003; Schratzenstaller 2003; Dethier and John 1998). The only comparative study about the New Members (Jacobs *et al.* 2003) reports the (forward) effective average tax rates (EATRs) for domestic investments.[7] Looking at Table 1.10, there is a wide range of EATRs within the New Members, from the low 19.37 percent in Hungary to 24.73 percent in Poland.

The average EATR in the selected New Members is 22.42 percent, about six percentage points lower than the European average (EU Commission 2001). Compared with the main EU countries, overall the New Members appear to have a significant advantage. The advantage increases considerably if the effects of tax incentives are considered (as shown in the last column of Table 1.10, the average EATR decreases from 22.42 percent to a low 16.56 percent).

As in EU countries, debt appears to be the most tax-efficient source of financing, followed by retained earnings. However, on average, the advantage of debt over equity is lower in the New Members than in the EU as a result of the lower statutory tax rates. The effective tax rate on retained earnings and on new equity is the same for all countries, with the exception of the Czech Republic and Estonia. In the Czech Republic, the EATR on new equity is lower as a result of the tax credit on distributed

Table 1.10 Average effective tax rates on domestic corporate investments in New Members

	Average for each source of finance				Average for each asset			Overall average with tax incentives
	Overall average	Retained earnings	New equity	Debt	Buildings	Machinery	Inventories	
Czech Republic	24.18	28.90	26.40	17.30	21.60	21.10	24.90	16.40
Estonia	22.52	19.50	28.60	19.50	22.50	22.50	22.50	11.34
Hungary	19.37	21.70	21.70	14.80	23.20	17.60	17.40	17.05
Poland	24.73	27.90	27.90	18.50	25.30	27.30	23.90	23.92
Slovak Republic	22.10	25.00	25.00	16.30	21.30	20.90	23.30	11.19
Slovenia	21.60	24.50	24.50	15.80	20.70	20.20	22.10	19.44
New Members average	22.42	24.56	25.66	17.03	22.42	21.61	22.34	16.56

Source: Jacobs *et al.* (2003).

earnings, while in Estonia the tax rate on retained earnings is lower because they are exempt from taxation until they are distributed. The specific Estonian system (in terms of exemption of retained earnings) produces the effect (neutrality) that EATR on retained earnings and on debt is the same, and that the EATR does not change across different types of investments (buildings, machinery and inventories).

Notes

1 I would like to thank Luigi Bernardi, Maria Cecilia Guerra, Christopher Heady and Nicola Iacobone for helpful comments and suggestions. Any remaining errors are mine.
2 A clearer move toward fiscal decentralization in New Members appears when looking at more recent and general comparable data (OECD 2002).
3 According to the original plan (Government's 1998 White Paper) the tax rates would have been lowered from the schedule 19, 30 and 40 percent to 18 and 28 percent in 2002, with the elimination of the top marginal tax rate (IMF 2003).
4 Considering also the other accession countries, the highest tax rate is in Malta (35 percent), the lowest in Lithuania and Cyprus (15 percent). In Lithuania, the tax rate is even lower (13 percent) for SMEs.
5 In the new tax reform proposal, still not approved, the tax rate should be further reduced to 19 percent.
6 However, among New Members, the implicit tax rates on capital and business are only available for Estonia and Poland.
7 The study reports also EATRs about international investments, but only from the perspective of parent companies located in Germany.

References

Appel, H. (2003) 'The political economy of tax reform in central Europe: do domestic policies still matter?', paper presented at the Congress 'Tax Policy in EU Candidate Countries', Riga, 12–14 September.

Bernardi, L. and Owens, J. (eds) (1994) *Tax Systems in North Africa and European Countries*, Deventer & Boston: Kluwer.

Brekis, E. and Revina, I. (2003) 'Baltic states tax legislation and entrepreneurship', paper presented at the Congress 'Tax Policy in EU Candidate Countries', Riga, 12–14 September.

Bronchi, C. and Burns, A. (2000) 'The tax system in the Czech Republic', OECD Economics Department Working Papers 245, Paris: OECD.

Cavalcanti, C. B. and Li, Z. (2000) 'Reforming tax expenditure programs in Poland', World Bank, Policy Research Working paper 2465, October.

Cnossen, S. (1998) *Value-Added Taxes in Central and Eastern European Countries: A Comparative Survey and Evaluation*, Paris: OECD.

Cnossen, S. (2001) 'How should tobacco be taxed in EU-accession countries?', CESIFO Working Paper 539, Munich, August.

Cnossen, S. (2002) 'Tax policy in the European union: a review of issues and options', CESIFO Working Paper 758, Munich, August.

Čok, M. (2003) *Average and Marginal Tax Rates in Slovenia*, Slovenia: Economics Kardeljeva, Ljubljana.

Dabrowski, M. and Tomczynska, M. (2001) 'Tax reforms in transition economies. A mixed record and complex future agenda', Center for Social and Economic Research, Studies and Analyses, 231, Warsaw.

Dethier, J. and John, C. (1998) 'The taxation of capital income in Hungary from the perspective of European integration', *mimeo*, April.

Dobrinsky, R. (2002) 'Tax structures in transition economies: a comparative perspective vis-à-vis member states', paper presented at the East–West Conference 'Structural Challenges and the Search for an Adequate Policy Mix in the EU and in Central and Eastern Europe', Vienna, 4–5 November.

EU Commission (2000) *Structure of the Tax Systems in Estonia, Poland, Hungary, the Czech Republic and Slovenia*, Brussels: European Commission.

EU Commission (2001) *Company Taxation in the Internal Market*, SEC (2001) 1681, Brussels: EU Commission.

Eurostat (2000) *Structures of the Taxation Systems in the European Union, 1970–1997*, Brussels: European Commission.

Eurostat (2003) *Structures of the Taxation Systems in the European Union, 1995–2001*, Brussels: European Commission.

Gandullia, L. (2004) 'A comparative view of selected European countries', in Bernardi, L. and Profeta, P. (eds) *Tax Systems and Tax Reforms in Europe*, London: Routledge.

Holeckova, J., Vitek, L. and Pubal, K. (2003) 'Distorting effects of taxation on assets and source of finance: effective tax rates in the central and eastern European countries during transition', paper presented at the Congress 'Tax Policy in EU Candidate Countries', Riga, 12–14 September.

IMF (1999a) 'Hungary: selected issues', IMF Staff Country Report 99/27, Washington, DC: IMF, April.

IMF (1999b) 'Republic of Poland: Selected Issues', IMF Staff Country Report 99/32, Washington, DC: IMF, April.

IMF (2003) 'Republic of Poland: selected issues', IMF Staff Country Report 03/188, Washington, DC: IMF, June.

Jacobs, O., Spengel, C., Finkenzeller, M. and Roche, M. (2003) 'Company taxation in the new EU member states', Study by Ernest & Young and the Centre for European Economic Research (ZEW), Frankfurt am Main/Mannheim, November.

Lenain, P. and Bartoszuk, L. (2000) 'The Polish tax reform', OECD Economics Department working papers 234, March.

Martinez-Serrano, A. and Patterson, B. (2003) 'Taxation in Europe: recent developments', European Parliament, Directorate-General for Research, Working Paper Economic Affairs Series, ECON 131 EN, January.

Martinez-Vazquez, J. and McNab, R. (1997) 'Tax reform in transition economies: experience and lessons', International Studies Program, Georgia State University, Working Paper 97-06, July.

Martinez-Vazquez, J. and McNab, R. (2000) 'The tax reform experiment in transitional countries', *National Tax Journal*, 53: 2, 273–98.

McLure, C. (1992) 'A simpler consumption-based alternative to the income tax for socialist economies in transition', *World Bank Research Observer*, 7: 2, 221–37.

Meussen, G. (2003) 'The EU-fight against harmful tax competition: developments in light of the enlargement of the EU with 10 candidate Member States', paper presented at the Congress 'Tax Policy in EU Candidate Countries', Riga, 12–14 September.

Miklos, I. (2004) *Fundamental Tax Reform in Slovakia*, Bratislava, March.

OECD (1991) *The Role of Tax Reform in Central and Eastern European Economies*, Paris: OECD.

OECD (1995) *Taxation of Foreign Direct Investment in Central and Eastern Europe*, Paris: OECD.

OECD (2002) *Fiscal Decentralization in EU Applicant States and Selected EU Member States*, Paris: OECD.

OECD (2003a) *Revenue Statistics 1965–2002*, Paris: OECD.

OECD (2003b) *Taxing Wages 2001–2002*, Paris: OECD.

OECD (2004) *Economic Survey: Slovak Republic*, Paris: OECD.

Raju, O. (2003) 'Estonian experiment in tax policy: abolition of corporate income tax', paper presented at the Congress 'Tax Policy in EU Candidate Countries', Riga, 12–14 September.

Schaffer, M. E. and Turley, G. (2001) 'Effective versus statutory taxation: measuring effective tax administration in transition economies', European Bank for Reconstruction and Development Working Paper 62, May.

Schratzenstaller, M. (2003) 'The effective tax burden on company profits in Poland in comparison to the European Union. Some methodological considerations and empirical results', paper presented at the Congress 'Tax Policy in EU Candidate Countries', Riga, 12–14 September.

Stepanyan, V. (2003) 'Reforming tax systems: experience of the Baltics, Russia, and other countries of the former Soviet Union', IMF Working Paper 173, Washington, DC: IMF, September.

Tanzi, V. (1975) 'Should we tax corporations?', in Bird, R. and Oldman, O. (eds) *Readings on Taxation in Developing Countries*, third edition, Baltimore: Johns Hopkins Press.

Tanzi, V. (1992) *Fiscal Policies in Economies of Transition*, Washington, DC: IMF.

Tanzi, V. (ed.) (1993a) *Transition to Market. Studies in Fiscal Reform*, Washington, DC: IMF.

Tanzi, V. (1993b) 'Financial markets and public finance in the transformation process', in Tanzi, V. (ed.) *Transition to Market: Studies in Fiscal Reform*, Washington, DC: IMF.

Tanzi, V. (1994) 'Taxation in developing countries', in Bernardi, L. and Owens, J. (eds) *Tax Systems in North Africa and European Countries*, Deventer & Boston: Kluwer.

Tanzi, V. and Tsibouris, G. (2000) 'Fiscal reform over ten years of transition', IMF Working Paper 113, Washington, DC: IMF.

Van den Noord, P. and Heady, C. (2001) 'Surveillance of tax policies: a synthesis of findings in economic surveys', Economic Department Working Paper 303, Paris: OECD.

2 Main tax policy issues

Luigi Bernardi and Mark Chandler

2.1 Executive summary[1]

The main purpose of taxes is to finance public spending. Hence, it is worthwhile scrutinizing the size and the scope of government in New Members, before considering their tax structure. On this topic, it has often been argued that governments in some transition economies, such as the New Members, are too big relative to their tax capacity and the need not to interfere with economic development. On average, public expenditure/GDP ratio is at present not far from 42 percent in the New Members. This figure is just below what is observed for far higher income countries and well over the level reached by other transition economies at the same level of per capita income.

However, one must notice the lack of robustness that characterizes all empirically estimated relationships between tax or spending/GDP ratio and per capita incomes. Usually, a statistically significant fit does exist but a scatter plot is very dispersed. The correlation looks still weaker inside the worldwide sub-sample of transition economies. Hence – not surprisingly – other variables contribute to explaining a higher/lower than 'normal' level of public spending. Actually many factors – economic, political and social in nature – seem to be working to pull up spending in the New Members.

By better focusing our attention on the problem, we observe however that, in transition economies, large spreads in public spending are almost entirely due to the public sector's engagement in the provision of welfare treatments and services. Once more the particular situation of New Members should call for a relevant public intervention in the welfare area. However, in some New Members there has been a move towards partially funded private pension schemes and itemized social insurance funds targeted to single risks. Time will tell what has been the best chosen way.

After the first years of transition to a market economy, and excluding the period around the Russian crisis of 1997, New Members' rates of growth have generally been satisfactory enough, and apparently they were not curbed by too cumbersome governments. Notwithstanding their bigger governments, New Members outperformed both CIS and Latin America countries, while only the catching-up 'Asian tigers' did better. However, both statistical evidence and economic theory suggest that there exists a negative, although weak, link between the level of taxes and public spending on one side and growth rates on the other. Therefore, non-minimal and well-targeted tax cuts could contribute to further enhancing growth, which indeed would help to reduce the current painfully high unemployment. Some scaling down of public expenditure is hence called for. Detailed analyses on the issue mainly suggested the need to redirect and better target social programs, to make more efficient use of resources in education, health and public administration and finally to strengthen budgetary procedures.

According to authoritative opinions, total fiscal pressure is also too high on average in the New Members and should not exceed about 30 percent, a level more consistent with the New Members' tax capacity and which is more supply friendly, but which stays around eight points under the figure of the last few years. Furthermore, the tax mix should be changed. Direct taxes look comparatively low with respect to indirect taxes. Social contributions remain very high. At a first check, we find that total fiscal pressure may go down, although perhaps by some points less than the above-quoted normative prescription. This is the case if one wants to avoid the disruption of public contributions to welfare treatments and services. By adding up some increase in direct taxes to the scaling down of total expenditures and taxes, a basket of (tentative) about six-to-seven GDP points might be allocated to the higher priority tax cuts. Where they are to be allocated is not a question to answer immediately.

According to the structure of taxation by economic function and to implicit rates, the trade-off between efficiency and equity in taxation not only arises but also appears particularly binding. From the point of view of efficiency, the New Members' tax structure overburdens labor and hits to very different degrees the various (productive and rent) components of capital and business (i.e. national accounting operating surplus). From the point of view of equity, consumption taxes stay high, are traditionally considered as regressive and may be particularly painful in New Members, because of the – low – level and the – uneven – distribution of personal incomes.

In these circumstances, it is quite difficult to strike a welfare maximizing balance between efficiency and equity. A somewhat formal solution would be to divide equally the resources' basket between efficiency – lighter tax wedge on employed labor, via a cut in social contributions – and equity – income tax enlargement and consumption tax squeezing.

This chapter also separately examines the four main categories of taxation in the New EU Member states. The first of these is personal income tax. Although some countries have clearly attempted to implement a uniform taxation of income, they remain in the minority. We discuss several explanations for the non-uniform taxation of income in these former command economies. The special interest explanation may explain why taxation of income from profits is lower than taxation of income from labor when social security payments are accounted for. Another plausible explanation is the attempt to minimize tax evasion and take account of the limited capacity of tax authorities in these countries. Making income tax more progressive is a debated issue, and the solutions adopted by single New Members vary considerably, on economic, social and political grounds. Progressivity is very low in some of the states and this appears to be determined by a combination of factors, including neighbors, expectations of taxpayers, and the ability of high earners to cooperate effectively to pursue their interest against progressivity. An alternative is to widen the base via the inclusion of incomes that, at present, are generally exempt or just slightly taxed and – even more – through the recovery of tax evasion, particularly from the hidden economy.

The taxation of corporate income has also been imaginative in the New Member states. Estonia abolished it in 2000 and others have reduced the rates substantially. Estonia's radical action does not appear to have been a major constraint on the collection of personal income tax. However, reductions in corporate income tax are only weakly correlated with the capacity of entrepreneurs to speed the economic catch-up of New Member states with the rest of the EU. Poland, for example, offers the least freedom for businesses among New Member states, and yet has the most lenient taxation of profit relative to labor income. Dynamic efficiency requires that mild taxation of corporations should be maintained, to favor the enlargement of entrepreneurship and to attract FDI also after the privatization decade. However, corporation (or at least dividends) tax should not vanish, as it should impede the diffusion of avoidance activities.

The – painfully increasing – harmonization of excises to EU standards is mandatory, just lightened by a long transition period. VAT structure hence becomes the only degree of freedom to relieve consumption taxation. Exemptions and reduced (perhaps in few cases also negative) rates should also therefore be well targeted according to the empirical evidence of Engel's curves. Additionally, as to equity, we have already noticed that New Members have to redirect their social programs. Therefore, welfare programs that are effective in relieving the living conditions of the poor should be more equity improving. From this point of view, implanting a social safety net is the main step.

By comparing the efficacy of VAT with that of personal income tax in the region we find the tax base of VAT is at least 80 percent larger than that of personal income in these countries. This implies that replacement of personal income taxation with VAT on the margin may yield unusually large efficiency gains. We also compare the efficacy of VAT collection across the region, and find that the Visegrad region performs less well than the Baltic states. We should be careful with such comparisons, however, since it is likely that the Baltic states suffer from relatively large under-recording of GDP, and this would bias their recorded VAT efficacy upwards.

Radical changes to the social security system in several New EU Member states have left their populations somewhat more at risk regarding their pensions due to the instability of the financial markets. This may be understandable given the instability of collective institutions over the longer term in this region, and the resulting low trust in such constitutions among the population. However, it is interesting to observe that the nations that would be commonly held to be the most capitalism savvy, the Czech Republic and Slovenia, have retained the collective pooling of risk common in the rest of the EU.

2.2 The size and scope of government

It has often been argued that government in some transition economies, such as the New Members, is too big relative to their tax capacity and the need not to interfere with economic development. A clear updated version of this argument, particularly useful for our purposes, has recently been presented by Mitra and Stern (2003) (see also Begg and Wyplosz 1999). These authors observe that, after the shift to a market economy, the share of public expenditures in CSB countries (Central, Southeastern Europe and Baltic states, including all the New Members) has decreased but just by about five points of GDP, from about 47 percent in 1992 to near 42 percent in 2000. This share is about five points higher than the corresponding value on the trend line which fits a set of public expenditure/GDP ratios against corresponding per capita incomes for a sample of near 50 developed and developing countries in 2000. Furthermore, the level of public expenditure in CSB countries is just 0.5 points under the value observed for high-income OECD countries, while it is about 13 points higher than the corresponding value of CIS (Commonwealth of Independent – i.e. post USSR – States), which decreased by almost 20 points from 1992 to 2000.[2] A broad discussion of the previous argument can be synthesized around the following three main issues.

Public expenditure/GDP ratio and per capita income

The econometric performance of Mitra and Stern's (and also of other authors') relationship between public expenditure/GDP ratios and per capita incomes does not look very robust: the resulting R^2 is not higher than 0.3.[3] The highest-income countries show an expenditure/GDP ratio variable within a range from 25 to 55 percent, with the lowest-income countries within a range from 15 to 50 percent.

We briefly go further on the topic. Table 2.1 shows a more definite, albeit small, sample of transition economies pertaining to main world

Table 2.1 Government revenue/GDP percentage ratios, per capita incomes and rates of growth – selected transition economies: year 2000

	Revenue/GDP	*Per capita GDP*	*Growth*
New members			
Czech Republic	41.1	4940	2.9
Estonia	38.7	3510	6.4
Hungary	44.0	4550	3.8
Poland	40.4	4100	4.1
Slovenia	43.3	9160	4.8
CIS			
Belarus	44.3	860	5.8
Kazhakstan	19.6	1230	1.7
Russia	37.0	1730	3.5
Turkmenistan	23.4	850	1.8
Ukraine	34.2	640	6.0
Latin America			
Brazil	32.9	4310	0.8
Chile	19.3	4630	5.4
Colombia	16.2	2290	2.8
Mexico	12.1	4790	6.9
Venezuela	8.5	3150	3.2
East Asia			
China	16.5	780	8.0
Philippines	12.7	1050	4.0
India	15.6	440	7.2
Malaysia	20.1	3390	8.3
Thailand	14.2	2010	4.4

Sources: New Members and CIS countries, Mitra and Stern (2003); Latin America: Martner and Tromben (2003); East Asia and growth rates: *UN Statistical Yearbook*, 2002.

Notes
Per capita GDP values are in US$ at 2000 exchange rates and not PPP corrected. Some data refer to 1999.

areas. Tax (= more or less spending)/GDP ratios may be contrasted to per capita GDP. High values of taxes to GDP ratios are reported for all New Members, where the per capita incomes stay almost always at the mean values[4] usually reported for transition economies and not far from their own average. At broadly comparable levels of per capita income, Latin American countries show very large differences across countries in the tax/GDP ratio. In any case, the specific ratios stay well below New Members' values. CIS countries' tax/GDP ratios are also widely dispersed. There is no discernible and statistically significant correlation between per capita incomes, which stay well below both those of New Members and of Latin American countries. Low per capita incomes are also shown by East Asian countries, with the exception of Malaysia, and in this area tax/GDP ratios are generally quite low.

Therefore, the multi-facet explanatory factors (Burgess and Stern 1993; Gupta *et al.* 2001) of the size and scope of government go well beyond the per capita income relationship suggested by Wagner's law (Wagner 1883), as has been recognized for a long time by the most authoritative literature (Musgrave 1969). Given this conclusion, we have then to notice that, broadly speaking, many factors might keep up the level of expenditure in New Members: the level of literacy, the relatively small size of the agricultural sector, the degree of urbanization, an ageing population, the long-term legacy of communist social aims on voters' preferences and lobbying activities, weak budgetary institutions and so forth.

More specifically however, the supposed over-sizing of New Members' governments is almost entirely due to the level of social security and welfare expenditures. According to Mitra and Stern's data, in New Members these programs together account for the 14.0 percent of GDP, against 15.6 percent observed in high-income countries, and just the 7.8 percent of CIS countries. Here, the welfare programs have been seriously cut in the post-communist era, particularly in Asian states. The remaining functional structure of public expenditure does not differ too much among country groups (including Education and Health, the latter with the exception of CIS countries, which cut it down to 2.2 percent of GDP in 2002). It is then the (public) provision of welfare services that makes the difference among the observed levels of public expenditure in transition economies. This is not an uncommon feature when one looks at a wider set of countries at various stages of development (Burgess and Stern 1993), including those with a high pro capita income (Richards *et al.* 1994).

Political economy views may give an initial explanation of the survival of wide welfare programs in East European transition economies (Milanovic 1999). It is commonly reported (Tanzi 1993a for all) that in almost any country an increase in poverty and a more unequal distribution of incomes occurred with the transition process. As a consequence, most social indicators went down and this stimulated electoral support for income maintenance programs intended to avoid the disruption of social cohesion.

Furthermore, population ageing shared by almost all New Members pushes social security and health care expenditures up further. Other factors seem to suggest the difficulty of scaling down education, health care and social protection programs in New Members (Heller and Keller 2001), as has been accomplished in other countries (Tanzi and Schuknecht 1997). A large proportion of the population is unemployed and/or poor and anyway requires public intervention against income and disability risk, as well as not being excluded from proper level of health care and education. New programs are required to meet the specific social risks of market economies (Kopits 1992). However it should be noticed that many, albeit not all, New Members are moving toward 'three pillars' pension schemes and itemized public insurance funds to cover other social risks. Pros and cons of this move are discussed at length later in the chapter.

A final remark is however necessary. Any suggestion to preserve the wide scope and aims of social programs and public services might be challenged by alleging the high level of corruption that characterizes the public sector in most transition economies, especially the post-communist ones. Generally, the answer to this must not necessarily be found in scaling down public activities to the level of the 'minimal state' (Burgess and Stern 1993). More precisely, it has been argued that corruption can be fought by speeding up structural reforms. Still, we must point out that almost all of our selected New Members stay at the top of the structural reforms index in transition economies, as well as at the bottom of the corruption ranking (Abed and Davoodi 2000).[5]

Size of government and economic performance

After the first years of transition to a market economy, and excluding the period around the Russian crisis of 1997, New Members' rates of growth have generally been satisfactory and apparently they were not curbed by too cumbersome governments. As shown in Table 2.1, at present the Czech Republic runs at a 3 percent increase in GDP yearly; Estonia and the other Baltic states perform far better at more than 5 percent yearly; Hungary stays around 4 percent, as substantially do Poland and Slovenia.

Transition economies of CIS countries as well as those of Latin America do not perform generally better, and a clear cut relationship with taxes to GDP ratios looks very difficult to find. 'Asian tigers' outperform all other transition economies' growth: here, as has been seen, the size of government is generally small (20–25 percent of GDP). A necessary caveat to be raised here is that the direction of causality in this relationship is quite uncertain, especially for transition economies. Furthermore, in Asian countries the level of income per capita is still low, thus somewhat reducing the demand for public goods. Economies are still passing through the catching-up stage. The households' cohesion of the peasant society survives. On the contrary, inside more urbanized societies, such as the New Members, the supply of public goods and the provision of welfare services might give a contribution not just to equity, but also to efficiency (Atkinson 1999).

More broadly speaking, cross-country correlation analyses (Agell *et al.* 1997)[6] as well as a diversified but converging stream of theoretical literature (Bernardi 2004)[7] came to the conclusion that there is a weak negative link between the level of taxes and public spending on one side and growth rates on the other. Therefore, only huge and well-targeted tax cuts can contribute to sustaining economic growth. Then, some cuts in public spending, together with a shift in tax bases should take place, for a total amount that should not be small. We return to this issue in the following sections.

More efficient and lower spending

New Members can be included in the group of transition economies that seem to do better in raising tax revenue as well as in spending it (Gupta *et al.* 2001), on the basis of selected indicators of governments' tax burden and spending benefits. This does not, however, imply that some social programs need not be revised, in order to perform better, to be less costly, and to become more appropriate with respect to the targets. There are three main strategies that could be jointly pursued, in order to decrease by some points the spending/GDP ratio, so to make possible an equivalent reduction of taxes.

i *Redirecting social protection* – The process (Kopits 1992) of adapting social security programs to the needs and constraints of a market economy must be still accomplished. Public pension and income maintenance plans should be better tailored to the emerging demographic decline[8] and to the persisting high level of poverty and inequality. Unemployment benefits should be targeted to the recovery of a work position and not only to a passive income support. A universal means-tested social security safety net is still lacking almost everywhere.

ii *More efficient resource use in education and health* – It has been convincingly reported that resources are not efficiently employed both in education and in health services (Gupta *et al.* 2001). Education is too concentrated in pre- and initial levels as well as in the top ones. Intermediate levels are suffering, especially considering that they must supply the new human capacities required by accelerating growth and the modernizing of both private and public services. Health requires a re-balancing between preventive and curative activities, a reduction of hospital beds and times of hospitalization. Both services look overstaffed.

iii *Public Administration, civil service and budgetary procedures* – As reported in other parts of this research, the present working of Public Administration looks generally poor and inefficient. Regulatory activities remain cumbersome. Corruption has been cut but not eliminated. Public employment must still be downsized to the more limited dimensions required by the aims of government in a market economy. Public pay is in turn comparatively high. However, improving all these aspects is not an easy task. Well-established vested interests and powerful lobby groups may resist any reform. They will be more easily subdued when hopefully stronger budgetary procedures will progressively enter into force, both at the central and local levels of government.

2.3 Taxation structure and main effects

Taxation level and structure

Mitra and Stern (2003) have also outlined something like an 'optimal' tax level and structure that would not damage efficiency and growth (see also Buiter 1997). The total fiscal pressure and tax mix are basically set according to the level of per capita income: here we consider suitable figures for the average New Member. The income tax basis accounts for about half of GDP, which is a small figure, mainly due to the difficulties in taxing widespread small informal businesses. Given a (not low) average net rate of 20 percent, the yield could stay around 8 percent of GDP. International competition would suggest, in turn, not raising corporation tax over two to three points of GDP.

VAT should be limited to about 7 percent of GDP: it would be difficult to enlarge its basis, when both the tax and the administration are new; too high rates might be distortionary. Excise duties may total an average of 2.5 percent of GDP: this burden is already heavy considering that they are levied on a tax basis, which amounts to about 5 percent of GDP. Social contributions should not stay over a level of around 11 percent of GDP, in order not to exert a disincentive effect on labor supply and not to promote the shadow economy. To sum up, according to Mitra and Stern's view, the total fiscal pressure should not exceed about 30 percent as the average of New Members, i.e. around eight points under last year's figure. Mitra and Stern continue by observing that the Eastern European tax-mix looks more similar to developing than to the developed countries' model and is imbalanced both on efficiency as well as on equity grounds. Direct taxes look comparatively low with respect to indirect taxes. Social contributions remain very high. Their present level would be a legacy both of the communist era and of the need to preserve social cohesion during the first years of transition, by means of largely diffused social transfers. Therefore, the authors' suggestion is to update the tax mix, through an increase in the share of direct taxes, particularly personal ones, balanced by a reduction of domestic indirect taxes[9] and social contributions.

We may try a first check of Mitra and Stern's suggestions, by looking at the data in Table 2.2. It should be possible to find some room to increase income tax, especially by enlarging its basis. Corporations should not be taxed more heavily, and possibly less, to attract FDI. On the contrary, some burden could be imposed on capital incomes and gains as well as on immovable wealth, which at present are widely exempt or hit very little.

On average, the New Members' VAT level does not differ much from the 'optimal' value. Excise duties will trend upwards as a consequence of a progressive harmonization to the EU's levels. Other indirect taxes (not considered by Mitra and Stern) should be somewhat reduced, especially the (low) remaining custom duties, but will continue to give some GDP

Table 2.2 Taxes/GDP percentage ratios: selected New Members and EU 15 (late 1990s) and 'optimal values'

	Czech Republic	Estonia	Hungary	Poland	Slovenia	Unweighted average	'Optimal values'	EU 15
Direct taxes, of which	9.0	11.1	8.7	11.2	7.8	9.6	10.5	13.7
Income tax	5.2	8.5	6.5	8.3	6.6	7.0	8.0	9.3
Corporation tax	3.7	2.6	2.2	2.9	1.2	2.5	2.5	3.0
Indirect taxes, of which	12.4	14.3	16.3	14.4	18.9	15.3	9.5	13.9
Value added tax	6.6	8.8	7.9	7.9	9.1	8.1	7.0	7.0
Excise duties	3.7	3.8	4.2	3.9	4.4	4.0	2.5	3.5
Total taxes	21.4	25.4	25.0	25.6	26.7	24.8	20.0	27.6
Social contributions	16.9	12.1	13.9	12.2	13.8	13.8	11.0	15.0
Total fiscal revenue	38.3	37.5	38.9	37.8	40.5	38.6	31.0	42.6

Sources: EU Commission (2000) for New Members and Eurostat (2000) for EU. Mitra and Stern (2003) for 'optimal values' (see text).

Notes
Data from New Members differ from those in Table 2.1, because of the change in source and reference year.

points of yield (non-consumption and stamp taxes). Therefore, as a tendency, indirect taxes on the whole seem to be destined to remain around their present level. Some cut should be required to lighten their worsening inequality level.

Social contributions stay some points over the 'optimal value' and are still higher than the level suitable to deter the underground economy and to relieve unemployment, by reducing the tax wedge on labor (Tanzi 1993b).

To conclude, the aforementioned expenditure cuts should allow a reduction, by some points, of the total fiscal pressure, even if the target suggested by Mitra and Stern seems difficult to reach without disrupting the previously discussed public support welfare programs and services. By adding up some feasible enlargement of direct taxes, the bundle for tax cuts does increase. Where should they be concentrated? A brief deepening of the analysis seems worthwhile to find a proper answer.

Taxation by economic function and implicit rates

The structure of taxation by economic function and according to implicit rates may give a clearer picture of the efficiency and equity effects of the tax burden, rather than the simple classification by institutional items we have considered up to now.

i   *Efficiency* – According to a traditional rule, growth-enhancing taxes should be mainly imposed on consumption and rents, while leaving productive factors less hit. Table 2.3 shows that, by economic function, New Members' consumption taxes stay on average around 13 percent, within a max-min interval of about ±2 percentage points. Still according to economic function, EU 15 consumption taxes are somewhat lower than those in New Members. The difference becomes smaller by considering implicit rates. Both these results are mainly due to the higher propensity by New Members to consume in comparison with that of the EU. Employed labor is heavily hit in New Members, according both to the taxation structure by economic function, and to implicit rates. Average values of both figures do not vary much among countries and stay a very few points below EU ones. Finally, taxes on capital and business give a yield in GDP terms that is more than one third lower than the EU average. This wide gap is mainly due to the shadow economy's wide evasion and to the generous exemptions allowed to financial capital incomes. To sum up, from the point of view of efficiency, the New Members' tax structure overburdens labor and hits, to a very different degree, the various components of capital and business (i.e. national accounting operating surplus). On the contrary, notice that consumption taxes stay at a comparatively high level.

Table 2.3 Structure of taxation by economic function and implicit rates in New Members and EU 15 (late 1990s)

	Czech Republic	Estonia	Hungary	Poland	Slovenia	Average New Members	EU 15
Economic functions % GDP							
Consumption	11.2	12.7	13.8	13.0	16.0	13.3	11.4
Labor employed	18.5	19.8	19.9	14.0	20.1	18.5	21.2
Labor self-employed	2.9	1.3	1.2	5.1	–	2.6	2.3
Capital and business	5.7	0.3	5.0	4.2	4.4	3.9	7.5
Implicit tax rates							
Consumption	15.6	15.5	18.9	16.3	21.0	17.5	16.8
Labor employed	38.6	39.4	41.9	37.2	38.4	39.1	41.9
Capital and business	–	–	–	–	21.5	–	31.1

Sources: EU Commission (2000) for selected New Members and Eurostat (2000) for EU 15 (1997 unweighted average).

Notes
Total taxation according to economic function is over Total fiscal revenue in Table 2.2, because of some double counting.
Implicit rates for capital and business are available only for Estonia and Slovenia.

ii   *Equity* – Consumption taxes are traditionally considered as regressive. In New Members they may be particularly painful, because of the low level of per capita income, the wide share of unemployed and low pension drawers, as a consequence of the dismantling of consumption subsidies. Taxes on labor are not as heavy. They are paid only by working people, and they largely finance welfare programs from which these people benefit. Thus, the trade-off between efficiency and equity in taxation does not just arise but appears particularly binding.

Some more issues on the efficiency–equity trade-off

In these circumstances, it is quite difficult to strike a welfare maximizing balance between efficiency and equity. Inequality in the distribution of incomes increased during the years of transition, and thus redistributive policies are required (Tanzi and Tsibouris 2000; see also Aghion and Commander 1999). Can tax system contribute to these policies, without damaging efficiency? A first step could be to reduce the high levels of social contributions, leaving room for an increase in personal income tax, and in order to partially finance social programs, as we have already suggested.

Performing this step by making income tax more progressive is a debated issue, and the solutions adopted by single New Members vary considerably, on economic, social and political grounds. One should also consider the need to make the tax as simple as possible, to avoid unaffordable difficulties of administrative enforcement (Tanzi 1993a; Bernardi and Majocchi 1994). Furthermore the redistributive effects of steeper graduated tax rates should not be over-evaluated just because incomes are highly concentrated around their (low) modal value. To summarize, a higher contribution of personal income tax to redistributive policies rests on two main conditions: a certain substitution of it for social contributions and the enlargement of its basis. The latter may be performed via the inclusion of incomes that at present are generally exempt or just slightly taxed[10] and – even more – through the recovery of tax evasion, particularly from the hidden economy.[11] A more uniform treatment of different incomes will also improve efficiency.

Efficiency requires the reduction of social contributions. In principle, they should be replaced not only by giving a more important role to income (and wealth) taxation but also without reducing the present heavy consumption taxes. However, this would be somewhat extreme, because of the stringent equity argument already dealt with. The current satisfactory New Members' rates of growth do not impose it. The resources' basket (tentatively about six-to-seven GDP points of an income tax increase and expenditure cuts) might be equally divided between efficiency – a lighter tax wedge on employed labor, via a social contributions cut – and equity – income tax basis enlargement and consumption taxes' squeezing.

The mandatory harmonization of excises to EU standards was already planned to take place gradually during a transition period of up to ten years, so as to avoid the reduction of living standards and the growth of illegal markets. The VAT structure – as to exemptions and reduced (perhaps in few cases also negative) rates – should also be well targeted according to the empirical evidence of Engel's curves. This is the only degree of freedom to lighten consumption taxation.[12]

Efficiency targets require that the mild taxation of corporations should also be maintained, to favor the enlargement of entrepreneurship and to attract FDI (Easson 1998; Funke and Strulik 2003), after the privatization decade and despite the complaints of neighboring EU countries (Germany especially). Low general rates are also the best way to allow the dismantling of too favorable regimes for offshore firms, which are contrary to the EU code of conduct for business taxation. However, corporation (or at least dividends) tax should not vanish, in order to impede especially the diffusion of avoidance activities.

We have already noticed that most New Members have already introduced or are planning to start reforms that are aimed at increasing the sustainability of welfare programs. We repeat now that many of these changes should be definitely applauded (e.g. the entitlements required for age pensions or the means test for other benefits); while some of them are very questionable (e.g. the diffusion and itemizing of contributions to public social program funds), and on some others the jury is still out (the shift to mixed PAYG-funded systems for pensions). All in all, welfare programs that are effective in relieving the living conditions of the poor should be more equity improving. From this point of view, a social safety net is the main step.

2.4 A closer look at the most critical features of the main taxes

Personal income tax

The standard prescription of orthodox economics is that the most efficient income tax is one that is uniform. The claim is that efficiency is highest when rates of taxation are the same across all types of income. This leads automatically to a further oft-quoted requirement that the tax base should be comprehensive, including all items that provide real income, since the tax cannot be uniform if some types of income are untaxed. However, in the vast majority of countries we observe that income tax is not as uniform as it could be, partly because the tax base is not comprehensive, but also for other reasons. We might have hoped that countries that largely created a tax system from scratch around 1990 would have had an opportunity to implement a uniform income tax. However, what we see in the New EU Member states today is far from this, and it is thus pertinent to ask why.

In order to consider this further it is necessary to review the assumptions on which the orthodox recommendation is based, especially given the normative nature of any discussion of efficiency. First, it is based on a Paretian definition of efficiency, with no attempt to make social welfare trade-offs with non-Pareto optimal states. Secondly, it is static, saying nothing about the impact of prior choices on economic decision-making. Thirdly, the prescription assumes that static economic (narrowly defined) efficiency is the primary goal of policy, disregarding social, political and other costs. A challenge to any of these three assumptions has the potential to provide a public interest explanation for departing from uniform taxation.

However, we must also recognize that narrow interests have played a role in the formation of tax policy in the New EU Member states. Following Olson (1965), the more narrowly a group can define itself, the more success we would expect it to have in reducing its tax burden. Hence we might expect taxation of capital gains to be relatively less burdensome than taxation of a more wide-ranging category such as labor income. To some extent this type of phenomenon may form part of the political costs of forming winning coalitions behind legislative programs, but it may also result from more structural inefficiencies in the political process. We might test this prediction against the taxation of dividends. To take into consideration the double taxation of this form of income, Table 2.4 lists the rates of corporate income tax and tax on dividends, calculates the combined rate and compares it with the general income tax rate.

The results are mixed. In five of the eight countries in this sample the combined dividend tax rate is lower than the top rate of income tax, and in only one case is it higher. Since we might expect shareholders to be in the top income tax bracket in most of these countries, that is a relevant comparison. However, it must also be noted that for individuals in the lowest income tax bracket, investing in shares, for example through their pension funds, implies higher tax rates than on ordinary income in five of the eight countries. This latter comparison has special relevance in Poland, since over 90 percent of taxpayers there are in the lowest tax bracket. In Estonia and, from the beginning of 2004, Slovakia, we observe the orthodox rule of equal tax rates across income types, achieved by not taxing profit at the corporate level in the former case and by non-taxation of dividends combined with equal corporate and personal income tax rates in the latter.

This picture changes considerably when we take into consideration social security contributions. Adding the social security taxation to the calculation of tax paid on labor income implies that labor income is taxed more highly than dividends in all countries. Only within the lowest personal income tax bracket in Slovenia is labor income taxed more lightly than dividends. There are two caveats to this finding. First, in many countries there is a cap on social security payments, hence the marginal rate of labor income taxation for top earners is only the top rate of personal income tax. Secondly, not all of the social security contribution is lost to

Table 2.4 Corporations, dividends and PIT rates in selected New Members

Country	CIT	Dividend	Combined tax on income from profit	Ordinary income PIT	Social security contributions		Combined labor tax
					Employer's	Employee's	
Czech Republic	15.5[a]	25.0[b]	36.625	15.0–32.0	35.0	12.5	44.9–55.9
Estonia	0.0[c]	26.0	26.000	26.0	33.5	1.0	45.1
Hungary	16.0	20.0	32.800	18.0–38.0	29.0	11.5	43.7–57.5
Latvia	15.0	0.0	15.000	25.0	24.1	9.0	45.0
Lithuania	15.0	15.0	27.750	33.0 (15.0)[d]	31.0	3.0	50.4 (37.1)
Poland	27.0	15.0	37.950	19.0–40.0	18.4	18.7	44.4–58.8
Slovakia	19.0	0.0	19.000	19.0	34.7–36.5	13.4	47.9–48.6
Slovenia	25.0	30.0	47.500	17.0–50.0	16.1	22.1	44.3–66.5

Sources: Corresponding country chapters of the book; Ernst and Young and Centre for European Economic Research (ZEW) (2003), p. 11; Yakimova (2002), p. 101; Čok (2004); MSI (2004); http://www.socmin.lt/?1845851012; http://www.cato.org/research/articles/tupy-040204.html; KPMG (2003); owns calculations.

Notes
a This rate only applies to dividends.
b Non-pension fund dividends.
c 26 percent on profits repatriated abroad.
d The lower rate applies to creative works.

the individual; some provides income in kind through increased unemployment, disability or pension insurance. This is in contrast to personal income tax payments, which provide no marginal benefits to the individual. However, it should be noted that, in most of the New Member states, it is young people who have proved the most entrepreneurial, and these persons' valuation of state social insurance is naturally low due to uncertainty over the future of the system.

Another example of non-uniform income taxation is the non-taxation of interest income in Latvia. Combined with the non-taxation of dividends in this country and the deductions for expenditure on education and health there is an apparent distortion in favor of investment in financial and human capital and against consumption. A counter-argument to this is that, since investments come from funds that are already taxed as income once, taxation of such investments would be a distortion in favor of consumption and it is the Latvian structure that is neutral. Perhaps the strongest critique of this Paretian efficiency view is that it ignores equity. We may object on equity grounds to a system that does not tax high incomes gained from investments, especially since we know that many of the assets were accumulated illicitly during the chaotic early independence years. And the equity view is not entirely divorced from efficiency: if we accept the diminishing marginal utility of income we might well expect that total social welfare would increase as we shift the tax burden from labor to investment income. Orthodox consideration of dynamics tends to assume that taxation of investment reduces economic growth to a sub-optimal level. However, to show this would require consideration of the size of positive externalities from one investment on returns or risk of another.

There may also be inefficiencies in the EU New Members' income taxation due to an oversight, providing ready opportunities for reform. Such an oversight can result from the weak public administration and government capacities in the former Soviet block countries. However, the rapid development of these economies likely contributes to the continuous creation of new areas for reform that are yet to be addressed, thus increasing the challenge for New Member state governments.

While the forgoing relates to the legal structure of taxation, the illegal evasion of tax has also had important consequences for universality in the New EU Member states. By putting payment of taxes on an *ad hoc* basis, or worse making it dependent on manipulation of the bureaucracy, evasion reduces the efficiency of the tax system considerably. The existence of this type of distortion in the tax system also opens up the possibility of a trade-off between legal distortions and evasion. Hence, in Lithuania, the income tax rate on creative work is 15 percent, in contrast to the 33 percent standard income tax rate. While this may be criticized for distorting the labor market in favor of non-standard labor contracts, it is clearly an attempt to take account of the relative ease with which individuals that create products independently can evade the income tax.

Progressivity is an issue on which the New EU Member states have found a surprising variety of solutions. While the orthodox Paretian efficiency position has demanded no progressivity, standard Western practice has implemented it on equity grounds and the 'ability to pay' theory. We might also argue for it on the basis of the benefit principle if we accept that higher income individuals benefit more from the state than lower income individuals.[13] It should be noted that all current income tax systems are to some extent progressive since they all have personal exemptions. However, among the New EU Member states, the three Baltic states and Slovakia have all now rejected multiple tax rates and, combined with very low personal exemptions, this means that their average income tax rates hardly vary across the income range. While there has been some debate on the introduction of multiple tax rates, particularly in Lithuania, these have so far not been supported by any Baltic government. Indeed, the trend appears to be in the opposite direction, with Slovakia's recent abandonment of multiple rates.

Although the equity argument would appear critical in the Baltic states at this time, there are a number of conditions of their transition that have perhaps contributed to the absence of multiple income tax rates there. First, for young people especially, the Baltic states might be seen as places where one's income level is very hard to predict, with plenty of opportunities for increasing it rapidly. Hence, even those on low income may prefer the dream of low tax on high income in the future. This, however, implies a surprising love of risk given the uncertainty level. Perhaps a more plausible explanation of this idea is that voters are generally optimistic about their opportunities to move up the income scale, although this is not something that seems congruent with most public opinion survey results. An alternative is that there is a public interest in encouraging entrepreneurs to earn high incomes by generating economic activity, thus creating a dynamic positive externality for all. This may be particularly acute in the relatively low income Baltic states. In addition, it may be an attempt to limit tax evasion, in recognition of the greater ease with which high income earners would evade, or even avoid, tax. This may be accentuated partly by the small size of the Baltic states, and also by their relative lack of capacity in tax collection, being the only New EU Members to have emerged from the USSR itself. Lastly, we should not ignore the influence of the special interest of high-income individuals. These form small enough groups in the Baltic states to be able to lobby governments effectively against any increases in their tax rates.

In contrast, the country with the most progressive income tax rates, and the largest range in its tax rates on non-exempt income, is Slovenia. This is also a small country, although within the size range of the Baltic states; hence, size does not appear to have been a crucial factor easing tax evasion and avoidance here. This suggests that neighbors may also be important here; Slovenia borders relatively high tax states, such as Croatia and Italy, whereas the Baltic states neighbor Russia, with its flat 13 percent income tax rate. However, we might also expect the arguments about the Baltic states to apply in reverse to Slovenia. Slovenia has, perhaps, a more stable social structure than the Baltic states, Slovenians may be more realistic about their chances to change their position in society, Slovenians may expect less positive externalities from entrepreneurs (possibly due to greater integration with other EU states), and may have more confidence in the tax authority's ability to impose high tax rates on them. Lastly there may be a more disperse group of high income earners in Slovenia and political institutions may be more adept at resisting interest group pressure.

Corporate income tax

It is well known that the role of corporate income tax, or profit tax, in the tax system has been controversial, at least since the development of Musgravian public finance, and this controversy has been played out graphically in the New EU Member states. We may recall that orthodox public finance theory criticizes the profit tax as a cause of the double taxation of dividends. This, it is often argued, compounds the injustice of taxing investment from income that has already been taxed, resulting in a triple taxation of such funds, before they are even spent. Furthermore, economists argue that the fiction of taxation of a 'legal person' only serves to hide the true burden of the tax on real persons. As we have already seen, Latvia and Slovakia have prevented the double taxation of dividends by making dividends tax exempt. Estonia took another course, abolishing the corporate income tax from the beginning of 2000 and taxing only profits distributed abroad, while leaving domestic dividends taxed at the same rate as ordinary income. This has, however, brought Estonia into conflict with the European Commission, since it implies prejudicial tax treatment of dividends paid to non-Estonian versus Estonian corporate shareholders.

Arguments in favor of taxation of corporations can be divided into the income measurement dilemma and the practical. The income measurement dilemma is that the retained profits of a corporation may give real benefit to its owners even if never distributed and the shares are never sold. Shareholders gain financial security and economic and social power through the increased strength of their company. Hence the only way to tax this real benefit would be at the corporate level. The practical argument is that, even in advanced EU members, Finance Ministries believe that without the corporate income tax the scope for avoidance and evasion of personal income tax and social security payments would be significantly higher, since the incentive for corporations to show employment expenses would vanish. With corporations no longer required to declare their expenditures, evasion would become significantly tougher for the authorities to prevent, possibly leading to a weakening of the personal income tax and social security system. In particular, if persons who incorporated themselves (e.g. doctors and lawyers) faced no profit tax, they would find it much easier to hide personal income from the tax authorities. Hence, we observe continued corporate income tax rates of up to 31 percent in the Czech Republic. Note that even at that rate the incentive to hide employment expenditure still exists; it is more financially advantageous to pay 31 percent on retained earnings than even the lowest 15 percent income tax rate on wages, due to the 35 percent social security tax on wage income in that country. This pattern is repeated everywhere so profit tax is only a partial offset to the cost of honestly declaring wages.

While the income measurement dilemma is of a more normative nature, it is potentially useful to ask whether the Estonian experiment in eliminating the corporate income tax for domestic investors has led to the damage to personal income tax collections predicted by the practical argument. While recent data on personal income tax revenue are not readily available for Estonia, the overall level appears to have held steady at about 8.5 percent of GDP from 1999 to 2002, despite a dip of about a percentage in the initial two years of reform.[14]

We know that there is a third, more fundamental, argument in favor of taxes on profit, however. A truly uniform tax system must not discriminate against labor income. However, labor income can also be interpreted as a return on investment in human capital. Much of that investment may not be financial but an investment of effort, for example while undergoing schooling. Hence, to completely remove taxation of income from financial investments while retaining it on investments in human capital would create a bias. It would mean that persons would have an artificial incentive to pay more attention to studying the stock market than to studying more traditional subjects that create real productivity. From a truly orthodox economic perspective there is no reason to tax returns on an investment of saved financial resources any differently from an equivalent return on an investment of leisure time.

The forgoing looks only at static welfare considerations, however. States have often felt that there are dynamic benefits from encouraging economic agents to shift to profit seeking activities rather than labor. An individual is likely to be more dynamic and flexible when involved directly in profit seeking activities than when working for labor income. This may spill over to faster growth in GDP for the state as a whole. In addition, since individuals are risk averse, while the state can afford to be risk neutral with regard to a particular investment, there may be good reasons to expect under-investment in more risky activities by individuals. The state can reduce taxation of profit to increase efficiency in both cases. How much optimal profit tax would then differ from tax on labor income would then vary from country to country depending on the types of profit seeking activities likely to be encouraged, the varieties of labor likely to be discouraged and their relative dynamism in the economy in question. Generally, we might expect that the optimal differentiation between labor income tax and profit tax would be negatively correlated with the flexibility of the labor market and institutional hindrances to business in the economy. However, flexibility of the labor market also improves the business conditions for entrepreneurs and thus the overall effect of this factor might be relatively weak.

Comparing the ratio of disposable income from profit and from wages across the New Member states we find labor taxed relatively the most in Poland, Latvia and Hungary.[15] If we include social contributions and look at the ratios of disposable income, the greatest disincentive to sell labor is in Poland, Slovakia and Hungary (see Table 2.5). The countries with the most even-handed treatment of dividends and labor income are the Czech Republic and Estonia. We may compare these data with the data from the Heritage Foundation on which countries have the greatest economic freedom, and thus the best conditions for entrepreneurial dynamism.[16] The Heritage Foundation data show starkly that Estonia is much more economically free than the other New Member states. Hence it is surprising that Estonia is one of the countries with the least tax incentive to switch from labor to profit seeking. This appearance may be illusory, however, since in Estonia investors may defer taxation by retaining earnings within the company, providing a greater tax bias against labor than is apparent from the tax rates alone. Conversely, Slovenia and Poland are estimated to be the countries with the least favorable business conditions. Hence it is surprising to see that Poland has the largest tax incentive to switch towards entrepreneurship. Slovenia has a middle-sized tax incentive against labor, again contradicting the expectation that such incentives are less useful in countries with less supportive business environments. Overall, then, the pattern is mixed with good reason to suppose that business lobbying that is not in step with the public interest drives some countries' reductions in profit tax.

There is also a question of international competition to lower corporate

Table 2.5 Disposable income of shareholders versus wage earners from equal total factor earnings in selected New Members

Country	Without social security	With social security
Czech Republic	0.75–0.93	1.15–1.44
Estonia	1.00	1.35
Hungary	0.82–1.10	1.19–1.58
Latvia	1.13	1.54
Lithuania	1.07 (0.85)	1.46 (1.15)
Poland	0.85–1.15	1.24–1.67
Slovakia	1.00	1.55–1.58
Slovenia	0.63–1.05	0.94–1.57

Source: See source for Table 2.4. Own calculations.

taxation. Some countries may be tempted to attract foreign investment by imposing a relatively low rate of tax on profit.[17] It is often argued that foreign direct investment has positive dynamic externalities for the economy by accelerating the introduction of more efficient management. Profits repatriated by foreign investors in Estonia are subject to a 26 percent tax, thus this small Baltic state cannot be accused of using the repeal of the profit tax to compete aggressively for foreign investment. This criticism could more logically be aimed at Latvia, Lithuania and Hungary, all of which have taxed profits at less than 20 percent for some time. There is some evidence that these low tax rates are having knock-on effects throughout the region. In 2004, there have been dramatic reductions in the profit tax rates in Poland and Slovakia, combined with a further easing in Latvia and Hungary. Whether these rates are moving below what would be optimal is difficult to say definitively, given the previous arguments justifying the presence itself of a corporate tax. The most extreme case is Poland, where profit seekers keep a 67 percent larger proportion of their earnings than is kept by top-income-tax-bracket individuals dependent on wages.

Value Added Tax and excises

It is worthwhile recalling that value added taxes, like income taxes, were originally seen as a way to tax total GDP. Rather than tracing income, VAT uses the value added at each stage of production as the tax basis. Hence it is revealing to compare the success of VAT in raising revenue with that of the income tax. This comparison is less precise in countries with multiple income tax rates. Moreover, the exemptions and deductions of the income tax and the exemptions of the VAT mean that the tax bases are not the same. However, from the orthodox economic perspective, all these differences are sources of inefficiency and not necessarily less pernicious than evasion of taxes. Hence it is still of interest to compare the efficacy of these two taxes in terms of revenue raised. Table 2.6 makes this comparison. To take the example of Lithuania, in 2000 its personal income tax and VAT each raised 7.6 percent of GDP despite the fact that the basic income tax rate was 33 percent while the VAT rate was only 18 percent. Hence, the average efficacy of a percentage of VAT was almost double that of a percentage of income tax. Any deviation of either of those taxes from a comprehensive tax on GDP is a source of inefficiency according to economic theory, whether that deviation results from legal or illegal activity. So this very raw number provides a strong argument in favor of shifting the balance of taxation from the personal income tax towards the value added tax in that country. In Hungary, by contrast, a significantly higher rate of VAT did not result in proportionately higher revenue and hence was not as demonstrably more efficacious than its multiple-rate personal income tax.

Table 2.6 Rates of PIT and VAT compared with their revenue as a percentage of GDP in selected New Members in 2000

Country	PIT rates	PIT revenue	PIT efficacy	VAT rate	VAT revenue	VAT efficacy	VAT/PIT efficacy ratio
Czech Republic[a]	10.0–40.0	5.2	0.13–0.52	22.0	7.6	0.35	0.6–2.7
Latvia	25.0	6.0	0.24	18.0	7.8	0.43	1.8
Estonia	26.0	7.7	0.30	18.0	9.5	0.53	1.8
Hungary[a]	20.0–40.0	7.0	0.18–0.35	25.0	8.6	0.34	1.0–1.9
Lithuania	33.0 (15.0)	7.6	0.23 (0.51)	18.0	7.6	0.42	1.8 (0.8)
Poland[a]	21.0–40.0	5.5	0.14–0.26	22.0	8.0	0.36	1.4–2.6
Slovakia[a]	17.0–42.0	5.2	0.12–0.31	23.0	7.6	0.33	1.1–2.8
Slovenia[a]	17.0–50.0	6.4	0.13–0.38	20.0	15.4	0.77	2.0–5.9

Sources: Yakimova (2002); Mitra and Stern (2003); country chapters of the book.

Note
a 1999–2000 average.

Perhaps a more robust comparison is to compare the success of VAT across countries. Here we see that the VAT efficacy, which is equivalent to the ratio of the VAT tax base to GDP, ranged from 33 percent in Slovakia to 77 percent in Slovenia. Slovenia stands out as a success story here, and underlines the room for other New Member states to improve. But it is interesting to note that the other more advanced countries in the group, the Visegrad countries, do not do well and are superseded by the Baltic states. Hence we may ask, why does Estonia do so well at collecting VAT and why does Hungary do so badly? One drawback of this simple approach is that it ignores the underestimation of GDP that results from tax evasion. Hence the Baltic states may appear to have higher VAT efficacy than the Visegrad countries only because the latter have done a better job at measuring GDP.

Excise taxation is an area of some controversy as the New Member states integrate into the European Union. During the accession negotiations the European Commission felt that the low excise duties in many accession states threatened the taxes of existing member states and demanded increases. This was clearly going to be politically unpopular in the accession states. Their governments' dilemma was increased by the fact that excise taxes had proved to be the most easily evaded and hardest to implement. In countries that border Belarus or the countries of former Yugoslavia, the opportunity for smuggling cigarettes, alcohol and petrol was high. Hence New Member states negotiated transition periods of up to 10 years, during which they would gradually increase excise duties to EU norms, while trying to clamp down on smuggling and evasion. Such excises can increase the efficiency of the taxation system by taxing goods with relatively low price elasticities of demand and negative externalities. However, a jump in taxation that leads to expansion of evasion will only serve to weaken the taxation system, along with other social institutions.

Social security contributions

As is well known, governments have long decided that some benefits should be allocated to individuals based on their tax history. Certain benefits would be conditional on the individual having paid taxes over a minimum period, others would also vary according to the amount of taxes paid. Governments started using this approach with regard to pension benefits, and have gradually extended it to other areas. Hence, the government provided a type of collective insurance of individuals against the 'risk' of reaching old age and viewed this differently to other benefits. There was a distinction between welfare 'Beveridgean' payments to ensure the elderly a minimum standard of living and 'Bismarkian' pension benefits based on how much an individual had paid in during their working years. Hence taxes paid for social security became viewed differently to other taxes that had no effect on the individual's eligibility for benefits.

This system raises a number of interesting questions that it is worthwhile to recall here, because they have been answered in different ways by the New Member states. The first question might be what is the government's role in providing these benefits? If individual benefits depend on individual premiums, why can't the private insurance market efficiently serve this demand? One answer to this for risk-averse individuals is that collective provision allows for more comprehensive risk pooling. Private insurance will seek to discriminate among individuals based on their riskiness, and individuals themselves will self-select insurance pools based on their knowledge of their own riskiness. To avoid the uncertainty generated by lack of knowledge of their future risk level, individuals rationally decide to organize the insurance collectively without heed to individual characteristics that affect risk. The collective has no incentive to discriminate, which private insurance companies would have even if they were legally forbidden from doing so. Another argument in favor of the collective provision of pensions is that it gives a benefit to middle-class voters, hence strengthening support for collective benefits that would otherwise go only to the poor. This may increase social welfare due to the diminishing marginal utility of income.

While the forgoing arguments seem to continue to garner support as a basis for social security systems, there is another that appears less widely respected, particularly in several of the New Member states. Individuals saving for their retirement are initially considering investments of 30 years or longer. This is a long enough period to see through several cycles of financial markets but not necessarily all. In the financial history of the twentieth century there have been 30-year periods during which stock market indices were lower at the end than at the beginning. Individual investors face even more risk in practice since their investment portfolios are unlikely to mirror stock market indices precisely. Hence, even over these relatively long periods, considerable financial risk remains for an individual. Collective provision of social security is a way to remove this risk.

However, in a number of New Member states the financial risk has been returned to the individual through implementation of the 'three pillar' pension system. This leaves in place a reduced basic pension based on pay-as-you-go contributions of current workers, but diverts some social security taxes to investment in individual accounts with returns dependent on the success of the fund the taxpayer decides to invest in. The third pillar then consists of favorable tax treatment of any additional non-mandatory investments the individual makes to these funds. The states that have implemented the three-pillar pension system include Hungary, Poland and the Baltic states (Lithuania significantly later and more cautiously than the other two), and most recently, Slovakia. Interestingly, the Czech Republic and Slovenia have resisted such moves, perhaps demonstrating the greater credulity of the populations of these more capitalism savvy nations to the vagaries of financial markets.

Another element of the experience of several New EU Member states has been the expansion of the public insurance principle to other benefits. It is perhaps natural that workers' accident compensation is related to their income at work and a similar case can be made for maternity leave and disability benefits. The level of social contributions tax rates depends on the generosity of the benefits relative to average wages and the dependency ratio of benefit recipients to taxpayers. It ranges from 26 percent of the total cost of employment in Latvia to 38 percent in Hungary. The high rate of social security tax in Hungary is partly governed by its low labor force participation rate, less than 60 percent until 2000 compared with over three quarters in Latvia. Social contributions are a larger proportion of the total cost of employment than the personal income tax in all New Member states, e.g. 38 percent versus a maximum of 24 percent, respectively, in Hungary. Thus, it is often social contributions that are primarily blamed for creating incentives for businesses to hide wage payments. Continuing the Hungarian example, it is preferable to pay 16 percent profit tax on a sum than show it as expenditure on employment and pay a minimum of 50 percent of it in tax, consisting of 38 percent social contributions and a minimum of 12 percent personal income tax.

As mentioned above, many analysts have traditionally not considered social contributions as taxes because they provide a direct benefit to the individual payer. However, we must recognize that social contributions are still involuntary levies collected by the state, and that many of their benefits may not be of practical use. In traditional pay-as-you-go pension systems, the contributions of workers made no difference to their benefits at the margin unless they were in their last ten years of employment. In the three pillar systems that have swept the region, many contributors might well heavily discount their expected returns based on the greater financial risk. Higher income individuals, especially, are likely to find state pension schemes, particularly in the relatively poor New Member states, inadequate and prefer private insurance for disability, unemployment and pensions. All individuals in these relatively unstable societies are likely to assign low probabilities to welfare benefits being available for them when needed. Hence, for a successful entrepreneur in the New Member states, who is likely to be young and have high income, social contributions payments may represent a true tax in the sense that they provide little expected benefit.

Notes

1 The authors thank R. Puglisi for careful reading and suggestions in a number of areas.
2 The PPP per capita income is evaluated at about US$9350 for CSB countries, $3850 for CIS countries, and $26,200 for high-income OECD countries. A wider picture about the decline of government size in transition economies may be found in Gupta *et al.* (2001).

3 Burgess and Stern (1993) show a similar estimated relationship for the ratio of taxes to GDP. Here also total explained variability is quite low ($R^2 = 0.03$); the constant term value is high; the coefficient associated with (log of) pro-capita income is higher than one and statistically significant at 5 percent. However this means that the countries' scatter plot is very dispersed, that public goods are superior goods, but the percentage average (not marginal) increase of expenditures or taxes/GDP ratio is less than for per-capita income, within any observed range. Also Gupta *et al.* (2001) give about the same results, for 148 countries, considering the period 1970–98.

4 The exception is Slovenia, whose per capita income reaches a value (>US$6000 per year) commonly ascribed to high-income countries.

5 The average value of the structural reform index for New Members is about 50 percent over the corresponding average of the other post-communist European and ex-USSR states. Corruption ranking performs more than twice better on average with respect to the same sample of other countries, the only worse exception being Latvia and Lithuania (in fact ex-USSR republics), but not Estonia.

6 A large number of such analyses were performed during the last 30 years. The emerging relationship between the level of taxes and public spending and GDP's rate of growth, all in all was found weak and unstable. It turned out that crucial control variables are the stage of a single country's development (if in the catching up phase or not) and the share of old people in the total population.

7 This holds true for labor market models, and for both exogenous and endogenous growth models.

8 See later in this chapter for a discussion concerning the alternative of public PAYG or of partially private funding pension schemes.

9 A similar suggestion might be found also in Burgess and Stern (1993) both for developing and transition countries.

10 Here we may anticipate that labor income generally is more heavily taxed (including social contributions) than saving vehicles. This is also a specific case of equity-efficiency trade-off.

11 This task should be accomplished through a large recourse to presumptive and minimum taxes (Tanzi 1994).

12 Notice however that VAT outperforms PIT as 'productive' efficiency in almost all New Members.

13 This argument is based on the idea that it is the state that guarantees the institutions of private property that give rise to the current distribution of income.

14 See Chandler *et al.* (2002) and Research Center of the Institute for Privatization and Management (2003).

15 These comparisons are based on the top rates of labor income taxation.

16 Miles *et al.* (2004).

17 This issue is discussed at length elsewhere in this book.

References

Abed, G. T. and Davoodi, H. R. (2000) 'Corruption, structural reforms, and economic performance in the transition economies', IMF Working Paper 132, Washington, DC: IMF.

Agell, J., Lindh, T. and Ohlsson, H. (1997) 'Growth and the public sector: a critical review essay', *European Journal of Political Economy*, 3, 33–52.

Aghion, P. and Commander, S. (1999) 'On the dynamics of inequality', *Economics of transition*, 7: 2, 275–98.

Atkinson, A. B. (1999) *The Economic Consequences of Rolling Back the Welfare State*, Cambridge, MA: The MIT Press.

Begg, D. K. H. and Wyplosz, C. (1999) 'How big a government? Transition economy forecast based on OECD history', paper presented at the fifth Dubrovnik Conference on transition economies, Dubrovnik, June.

Bernardi, L. (2004) 'Rationale and open issues of more radical reforms', in Bernardi, L. and Profeta, P. (eds) *Tax Systems and Tax Reforms in Europe*, London: Routledge.

Bernardi, L. and Majocchi, A. (1994) 'North Africa's taxes and Europe: present status and main issues', in Bernardi, L. and Owens, J. (eds) *Tax Systems in North Africa and European Countries*, Deventer & Boston: Kluwer.

Bernardi, L. and Owens, J. (eds) (1994) *Tax Systems in North Africa and European Countries*, Deventer & Boston: Kluwer.

Bernardi, L. and Profeta, P. (eds) (2004) *Tax Systems and Tax Reforms in Europe*, London: Routledge.

Buiter, W. H. (1997) 'Aspects of fiscal performance in some transition economies: explaining the differences', IMF Working Paper 97/31, Washington, DC: IMF.

Burgess, R. and Stern, N. (1993) 'Taxation and development', *Journal of Economic Literature*, 2, 762–830.

Chandler, M., Jekaterina, R. and Vetlov, I. (2002) 'Growth: experience of and prospects for the Baltic economies', Working Paper, July. http://www.cerge-ei.cz/pdf/gdn/grp_final_baltics.pdf.

Čok, M. (2003) *Average and Marginal Tax Rates in Slovenia*, Slovenia: Economics Kardeljeva, Ljubljana.

Easson, A. (1998) 'Tax competition heats up in Central Europe', *Bulletin of International Bureau of Fiscal Documentation*, May, 192–97.

Ernst and Young and the Centre for Economic Research (ZEW) (2003) *Company Taxation in the New EU Member States*, Mannheim.

EU Commission (2000) *Structure of Tax Systems in Estonia, Poland, Hungary, the Czech Republic and Slovenia*, Brussels: EU Commission.

Eurostat (2000) *Structures of the Taxation Systems in the European Union, 1970–1997*, Brussels: EU Commission.

Funke, M. and Strulik, H. (2003) 'Taxation, growth and welfare: dynamic effects of Estonia's 2000 income tax act', Discussion Paper 10, Helsinki: Bank of Finland, Institute for Economies in Transition.

Gupta, S., Leruth, L., de Mello, L. and Chakravarti, S. (2001) 'Transition economies: how appropriate is the size and scope of government?', IMF Working Paper 55, Washington, DC: IMF.

Heller, P. S. and Keller, S. (2001) 'Social sector reform in transition countries', IMF Working Paper 35, Washington, DC: IMF.

Kopits, G. (1992) 'Social security', in Tanzi, V. (ed.) *Fiscal Policies in Economies of Transition*, Washington, DC: IMF.

KPMG (2003) 'A new Slovak social security system to be introduced', http://www.kpmg.sk/dbfetch/52616e646f6d4956a7c80a06692e5926aac82a8e2dd6df71/newsflash_november_03_en.pdf%22.

Martner, R. and Tromben, V. (2004) 'Tax reforms and fiscal stabilization in Latin American countries', United Nations, CEPAL, Santiago de Chile, June.

Milanovic, B. (1999) *Income, Inequality and Poverty during the Transition from Planned to Market Economy*, Washington, DC: The World Bank.

Miles, M. A., Fuelner, E. Jr. and O'Grady, M. A. (2004) *2004 Index of Economic Freedom* (Heritage Foundation and *Wall Street Journal*). http://www.heritage. org/research/features/index/downloads.html.

Mitra, P. and Stern, N. (2003) 'Tax systems in transition', WB Working Paper 2947, Washington, DC: The World Bank.

MSI (2004) *Income Tax Changes in Slovakia*, March 2004. http://msi-network. com/content/technical_article_alixfrank_slovakia_tax.asp.

Musgrave, R. A. (1969) *Fiscal Systems*, New Haven and London: Yale University Press.

Olson, M. (1965) *The Logic of Collective Action*, Cambridge: Harvard University Press.

Research Center of the Institute for Privatization and Management (2003) 'Personal income tax reform in Belarus', P/9/03. http://www.ipm.by/pdf/PP903e.pdf.

Richards, J., Watson, G. and Brown, D. M. (1994) *The Case for Change: Reinventing the Welfare State*, Toronto: C.D. Howe Institute.

Tanzi, V. (ed.) (1993a) *Transition to Market. Studies in Fiscal Reform*, Washington, DC: IMF.

Tanzi, V. (1993b) 'Financial markets and public finance in the transformation process', in Tanzi, V. (ed.) *Transition to Market: Studies in Fiscal Reform*, Washington, DC: IMF.

Tanzi, V. (1994) 'Taxation in developing countries', in Bernardi, L. and Owens, J. (eds) *Tax Systems in North Africa and European Countries*, Deventer & Boston: Kluwer.

Tanzi, V. and Schucknecht, L. (1997) 'Reforming government: an overview of recent experiences', *European Journal of Political Economy*, 13, 395–417.

Tanzi, V. and Tsibouris, G. (2000) 'Fiscal reform over ten years of transition', IMF Working Paper 113, Washington, DC: IMF.

Wagner, A. (1883) *Finanzwissenshaft*, Leipzig: Winter.

Yakimova, I. (2002) 'Bulgaria', Working Paper. http://www.cerge-ei.cz/pdf/gdn/ grp_final_bulgaria.pdf.

3   The political economy of taxation and tax reforms

Paola Profeta[1]

3.1 Introduction

Political economy arguments are at the centre of the debate on the transition process from communist to market economies that took place in most EU New Members. They have been used to explain or justify many aspects of the transition, to characterize the different performances across transition countries, and to discuss the strategies of the economic reforms.

In this chapter, I will focus on the main political economy arguments related to the issue of taxation in New EU Members countries. I will analyze how political economy arguments can explain and justify many aspects of tax systems and tax reforms in New EU Members (as described in Chapters 1 and 2 of this book), how they can explain some differences across transition countries, and what is their role in shaping tax reforms.

From a tax policy perspective, new and more efficient instruments of taxation were introduced with the transition (for instance, VAT) while the major existing problems concern how to raise revenues, the definition of the role of government and the relation between levels of government, tax administration and taxation of small enterprises, a closer harmonization with EU tax systems. A general problem concerns the definition of a fiscal institution, including tax administration, which represents an endogenous outcome, since institutions are a product of the transition process. I will focus on these issues and provide a political economy perspective.

Political economy arguments are at the centre of both the positive and the normative sides of the analysis of the political economy of transition reforms. The normative side focuses on the political constraints faced by the reformers. There exist ex ante constraints related to the conditions for a reform to be feasible and accepted – and ex post ones, related to the conditions for a reform to be maintained and not reversed after its implementation and after the outcome is observed. The positive side focuses on the action of special interest rent seeking groups, which, depending on the economic, social and political initial conditions of reforms, have a different impact on the reform process. There is also a wide debate about the political economy desirability of big bang/shocking reforms *versus* gradualist reforms. I will analyze these issues in the context of tax reforms.

This line of analysis belongs to the *political economics* literature, a more general and fundamental field of economic research, based on the interplay between economic problems and their political determinants (see Persson and Tabellini 2000). The political economy of transition has been largely studied by Roland (2001, 2002). The political economy of taxation has been previously studied by Hettich and Winer (1999) and Profeta (2004). While many suggestions can be derived from studies of various authors, especially at the World Bank and the IMF, there is not a comprehensive analysis of the political economy of taxation focusing on New EU Members countries.

This chapter is organized as follows: first it examines issues on the political economy of tax systems in New Members countries. Second, it analyzes tax reforms in New Members countries, from both a positive and a normative side. This is followed by a conclusion.

3.2 Issues on the political economy of tax systems in New EU Members

This section starts with some information on the politics of the New EU Members analyzed in this book. Then, it addresses, from a political economy view, some of the main problems faced by these countries: how to raise revenues, to redefine the role of government and of different levels of government, to build a new fiscal institution, to administer taxes and to tax small enterprises.

Some facts

It is useful to start with some information on the political systems in the New EU Members. This section shows that these countries are characterized by a general political instability, measured at different levels.

All these countries have opted for a parliamentary regime, the main form of government in Western Europe. Roland (2002) shows that Hungary and Slovenia have been very stable, with an average time between elections respectively of 48 and 47 months, while this time has been 32 months in the Czech Republic, 36 in Estonia and 36.5 in Poland. Average government duration has, however, been low (18.2 in the Czech Republic, 12.9 in Estonia, 17.9 in Poland, 23.3 in Slovenia) with the exception of Hungary (48). Government duration between the two most recent elections has, in general, been longer (24 in Poland and Slovenia, 48 in Hungary) with the exception of the Czech Republic (12) and Estonia (12), reflecting political tensions or instability. The average number of parties in government ranges from 2.2 in Estonia to 2.7 in Hungary, 3 in Slovenia, 3.2 in the Czech Republic and 3.4 in Poland, with a high percentage of right-wing parties in government. There is a huge variation in the re-election of incumbents: 50 and 100 percent of re-elected governments respectively in the Czech Republic and Slovenia, while zero in the other three considered countries.

How to raise revenues

Pre-transition countries were characterized by three major sources of taxation: turnover taxes, enterprise taxes and payroll taxes. The taxation of resources and indirect subsidies were implicit in the state allocation of under-priced resources. During the transition, corporate income taxes fall, due to the loss of revenues from profits of publicly owned enterprises under the price liberalization, the diffusion of tax exemptions and tax arrears, and the use of harder budget constraints. This led to a decrease of the importance of income taxes, although personal income taxes increased, and a general decrease of tax revenue as percentage of GDP. At the same time, indirect taxes (VAT, sales, turnover taxes and excises) increased in their importance. As a general trend, the evolution of the share of tax revenue to GDP and the share of major taxes on GDP in transition countries appears to be U-shaped, reflecting both the loss of traditional profit, turnover and payroll tax revenues and the difficulties in tax administration (Mitra and Stern 2003).

The transition implies a movement from a system where the government decided first, before citizens had access to the resources of the economy, to one with a reduced role of the public sector, where the government needs to collect revenues before spending. This means that New EU Members countries need to build a fiscal system based on new and more efficient instruments of taxation, for instance by increasing the share of direct taxes, personal income taxes, with respect to the share of revenue from domestic indirect taxes. However, the way in which revenues can be raised represents a major problem. This is an issue where political factors interplay with economics arguments to design the current status of the fiscal systems. To raise revenues, i.e. to collect taxes, a political will is necessary, which is based on the support of citizens as voters (Burgess and Stern 1993). However, to agree on policy decisions aimed at changing the composition of revenues, people need to believe and trust the efficacy and the fairness of the system. In absence of this belief, people may choose not to support the policy, or not to pay. Thus, an adequate tax administration is necessary to guarantee an efficient extraction of resources. How the political system affects the ability to extract resources is a crucial issue. These countries risk being stuck between the need of increasing revenues, the weakness of tax administration and the political difficulties of changing the status of tax policy in the absence of public positive beliefs in the system.

The role of government

A related issue concerns the new role of government in New EU Members countries.

Data from Gupta *et al.* (2001) show that, on average, government spending as a percentage of GDP in New EU Members countries has declined since the early 1990s. As a consequence, these governments are smaller than those in Western European countries (Tanzi and Schuknecht 1997). However, this reduction in government spending does not necessarily imply a reduction of the role of government, but rather represents the answer of the government to its limited revenue-raising capacity and a shift of resources across different uses and functions. As explained before, in the new system, the government needs to collect revenues before spending. This revenue constraint is affected by the economic development of the country and the level of its tax administration. After being taken, the decisions over spending plans are difficult to change, especially if they concern expenditures involving long-term commitment and a large number of beneficiaries (such as pensions, health, public unemployment). Since New Members countries have, in some cases, economic conditions (per capita income and economic structure) closer to developing countries than to industrial countries (see Tanzi and Tsibouris 2000), we expect that in these countries taxes cannot stay as high as their current levels and they will start to fall. As a consequence, governments need to be realistic when committing to expenditure programs, by reducing their programmed levels accordingly. However, Gupta *et al.* (2001) find that this reduction of government spending has not been sufficient in many New EU Members countries, where the level of government spending still remains quite high, owing to rising indebtedness, a heavy regulatory burden and the prevalence of non-cash transactions. At the same time, this reduction of government spending has not been appropriate: governments in many New EU Members have now to provide services, such as kindergartens, health care centres and housing, that were previously the responsibility of the state-owned enterprises, and they have to provide subsidies to meet social needs for groups negatively affected by economic reforms. As a consequence, an appropriate definition of the role of the new governments is still needed. In this respect, political economy determinants should be taken into account (Alesina and Perotti 1995): political economy constraints to reform, vested interests, preferences of regional groups, a strong tax administration and control are all elements that may affect the size and scope of governments.

Moreover, the role of government depends on the relations between the executive and the legislative branches of government. The political process that generates the legislature and creates the executive branch of government has an impact on this outcome. It is essential that the executive and the legislative branches have close views and that they are working under common, clear and well-defined rules, strategies and objectives, to contrast possible pressures by powerful political groups or figures in the legislative or the executive branch, aimed at reducing the tax liabilities of specific taxpayers or protecting tax arrears.

These difficulties may explain why some governments are more effective than others in the transition process. According to the *EBRD Transition Report 1998* among our countries, central and eastern European countries, such as Hungary, Poland, the Czech Republic and Slovenia, have been more successful in the transition, followed by Estonia and the Baltics.

The success of the transition process in the fiscal area also depends on both the allocation of fiscal responsibilities among the different levels of government and on the creation of well-working fiscal institutions. Both these issues have a political economy component, as I will show in the next two sections.

Levels of government

The definition of the role of government in fiscal issues implies the definition of the fiscal responsibilities of the subnational and national governments. This has to be done through clear and precise rules. In the absence of these rules, political interests can intervene, on top of economic considerations. The assignment of revenue is related to the assignment of expenditures: apart from the transfers they receive from the central government, subnational governments need adequate resources to pay the expenditures under their responsibilities, and they have to be forced to respect their budgets. In New Members countries it is often the case that fiscal arrangements between national and subnational governments are vague and local governments can act without control.

During the transition, several expenditure responsibilities (education, health and social welfare) are assigned to subnational governments, but without a clear definition of the basis for expenditure and revenue assignments. Revenue assignments and taxing powers were often maintained at national levels, with an inadequate system of intergovernmental transfers. This has led to intergovernmental fiscal imbalances, low efficiency of public services, and has limited the potential benefits from decentralization. Moreover, this has left a large space for discretionary fiscal behavior, including bargaining among the different levels of government and between the budget entities and their suppliers (such as utility companies) at the subnational level.

The main challenge for the leading reform countries, such as the Czech Republic and Hungary, is the definition of government responsibilities at the local level, including details over revenue and expenditure assignments. In these countries the role of intermediate levels of government is now relatively clear, but the role of the local governments is still problematic, with problems of fragmented or inefficient service delivery. Local governments need greater accountability, to collect their own sources of revenue and decide with greater autonomy over them.

A second challenge is represented by establishing clear, transparent and stable rules for transfer systems, which would avoid the process of negotiation based on political interests.

Finally, local governments should be monitored and their borrowing should be limited. Information and the capacity of subnational governments in public expenditure and debt management are necessary.

Fiscal institutions and tax administration

Fiscal institutions are necessary to have a successful transition of the fiscal system.

In the pre-transition period, taxes were mainly collected on the basis of negotiations between the enterprises and the government. There were no precise rules, codified tax law, well-defined tax bases and tax rates. As there were no explicit taxes, most individuals had no direct contacts with the tax authorities and they did not even know how much they were actually paying.

The transition made it necessary radically to change the tax system. The elimination of the planned economies implied that the government could not directly control quantities and prices to be taxed, and had to rely on tax declarations, which were not always correct due to large tax evasion. The main sources of revenues, such as tax on state enterprises, disappeared, while the number of new potential taxpayers largely increased due to the birth of private sector activities. In addition, corruption and bribes increased.

All these changes called for a radical reform of the tax system (Tanzi and Tsibouris 2000). A totally new, transparent tax system was necessary and new fiscal institutions were required. These new fiscal institutions, such as the tax administration, were essential to allow a correct functioning of the new tax system. Radical reform means that not only do the new fiscal institutions have to introduce new instruments of taxation, a transparent fiscal system, and a well-working tax administration, but also that they have to correct attitudes, incentives and relations. In particular, the new fiscal institutions have to strengthen enforcement and at the same time develop the taxpayer education and improve compliance. This means that taxpayers have to be informed about the need to pay taxes, and to be assisted in paying them, through the simplification of procedures.

However, these institutions had numerous difficulties. They were created lacking financial resources, specialized skills and technical knowledge and with no clear definition of strategies and objectives under a defined legal system. Moreover, it has to be stressed that political economy issues played a twofold important role in this respect. In fact, on one side, political interference by powerful groups in politics and economics posed an additional constraint to the activities of the newborn fiscal institutions, especially for the tax administration. On the other side, these institutions were created arbitrarily, rather than through a structured political process, and thus, owing to their lack of authority, they were even more exposed to these political interferences.

Tax administration in transition countries is highly politicized. Widespread tax exemptions, deferrals and arrears indicate that the tax system is politicized, firms bargain with the state to obtain tax concessions and so on. As a result, tax compliance is low and tax avoidance is high. An interesting study by Schaffer and Turley (2000) measures the effective tax administration in transition economies, by calculating the ratio between effective and statutory tax rates for 25 transition countries. This ratio is calculated for three taxes paid by the firm: corporate income tax (CIT), value added tax (VAT) and social security tax (SST). Huge differences between effective and statutory tax rates indicate tax compliance and collection problems. The authors find that, due to the greater politicization of the tax system, the shortfalls in effective tax yields in transition economies (calculated on 1997 data) are larger than a benchmark for mature economies (the 1996 average of the EU-15 countries) where tax systems are well established, the administrative capacity is stronger and tax arrears are tolerated less frequently. However, the leading transition countries (Poland, Hungary, Slovenia, the Czech Republic and the Baltic states) have effective/statutory tax-rate ratios similar to the EU average. Focusing on the countries analyzed in this book, for VAT, the Czech Republic and Hungary have an effective/statutory tax ratio of 0.40, Poland of 0.46 and Estonia of 0.68, while the EU-15 mean is 0.45. For SST, Poland shows a value of 0.76 followed by Hungary with 0.80, Estonia with 0.83, the Czech Republic and Slovenia with 0.94, while the EU-15 mean is 0.88. Finally, for CIT, Slovenia shows a value of 0.15, Poland of 0.20, Estonia of 0.22, the Czech Republic of 0.23, Hungary of 0.26, while the EU-15 mean is 0.24. This result contrasts with the values obtained for other transition countries largely behind in the transition process, which show lower values of the ratio of effective/statutory rates. In fact, the authors find that progress in transition, measured by an EBRD transition indicator, is positively correlated with effective tax administration. The authors also find that countries with larger bribes have less effective tax administration, owing to a highly politicized tax administration. In transition economies, it is not uncommon for firms to pay bribes to government officials in return for tax concessions and various favors. Obviously, the amount of these payments does not appear in government fiscal accounts. Interestingly, the EBRD (1999) and the World Bank construct a measure of the extent to which firms pay bribes to government officials: the average bribe tax in our analyzed transition countries ranges from 2.5 in Poland, to 2.8 in Estonia, 3.4 in Slovenia, 3.5 in Hungary and 4.5 in the Czech Republic. Again, these leading transition countries perform better than the other transition countries.

As stressed by Mitra and Stern (2003), this politicization of the tax administration should be avoided. Political will plays an essential role in the administration of tax policy at two different levels: (i) to support the hardening budget constraints and (ii) as a commitment to simplify procedures and tax regimes and to create an attractive investment climate. However, this does not imply that tax administration should be used for political ends, such as enforcing tax discipline on large taxpayers.

Taxation of small enterprises

A crucial issue in tax systems of New EU Members countries is the treatment of small enterprises. In this specific field, we find many issues have already been discussed regarding the weakness of tax administration, and its political determinants.

Small enterprises are a key sector in promoting growth and employment in transition countries. Mitra and Stern (2003) find a positive correlation between the number of small firms and the level of development of the country. A major challenge for governments of New EU Members is to create an attractive and competitive investment climate, which would give incentives to the activities of restructured and new enterprises. This challenge requires a clear political strategy. This strategy includes reducing excessively high tax rates for small firms, simplifying regulatory procedures and tax administration for small firms and eliminating tax exemptions that benefit powerful special interests. All these measures would encourage compliance by small firms. A study by the EBRD (1999) finds that taxes and regulations are among the more important obstacles to the development of new enterprises in transition countries. Among the New EU Members, Poland and Hungary have less complex systems of tax on business. However, tax incentives for new enterprises are currently almost zero in all countries, because of harmonization with the EU systems.

3.3 Issues on the political economy of tax reforms in New EU Members countries

This section addresses general issues of the political economy of transition reforms, from a normative and a positive side.

The normative side: political constraints

The normative side focuses on the political constraints faced by the reformers.

Following Roland (2002), these political constraints can be of two types: (i) feasibility constraints, also called ex ante political constraints, that can block decision-making and prevent reforms from being accepted, and (ii) ex post political constraints, that can reverse a reform after its implementation. These two types of constraints are not the same in the presence of uncertainty and reversal costs. In reforming transition countries, aggregate (concerning the economic effects of reform programs) and individual (concerning the identity of the winners and losers of the reforms) uncertainty and reversal costs play a crucial role. The final output of the transition process is uncertain and the political constraints are different if this outcome will be a positive result, or at least an improvement with respect to the status quo, or if it will be a negative result, since in the latter people may want to reverse a reform. Uncertainty may imply that a majority will oppose a reform even though ex post it could have benefitted from the reforms (see Fernandez and Rodrik 1991). Reversal costs make it more difficult to start a reform. A sequence of politically feasible reforms is more difficult in the presence of uncertainty. In this case, gradualist reform packages have higher ex ante feasibility and higher ex post irreversibility of enacted reform than big-bang strategies, which involve high reversal costs (Dewatripont and Roland 1995). In fact, countries such as the ones analyzed in this book, which have followed a gradual reform process, by starting transition early, growing and then facing the prospect of entry into the European Union, have been more successful in the transition process.

To relax the ex ante political constraints and start a reform under the status quo, it is necessary either to design a reform, which compensates the losers, and credibly commit to this design, or to make only a partial reform. Focusing on tax reforms, the design of a reform package, which includes compensating transfers, seems quite difficult. Compensation by redistributive transfers would be feasible only if distortionary costs of collecting revenues were not very high and enforcement of tax collection were guaranteed, both conditions being quite far from the picture of the tax systems in New EU Members countries described in section 3.2. Such kinds of compensations also need the commitment of decision makers, whereas it is unlikely in these countries that the coalition in power today could commit to continuation of these policies by future coalitions. These difficulties may explain why partial reforms are more easily implemented, although they have the risk of creating rents for given groups that will be threatened by further reforms (see the following subsection), and thus create opposition to further reforms. The sequence of reforms is also important, since more popular reforms at the beginning may build support for further, initially less popular, reforms.

Reforms supported by broader coalitions are more likely to be ex ante politically feasible. These reforms are also more likely to be ex post politically feasible, since if they are accepted by broader coalitions, they will be reversed with more difficulty. However, there may exist a trade-off between political constraints and graduality of reforms: if ex ante political constraints are less important, a less gradual reform may ensure more irreversibility. Again, starting with more popular reforms is preferred, to avoid support for reform reversal.

Roland (2001) argues that the political constraints to reform have been less strong in Central Europe than in other transition countries, such as the former Soviet Union. He argues that geopolitical factors play an important role: transition represents an opportunity for many countries, including the ones analyzed in this book, to shift from being a satellite country of the Soviet empire to being anchored to the European Union, adopting its political and economic system. People do not see this event as a traumatic experience, as for instance in Russia, but rather as a liberation. Governments such as the Czech Republic's, Hungarian and Polish entered a 'transition tournament', trying to show they were the most advanced transition country, in order to attract investments. This created favorable political support for reforms, especially in the field of taxation, which are essential for the development of foreign investments and new enterprises.

The positive side: the role of interest groups

In New EU Members, politically powerful special interest groups and rent seeking play an important role in tax reforms (Roland 2002; Burgess and Stern 1993). The support of powerful lobbies may be essential to implement specific reforms, which would never be approved by the majority of people. In particular, owners of privatized enterprises, who represent a minority and are thus not likely to be pivotal in elections, may have incentives to organize as a lobby and exert their economic and political power to obtain tax advantages for their firms, as happened in many cases (see section 3.2).

New rich individuals benefit from many tax advantages and tax exemptions. Corruption is strictly related to the action of these groups.

It can be noticed that the action of powerful social networks, such as the Catholic Church and the Solidarity Trade Union in Poland, have been important in countering the Communist Party and in creating social support for the transition. In other countries, where these social networks did not exist, oligarchs and insiders emerged as a more powerful political and economic force.

The question of rent seeking is also related to the distribution of wealth and power. The transition process increased inequality with political and economic consequences. The increase in inequality affected the political decision-making through different political channels, which go beyond the median voter theory, including the relative role of electoral politics and special interest politics, and the policy and political coalition formation process. A vicious circle emerges when a few rich individuals are politically powerful: they can influence reforms in their favor, which in turn creates persistence for their economic and political power.

3.4 Conclusions

New EU Members are experiencing fundamental changes. Tax systems and tax reforms represent one of the major challenges that these countries have to face. In these countries, politics and economics strictly interact in all sectors of the society, including taxation. Many problematic issues of taxation and tax reforms in transition countries are related to political determinants, such as the definition of the role of government and the relation between levels of government, the definition of a fiscal institution, including tax administration and taxation of enterprises. In particular, tax policy improvements have been substantial, while tax administration remains weak and fragmented, hence representing a crucial constraint to revenue collection and to the general working of the tax system. Political economy factors are behind this lack of efficacy of the tax administration.

Political constraints are fundamental both to start and implement tax reforms (ex ante political constraints) and to maintain such reforms (ex post political constraint). Majority voting models do not capture the essential elements of the political process to determine tax reforms in these countries, such as the action of the rent seeking interest groups and of the economically and politically powerful lobbies that emerged from the transition process. A natural extension of this chapter would be to compare more appropriate political economy models to analyze specific economic reforms in transition versus developed countries. I would expect that lobbying models perform better in the case of transition countries than the more common median voter models, especially in sectors such as taxation, characterized by a strong influence of powerful interest groups.

Note

1 Department of Public Economics, University of Pavia, Italy. E-mail: paola.profeta@unipv.it.

References

Alam, A. and Sundberg, M. (2002) *A Decade of Fiscal Transition*, Washington, DC: The World Bank.

Alesina, A. and Perotti, R. (1995) 'Political economy of budget deficits', Staff Papers, IMF, 42: 1–31, Washington, DC: IMF.

Burgess, R. and Stern, N. (1993) 'Taxation and development', *Journal of Economic Literature*, 31, 762–830.

Dewatripont, M. and Roland, G. (1995) 'The design of reform packages under uncertainty', *American Economic Review*, 85, 1207–23.

European Bank for Reconstruction and Development (1999) *Transition Report 1998*, London: EBRD.

Fernandez, R. and Rodrik, D. (1991) 'Resistance of reforms: status quo bias in the presence of individual-specific uncertainty', *American Economic Review*, 81, 1146–55.

Gupta, S., Leruth, L., de Mello, L. and Chakravarti, S. (2001) 'Transition economies: how appropriate is the size and scope of government?', IMF Working Paper, 55, Washington, DC: IMF.

Hettich, W. and Winer, S. (1999) *Democratic Choice and Taxation*, Cambridge: Cambridge University Press.

Mitra, P. and Stern, N. (2003) 'Tax systems in transition', WB Working Paper 2947, Washington, DC: The World Bank.

Persson, T. and Tabellini, G. (2000) *Political Economics. Explaining Economic Policy*, Cambridge, MA: MIT Press.

Profeta, P. (2004) 'Public finance and political economics in tax design and reforms', in Bernardi, L. and Profeta, P. (eds) *Tax Systems and Tax Reforms in Europe*, London: Routledge.

Roland, G. (2001) 'Ten years after . . . transition and economics', IMF Staff Papers, 48 Special Issue: 29–52, Washington, DC: IMF.

Roland, G. (2002) 'The political economy of transition', *Journal of Economic Perspectives*, 16: 29–50.

Schaffer, M. and Turley, G. (2000) 'Effective versus statutory taxation: measuring effective tax administration in transition economies', Working Paper 347 William Davidson Institute at University of Michigan.

Tanzi, V. and Schuknect, L. (1997) 'Reconsidering the fiscal role of government: the international perspective', *American Economic Review, Papers and Proceedings*, 87, 164–8.

Tanzi, V. and Tsibouris, G. (2000) 'Fiscal reform over ten years of transition', IMF Working Paper 113, Washington, DC: IMF.

4 Fiscal policy in the accession countries

Fedele de Novellis and Salvatore Parlato

4.1 Introduction, contents and main conclusions

The analysis of the future framework that will prevail in an enlarged Europe must encompass several aspects concerning the macroeconomic and public finance characteristics of the accession countries, their first best strategy in managing the transition towards the Union, and the weak points that emerge in the design of fiscal rules governing the EU 12 zone. Only by taking account of these elements is it possible to discuss and propose some guidelines for the design of new rules that fit the needs of a very heterogeneous and decentralized group of countries.

Even though the accession countries do not represent a homogeneous group, it is still possible to remark on some aspects of their macroeconomic structure. They are generally small and open economies, so that most of the shortcomings of financial and market liberalization apply to these countries, i.e. a critical exposure to financial and currency crises. With respect to this point, an optimal policy should avoid, at first glance, a prolonged transition time before the adoption of the euro. With respect to macroeconomic figures, the New Members countries show, and will show in the future, GDP growth and inflation rates higher (and more volatile in the past years) than those experienced in the early EU countries. This will happen both for catching-up and Balassa effects. Giving the hypothesis of a single monetary policy, a corollary to the previous assumption is that accession countries will benefit from low real interest rates. A non-secondary aspect in defining a fiscal rule concerns the public finance of these states, since they are generally low debt, high deficit and high capital expenditures countries.

All these elements must be taken into account in the design of the optimal fiscal rule governing both the transition and the steady state phases of an enlarged Europe. Given the excessive output volatility shown in the past, fiscal rules based on output gap measures could be unfeasible or too weak as constraints in the short run, even if appropriate in the steady state hypothesis, when output volatility could be removed in the calculation of output gaps. Furthermore, rules based on debt sustainability would not have an effective binding effect during the transition, since almost all countries will enter the EU with a very low starting debt-to-GDP ratio.

Therefore, the trade-off between a transition-focused and steady-state-focused rule is evident. The softer the budget constraints in the transition, the higher the risk of weak sustainability in the long run. Then the fiscal rule should be coherent with the general macroeconomic strategy that will be adopted to manage the enlargement. If the enlargement is conducted with a strategy of long transition, then fiscal rules must be soft constraining to avoid financial turbulence to the accession countries, i.e. fiscal rules based on the debt concept should prevail.

Conversely, a no-transition strategy would not necessitate, by the definition of rules that will soften the transitional period. Therefore, nominal ceilings to the deficit-to-GDP ratio could be maintained as binding constraints for national fiscal policies, and cyclically adjusted measures moderately used to address the decisions of the (enlarged) European Commission in its judgements with respect to the rule. In short, a no-transition hypothesis should be accompanied by the adoption of the actual Stability and Growth Pact (SGP). Therefore, the question is whether the SGP is a good fiscal rule for the EU 12 countries or it requires a substantial revisiting.

The implementation of the SGP started in a favorable situation of high growth with the belief that all divergence phenomena should have been removed in a few years, without generating a significant role for the asymmetric effects of SGP during the transition. Problems started with the economic slowdown of late 2000. The need for reforming the SGP became increasingly obvious in the course of 2002, when some (the most important) countries experienced a pro-cyclical policy mix due to extremely simple and homogeneous rules for the European Union, which is instead still heterogeneous and characterized by persistent inflation differentials (Creel and Le Cacheux 2003; De Novellis and Parlato 2004). The violation of the deficit ceiling of 3 percent on GDP by half of all EU countries expected for 2004 (European Commission 2004) has made the debate on the rewriting of the pact deferrable no longer. Furthermore, the persistence of low GDP growth in Europe has renewed the hard criticism about the consistency of the SGP with policies aimed to stimulate growth. Then the choice of a fiscal rule for accession countries passes through the reform of the SGP, since the latter could not be used in its actual form as suggested above. The paradox relies on the fact that, although the SGP could be shown to be an optimal fiscal rule, it could not necessarily work in the EU 15 (or 25) group since the EU does not converge spontaneously in the medium term towards an (optimal) economic union. To reach a solution for the design of a fiscal rule in an enlarged Europe, it is necessary jointly to treat the problems that characterize the EU 15 and the accession countries. The optimal fiscal rule, on one hand, should be able to ensure more flexibility to the EU 15 countries, given the existing inflation differentials, and to free resources to finance capital public expenditures, in order to promote growth both in EU 15 and in New Members countries; on the other hand, it should be able to impose fiscal severity and ensure fiscal sustainability of each member state and of the enlarged area as a whole, once it is established that a non-transitional period is required for the accession countries to join the euro.

Posed in these terms, the proposal that arises implies an internal revisiting of SGP, by adopting a multiple targeting criteria in the spirit of Maastricht accession criteria. Specifically, the rule of 3 percent should still be maintained but weighted by the level of debt-to-GDP ratio and, where available, by the cyclical adjusted primary balance. Moreover the new SGP should be addressed towards a golden rule conditional on debt-to-GDP ratio, in order to promote public investments without risking the fiscal sustainability in the long run. The rationale underlying this setting would resemble that used in the conduction of monetary policy by the ECB. As the European Central Bank (ECB) uses two pillars in conducting monetary policy in EU 12 – one simple and easily accountable (the 2 percent limit of inflation rate), the other not defined but considered (money growth) – the 'enlarged' European Commission could adopt a similar strategy, by declaring the 'targets' in terms of deficit and the debt-to-GDP ratio, but not revealing *ex ante* in which way it evaluates the sustainability of national public finances. Given a deficit and a debt-to-GDP ratio, sustainability would depend on judgements about GDP growth, the composition of revenues and expenditures, the launch of structural reforms, and so forth.

If the ECB has been successful in conducting monetary policy without curbing inflation under 2 percent, the European Commission in the same way could ensure fiscal stability, allowing some countries to breach the 3 percent limit. Of course, this proposal would involve some procedural adjustment in order to make the Commission more accountable and more powerful in its role, but this would seem to be an unavoidable price to grant stability, flexibility and co-ordination to fiscal policy in an enlarged Europe.

4.2 Growth and inflation in the accession countries

From the beginning of the 1990s, the accession countries shared a common economic development. With the start of the transition period they experienced a deep recession, followed by a period of rapid growth starting from the middle of the past decade. At the end of the 1990s they also suffered because of the Russian crisis. More marked were the negative impacts on Baltic countries, which however recovered rapidly in the following two-year period. Even though, at the beginning of the new decade, the phase of deceleration of the international cycle weakened the performance of these countries, starting from 2003 they have already shown a cyclical recovery, in spite of the economic weakness of the demand in the Western Europe economies.

Regardless the evolution of the cycle, these economies have experienced high growth rates since the second part of the 1990s, although, as shown in the Table 4.1, the rhythms of growth were rather differentiated.

All in all, the economic performance observed during the 1990s can be evaluated positively, once we take into account the not easy macroeconomic environment outside these economies. The Western European countries, especially Germany, that could have offered a support to growth, showed a weak internal demand. The difficulties of the Russian economy must be included, as that experienced high output volatility during the last decade.

It is too soon to draft a definitive judgement on the results of the first phase of the transition, the evidence being still mixed. First, countries that joined EU in 2004 show, on average, high rates of development, higher than those observed in other transition economies.

The second aspect is related to the high output volatility. This instability comes partly from the specific shocks coming from the Russian crisis at the end of the 1990s, but is largely due to widespread changes occurring in the productive structure at the beginning of the decade. During the 1990s a reduction in output growth dispersion among different economies was also observed. Therefore, the high output volatility does not necessarily constitute a structural feature of these economies.

Third, and strictly connected to the previous aspects, it is difficult at the moment to quantify, on the basis of the most common techniques, the growth trend that characterizes these economies. As a consequence of the measurement of the dimension of the cyclical component of the growth being extremely uncertain, it is hard to impose fiscal targets based on structural balances to these countries.

As concerns prices dynamics, the general tendency with respect to the 1990s was clearly declining. As open and small economies, the accession countries are exposed to exchange rate volatility. Therefore, it is straightforward to notice how any policy aimed at curbing inflation must be focused on the control of the exchange rate. In this case it is important to recognize that, especially for the Baltic countries, even if the euro constitutes the most important currency as a reference for fixing the exchange rate, the Russian ruble could have an important role in influencing the domestic prices. This factor could represent a further element of instability once New Member states adopt the euro as their national currency.

However, in the last few years monetary and exchange rate policies were not entirely successful in curbing inflation, thus implying a real appreciation of the exchange rate. Such a phenomenon reflects the high productivity achieved in the tradable sectors, which entails the so-called Balassa effect. The economies experience a rise in price dynamics

Table 4.1 Selected economic indicators for accession countries

Year	Poland	Hungary	Czech Republic	Slovak Republic	Slovenia	Estonia	Latvia	Lithuania
(a) Gross Domestic Product – year on year percentage change								
1996	6.0	1.3	4.3	5.7	3.5	3.9	3.7	4.7
1997	6.9	4.6	−0.8	5.6	4.6	9.8	8.4	7.0
1998	4.8	4.8	−1.1	4.1	3.8	4.6	4.8	7.3
1999	4.1	4.2	0.5	1.3	5.2	−0.6	2.8	−1.8
2000	4.0	5.2	3.2	2.2	4.6	7.3	6.8	4.0
2001	1.0	3.8	3.1	3.3	2.8	6.5	7.9	6.5
2002	1.4	3.3	2.0	4.4	2.9	6.0	6.1	6.8
94–04 average	4.5	3.5	2.1	4.2	4.1	4.4	5.8	5.4
(b) Consumer prices – year on year percentage change								
1996	19.9	23.5	8.8	5.4	9.9	23.1	17.5	24.6
1997	14.8	18.3	8.4	6.2	8.3	10.6	8.5	8.9
1998	11.6	14.1	10.7	6.7	7.9	8.2	4.6	5.1
1999	7.3	10.0	2.1	10.6	6.1	3.3	2.4	0.8
2000	10.1	9.8	3.9	12.0	8.9	4.0	2.7	1.0
2001	5.5	9.2	4.8	7.3	8.5	5.8	2.5	1.3
2002	1.9	5.3	1.8	3.3	7.5	3.6	1.9	0.3
2003	0.8	4.7	0.1	8.5	5.6	1.3	3.0	−0.8

(c) Current account – as a percentage of GDP

Year								
1996	-2.3	0.6	-7.1	-9.6	0.3	-9.2	-5.5	-9.2
1997	-4.0	-1.4	-6.7	-8.5	0.3	-12.1	-6.1	-10.2
1998	-4.4	-4.7	-2.2	-9.0	-0.6	-9.2	-10.7	-11.9
1999	-8.1	-5.1	-2.7	-4.9	-3.5	-4.7	-9.8	-11.2
2000	-6.1	-6.2	-5.3	-3.7	-2.9	-5.7	-6.9	-6.0
2001	-2.9	-3.4	-5.7	-8.5	0.2	-6.1	-9.5	-4.8
2002	-2.8	-3.9	-6.5	-8.1	1.7	-12.3	-7.8	-5.3
2003	-3.1	-6.0	-6.9	-2.2	–	–	–	–

(d) External debt – as a percentage of GDP

Year								
1996	35.3	61.9	36.7	38.8	21.1	35.2	41.0	30.5
1997	36.6	53.3	40.8	48.5	22.6	55.5	49.0	34.3
1998	37.3	58.0	42.7	55.9	25.1	56.0	50.9	34.9
1999	42.2	61.1	41.6	53.4	26.9	55.4	57.5	42.6
2000	42.4	65.6	42.1	56.3	32.8	58.5	65.6	43.7
2001	39.2	65.0	39.1	56.5	34.4	58.8	72.6	44.4
2002	43.5	55.4	37.8	55.7	40.0	72.3	83.0	45.0

Sources: OECD, EBRD.

notwithstanding a stable competitive position, as the productivity differential in the tradable sectors is higher than that registered in the no-tradable sectors. This phenomenon could well persist when the euro is adopted, thus entailing a systematic inflation differential compared with the other European countries and a constant real appreciation of the exchange rate. In Figures 4.1(a)–(c) two real exchange rate measures based on consumer prices and on the manufacturing unit labor cost are represented. The cumulative distance between the two variables is caused by the part of the real appreciation of the exchange rate deriving from the Balassa effect and thus is not attributable to a loss of competitiveness for the sector exposed to the competition.

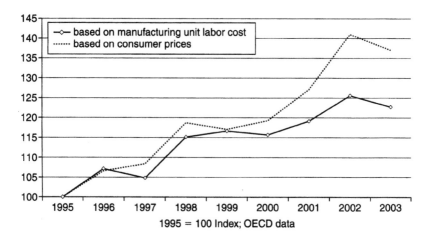

Figure 4.1(a) Real exchange rates – Czech Republic.

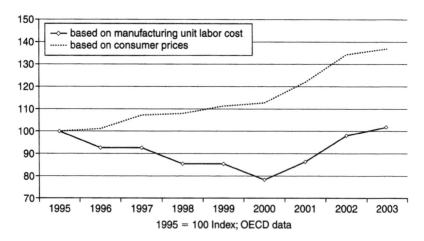

Figure 4.1(b) Real exchange rates – Hungary.

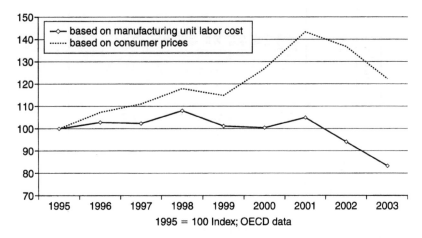

Figure 4.1(c) Real exchange rates – Poland.

Finally, the accession countries have generally shown during the last few years – with the exception of Slovenia – high current account deficits so that they have accumulated high levels of foreign debt. Generally it is normal that current accounts register some deficits in the economies in the early development stage, as they attract foreign capitals to compensate for insufficient internal savings to finance investments. If such development materializes, there are no problems for repaying external lenders and the foreign debt is not a concern. Nevertheless, it remains difficult to evaluate whether the competitive position or the sustainability of the current account deficit could influence the opinions of financial markets, thus putting under pressure the debt sustainability. Such characteristics expose these countries to the risk of a currency or financial crisis.

Starting from the tendencies that emerged in the last decade, we are able to propose a rapid description of some structural features of the accession countries and to compare them with the Western European countries. In particular, Table 4.2 shows the relevant levels of income and prices for these countries.

The implicit relative prices are calculated on the basis of the relation between the GDP expressed in terms of effective nominal exchanges, and GDP expressed in terms of Purchasing Power Parity. The accession countries are compared with the Eurozone. Generally, the correlation between the relative levels of per capita GDP and the relative prices is maintained. The accession countries present levels for both variables that are relatively low, but are higher than those of the other three Eastern European economies included in the table. Only Slovenia presents per capita income and relative price levels close to those of some countries of the Eurozone, such as Greece and Portugal.

Table 4.2 Per capita GDP and relative price level

| | Per capita GDP | | | | Relative price levels | |
| | Current prices and exchange rates | | Current prices and PPP exchange rates | | | |
	1995	2003	1995	2003	1995	2003
EU 15	98.6	103.3	100.4	102.1	98	101
Euro area	100.0	100.0	100.0	100.0	100	100
Estonia	10.6	23.3	31.2	43.0	34	54
Latvia	7.6	16.0	26.3	37.3	29	43
Lithuania	7.3	19.1	31.0	42.2	23	45
Poland	14.0	20.3	35.1	42.8	40	47
Hungary	18.4	30.3	44.9	56.3	41	54
Czech Rep.	21.5	32.9	63.3	63.9	34	51
Slovak Rep.	15.4	23.2	40.4	50.0	38	46
Slovenia	42.4	52.2	61.3	70.3	69	74
Malta	36.6	44.9	63.2	65.7	58	68
Cyprus	57.7	71.0	74.9	78.8	77	90
Total AC – 10	16.4	25.0	41.3	49.1	40	51
Total EU – 25	84.8	90.6	90.5	93.5	94	97
Romania	6.7	9.5	27.6	28.4	24	33
Bulgaria	6.6	9.7	28.2	28.8	24	34
Turkey	11.7	12.9	27.3	25.4	43	51

Sources: calculations on EC AMECO database.

The brief analysis of economic features of these countries allows us to point out some stylized facts, which will be useful for drawing indications about the perspectives of these economies. The tendencies of the last few years showed a sustained path of development for the accession countries, indicating that a catching up process is happening. This allows us to forecast a phase of high growth for the next few years. Notwithstanding this, extreme caution is necessary before drafting indications about the dynamics of potential output. In fact, the development path observed during the last few years was extremely unstable, mainly in the early stages of the transition. The GDP growth was accompanied by a gradual increase of the relative level of both the per capita GDP and the relative prices. Therefore, real exchange indicators show a tendency towards appreciation and the phenomenon seems to be persistent.

4.3 The optimal strategy to join the euro

The analysis in the previous section has shown that the target for nominal and real convergence entails internal conflicts. The catching up could require a phase with relatively high inflation, but the attainment of Maastricht criteria would impose on these countries restrictive economic policies aimed at reducing inflation. According to some studies, the priority would be attributed to the real convergence: the adhesion to the euro and the attainment of the parameters of Maastricht criteria should be deferred. An opposite view emphasizes that joining the euro could facilitate faster economic development. Therefore, the accession to the euro should be achieved quickly.

A long transition could have several advantages, if one considers that a real convergence could imply a reduction in the differences of the economic structures. Economic structures of the accession countries that are more similar to those of the Western Europe countries would allow a reduction of the risks of asymmetric shocks, and therefore make it easier for these countries to participate in the European single currency. Moreover, it must also be observed that the behaviors that the accession countries will exhibit in the next few years are difficult to appraise. For the following years, greater opportunities will be introduced into the European markets, but also greater exposure of local industries to competitive pressures. The transition could create a context of extremely elevated uncertainty (Issing 2003). In such conditions, it would seem more appropriate to maintain the availability of one economic policy instrument, such as the exchange rate.

On the other hand, the advantages of a no-transition strategy could be extremely high. First, as the differences among incumbent and New Members countries are very pronounced, the advantages of real convergence disappear, since the convergence would require an infinite horizon in which to be completed. Moreover, this implies that fulfilling the

Maastricht criteria would impose an excessive cost to the accession countries. Furthermore, if mechanisms such as the Balassa effect were in action, then a group of countries would experience inflation rates systematically higher than others, rendering such a policy partially incoherent. Finally, since curbing inflation should be inevitably based on pegging the exchange rate, such a policy could be difficult to implement in small and open economies where capital inflows play a significant role (Wyplosz 2003).

On the basis of these considerations, an alternative option should allow for an immediate access to the euro, without imposing restrictive policies aimed at fulfilling the Maastricht criteria, since a no-transition strategy would actually be incompatible with such requirements.

This exception would also be opportune, once taking into account that the monetary instability of the New Members countries would not be without effects for the other economies of the Union. The choice to delay the adhesion to the euro produces uncertain and risky outcomes. Another argument in favor of a fast entry to the euro is represented by the fact that the same transition towards the euro can be rendered more unstable from the lack of sufficient reputation of the national Central Banks, since in some cases their independence is not still complete. If a greater independence of the national Central Banks is required, as is essential for adhesion to the single currency (Padoa Schioppa 2002), this could be deferred for a long time. The road of the fast adhesion to the euro concurs also to encompass this type of problem.

There also exist intermediate options to loosen ties for the adhesion to the euro, although they are not easy to apply. As an example, the inflation requirement could be maintained, but in a less restrictive manner in order to take account of the catching-up stage. Moreover, it is clear that the adhesion to the euro could be facilitated if the structure of parameters were modified by rendering them less tight. The increased probability of adhesion would entail at least two benefits: on one hand it would stimulate virtuous policies, because of the greater probability of succeeding with them. On the other hand, these same policies would be less onerous, because they could be accompanied by a reduction in interest rates.

4.4 The fiscal position of the accession countries

The budget position of the accession countries is illustrated in the country chapters of this book. As is shown, the situation is not homogeneous and each country presents marked differences with respect to the other countries. In general terms, these are the main elements that emerge from the reading of the data.

The role of the public sector is large. The incidence of revenues and expenditures as a percentage of GDP is relatively high, compared with that of the EU countries, and higher than that observed in the other transition economies. This reflects a historical inheritance of the accession countries that, at the beginning of the transition, already presented a high weight of the public sector. Since the early stages of the transition, the weight of the public sector on the GDP has been drastically reduced by the wave of privatization of publicly held industries.

The reduction was evident in Hungary, where the amount of total outlays has been lowered, starting from the early 1990s, from around 60 percent of GDP to 50 percent at the beginning of the new millennium. In Poland, expenditures dropped from 54 percent to 46 percent of GDP in recent years. In both countries, however, data show that the reduction of the public expenditure has been interrupted in the last few years. In Poland, the recent increase in public expenditure is mainly due to growth in the current disbursement, in part offset by a reduction in the capital outlays. In the Slovak Republic the route of curbing expenditure is more recent: still in 2000 the expenditure reached the highest level, 65 percent of GDP, and then recorded a strong reduction in 2001 and 2002.

It seems that in the economies where the greater programs of expenditure cuts were experienced, a relaxation in the plans of reforms happened later. The strategies followed by the Czech Republic, Slovenia and the three Baltic countries are different. These countries, in fact, in the middle of the 1990s already presented small levels of public expenditure and, since then, they have not realized expenditure reductions. On the contrary, in the case of the Czech Republic, an increasing trend in public expenditure is observed, starting at the end of the past decade. The three Baltic economies share the same path: an upsurge of public expenditure occurred in 1998–99 and a strong reduction in the following years. This evolution, influenced by the Russian crisis, testifies to a strong reactivity of the budget to the cycle from the side of the expenditure.

As concerns interest expenditure, this can be approached from the 'property income paid by government' according to the definition proposed by the OECD. Interest payments on debt have been strongly reduced in Poland and Hungary, thanks to the fall of interest rates caused by the reduction of inflation. Interest expenditure has been low in the Czech Republic, a country characterized by a low level of the stock of public debt as a percentage of GDP, but it increased in the Slovak Republic, in line with the contextual increase of the debt-to-GDP ratio. Considering that the reductions of the expenditure involved much more than the expenditure in the capital account, we point out that the four greater economies experienced stable current primary spending as percentage of GDP, with the exception of the Slovak Republic, where a solid reduction has been realized.

Therefore, on the expenditure side of the budget, accession countries show a deterioration of composition, since capital outlays decrease while current ones remain stable or increase.

This is, above all, the case of Poland, where the level of the net capital outlays has been reduced on values close to 2 percent of GDP. In Hungary, this level of expenditure goes from values of 6–7 percent of GDP in the middle of the 1990s to values around 4.5 percent in the last few years.

Even if these values of capital expenditure are high on average, they show a problem in perspective. In fact, efforts to balance the budgets in order to join the euro could be concentrated on capital expenditure, thus preventing these economies from pursuing a welcome level of investments in infrastructures to accelerate the catching-up process.

The revenues show a not very different structure with respect to the euro countries. Dynamically, revenues show an evolution close to that of expenditures. However, their incidence on the GDP has reduced less than the expenditure did, thus favoring a deficit reduction. The reduction generally involved indirect taxes. Only Poland registered a fall in direct taxes as a percentage of GDP.

Generally, making reference to the reclassification of the OECD, the main divergence in the structure of revenues with respect to the euro countries regards the low level of the direct taxes on personal income. Conversely, indirect taxes are not low, even in comparison with euro countries. Hungary and the Slovakian Republic show a sufficient contained level of social contributions.

Since the revenue structure is similar to that experienced by European countries, one can suppose that accession countries' budgets would show, in the future, the same response to the cycle registered in Europe. Even if this were the case, the problem remains open of correctly measuring such elasticity given the high output volatility observed during the past. However, once this lack of stability is removed, it is arguable whether budget elasticity in accession countries will be very close to that of the European states.

The budget deficits are, on average, higher than in other European countries, but within the accession countries there is a certain differentiation. Some countries, such as Hungary and the Czech Republic, exhibit a rather high deficit, while others share more contained imbalances. The target of 3 percent of GDP is breached almost everywhere in the larger economies. Instead, it is achieved by Slovenia and the three Baltic countries. On average, the Central European countries show higher deficits than the Baltic countries, although the reverse is true when we consider economic growth. In particular, the Baltic countries have been heavily hit by recession due to the Russian crisis, but their fiscal position has been quickly strengthened in the successive phases of expansion of the economic cycle. The Central European countries instead have largely adopted pro-cyclical fiscal policies (Zogada 2003).

The main feature of fiscal position of the accession countries relies on the low levels of debt they share. It is worthwhile noting that the low levels of public debt widely reflect the initial conditions of the transition. Economies that exhibited an elevated public debt at the beginning of the

1990s, such as Poland and Hungary, still have a debt-to-GDP ratio higher than other countries. However, these are not exceptional values, and are reducing. Poland reduced its debt-to-GDP ratio from over 50 to 46 percent, while in Hungary the debt-to-GDP ratio declined from 80 percent in 1995 to 55 percent at the beginning of the current decade. Similarly, countries that initially had contained debt levels still have a low degree of indebtedness. An exception is constituted by the Czech Republic and the Slovakian Republic, which have shown an increasing debt-to-GDP ratio (Zogada 2003). In Slovenia and in the Baltic republics, the debt-to-GDP ratio is negligible.

4.5 The choice of fiscal rule

A binding starting point in selecting the fiscal rule that best fits the needs of New Members countries relies on the macroeconomic strategy pursued to join the euro. As stated above, the strategy to adopt the euro is twofold. One prescribes a prolonged transition, the other implies an instantaneous transition. Inevitably, the choice of a fiscal rule depends on the strategy that will be adopted. If joining the euro is subjected to the condition that the Maastricht parameters are satisfied, the optimal fiscal rule would be the one that ensures a soft constraint to budget policies in order to facilitate the transition. Conversely, if the euro is adopted without fulfilling any entry criteria, then the optimal fiscal rule should focus on a steady state by ensuring there is a balanced budget policy that is coherent with long-run equilibrium.

If this were the case, because the steady state is a situation in which countries have accomplished the transition towards medium-term positions of being close-to-balance, a fiscal rule will not provide a ready-made recipe for tackling the problems that countries with deficits still close to the upper ceiling face in the event either a cyclical downturn or a financial crisis. Such a fiscal rule should be devoted only to guaranteeing budget flexibility in a close-to-balance framework (in cyclically adjusted terms). On the contrary, if the transition period implies New Members countries are out of long-run equilibrium, then the budget flexibility allowed by a fiscal rule should be ensured regardless of the cyclical position or the budget condition of a country.

Therefore, the trade-off emerging from the above-discussed scenarios (long transition versus no transition) is between flexibility and severity of fiscal rules. The more flexible is the fiscal rule, i.e. it does not interfere with national fiscal policy whatever the economic shock, the less severe it will be in ensuring fiscal sustainability in the long run. Conversely, the more well suited the fiscal rule is for steady state equilibria, the less useful it will be to help governments avoid financial or currency crises that are generated by adverse shocks during the transition towards the euro. Given this framework, an optimal fiscal rule should maximize both flexibility and sustainability of fiscal policy conditional on the macroeconomic strategy that has been chosen, i.e. long transition or no transition.

Even though we do not provide an analytical derivation, it is still possible to draft some prescriptions on the optimal rule by using the above-described stylized facts regarding budget conditions, the economic structure and the cyclical position of candidates countries.

First, many of these countries share a high deficit-to-GDP ratio. This suggests that it is better not to impose on the New Members the condition that they have to fulfill the close-to-balance criterion, since it could never allow these countries to adopt the euro. In fact, they would be exposed too much to the risk of breaching the ceiling and thus incurring financial turmoil during the transition. For more fragile countries, such a strategy could entail a never-ending transition. Under this condition, there would be two feasible solutions: to eliminate the transition period, thus allowing the accession countries immediately to adopt the euro as their currency, or to change the target used in the fiscal rule. If the latter were the case, a shift from deficit to debt-to-GDP ratio as a target for fiscal rule could be optimal, given the low indebtedness shared by candidate countries.

Of course, this solution could entail a fiscal laxity by allowing the New Members countries to enlarge their public deficits. Moreover, given their actually high nominal GDP growth rates, such a solution would make the budget condition of accession countries very fragile in the medium term.

Therefore, after taking into account the above-discussed optimality of a no-transition strategy from a macroeconomic point of view, the best choice for accession countries seems to be the adoption of a fiscal rule based on deficit-to-GDP ratio. In order to allow an immediate entry into the Eurozone, the target on deficits could be substantially relaxed in the early stage of enlargement, with the fiscal sustainability ensured by high growth, low real interest rates and small debt-to-GDP ratios. Of course, the laxity of initial conditions should not prevent the fiscal rule imposing credible paths of deficit reduction in the medium term.

The choice of entry parameters softer than those used in the Maastricht Treaty would also be desirable as it reduces the risk of breaching the ceiling and thus lowers the risk that a disruptive capital flight hits the accession countries more than a legal penalty could do.

In the design of the optimal fiscal rule, the concept of structural balances also matters. The use of such measures is justified by the necessity to avoid national governments being induced to pursue pro-cyclical policies in order to respect the fiscal rules. Defining the budget targets in structural terms helps the automatic stabilizers to function freely when the economic is hit by an adverse shock, without easing fiscal control on national public finances.

The adoption of such indicators within the rule governing the fiscal policy in the accession countries would also be desirable, but the transition they experienced towards a free market signalled a structural break in the statistics. As a consequence, the authors do not have the data necessary to calculate output trends and to know rapidly effective GDP growth (they are frequently revised). Therefore, output gap measures, which are not univocally determined and subject to periodical revisions in the industrialized countries, are far from being unambiguous indicators to be used for the accession countries, at least in the early stages of the enlargement. Consequently, the use of structural balances as the target of fiscal rules could be greatly misleading. However, looking at structural balances as reference values could be a complementary strategy in evaluating whether fiscal rules are fulfilled based on nominal targets. Of course, once the problems in calculating output gaps are removed, a shift of the targets from nominal to structural balances would be desirable within the fiscal rule suited for the accession countries.

Finally, once the optimal fiscal rule has been defined as regards nominal targets and the speed to reach them, qualitative properties of the rule have to be investigated. One of the most recurrent criticisms against fiscal rules based on nominal deficit concerns the disincentive that they pose in developing public capital accumulation. To alleviate this problem, the so-called 'golden rule' has been proposed. According to the golden rule of deficit financing, borrowing is allowed to finance public investment. Implementing the golden rule requires establishing a dual budget separating investment spending from current spending.

The main advantages of the golden rule are those of spreading the burden of capital projects over the different generations of taxpayers benefitting from them and avoiding the efficiency loss caused by distortionary taxation, if the tax rate fluctuates over time. The lack of this possibility may negatively affect capital spending.

The problem is particularly relevant in the initial transition period, in which current generations have to tax-finance new projects, while also paying interest on past debts. However, this argument hardly holds for New Members countries, largely engaged in a catching-up process towards higher per-capita GDP levels.

According to Coricelli and Ercolani (2002), the enlargement of the EU should be a good occasion to modify the actual rules prevailing in the Eurozone for the *Early Comers*. However, there are a number of arguments against the introduction of the golden rule (Buti *et al.* 2003).

First, if applied to gross public investment, the golden rule would be an obstacle to deficit and debt reduction. In particular, given the ratio of public investment as a percentage of GDP, the long-run equilibrium level of government debt could be very high, especially in an environment of low inflation.

Second, what is important is overall capital accumulation in both private and public capital. For instance, a well-devised tax reform that, by lowering tax burden and distortions, leads to higher investment may be preferable to public investment. Moreover, there is no clear evidence in the empirical literature that investment in public infrastructure always leads to significant positive growth effects.

Third, a dual budget may distort expenditure decisions in favor of physical assets and against spending on intangibles. Moreover, the golden rule provides leeway for opportunistic behavior, as governments would have an incentive to classify current expenditure as capital spending.

Given these shortcomings in the use of a golden rule, the adoption of a not strictly binding target for nominal deficit on GDP, which encompasses the distinction between current and capital spending, does not have to be associated with discretionary power in pursuing such soft budget constraints. Otherwise, a soft target and high discretion would entail weak credibility of such a fiscal rule.

By combining all the above assertions and considering that a golden rule scheme could be designed to be internal to the actual SGP (Buti *et al.* 2003), the policy prescription which emerges for the accession countries is quite obvious. When a no-transition strategy is opted for, namely a entry strategy to the Eurozone which does not encompass the fulfillment of the Maastricht criteria, then the optimal fiscal rule for accession countries is the one actually in force in the EU, i.e. the SGP. In fact, all the figures composing the optimal fiscal rule constitute only internal adjustments of the SGP.

On this basis, the next step to evaluate whether a revised version of the SGP could be adopted to manage fiscal policy in an enlarged Union is to test how optimal is such a modified rule for New Members countries. This question would appear paradoxical, but recent events testify how difficult it has become to maintain in action the SGP without changing the Treaty.

The implementation of the SGP started in a favorable situation of high growth. Problems started to show with the economic slowdown of late 2000. The need for reforming the SGP became increasingly obvious in the course of 2002. The violation of the deficit ceiling of 3 percent on GDP by half of the total EU countries expected for 2004 (European Commission 2004) and the contextual launch of the enlargement of the Union to selected Eastern countries, namely the EEC countries, make the debate on the rewriting of the pact deferrable no more.

Since the design of a new pact appears unavoidable in order to correct the adverse effects shown in the past, and to prevent divergence phenomena for an enlarged Europe in the future, it is opportune to consider firstly the drawbacks on which the main criticisms of the pact rely.

Subsequently, it will be possible to verify whether the internal adjustments to SGP proposed above are coherent with such proposals, thus indicating the existence of a uniform effective fiscal rule for an enlarged Europe, or if differentiated fiscal rules are required among the Union.

4.6 The main shortcomings of the SGP

Generally a fiscal rule based on numerical targets is required to share some optimal properties that could be summarized by the so-called Kopits–Symansky's criteria.

According to these criteria, an ideal fiscal rule should be well defined, transparent, simple, flexible, adequate relative to the final goal, enforceable, consistent and underpinned by public finance reforms.

Quoting Kopits and Symansky (1998), as summarized by Creel (2003):

1   'a fiscal rule should be *well-defined* as to the indicator to be constrained, the institutional coverage, and specific escape clauses, in order to avoid ambiguities and ineffective enforcement';
2   'an essential characteristic of a durable fiscal rule is *transparency* in government operations, including accounting, forecasting, and institutional arrangements' in order to gain 'popular support';
3   'rules should be characterized by *simplicity* to enhance their appeal to the legislature and to the public';
4   'rules must be *flexible* to accommodate exogenous shocks beyond the control of the authorities';
5   'fiscal rules should be *adequate* with respect to the specified proximate goal';
6   'a fiscal rule should be *enforceable*. (There is) a need for constitutional or legal statutes, possibly accompanied by penalties for non-compliance and authority for enforcement';
7   'a closely related criterion is for a set of fiscal rules to be *consistent* internally, as well as with other macroeconomic policies or policy rules';
8   'most rules cannot last for long unless they are supported by *efficient* policy actions. [...] From this perspective, [...] a fiscal rule may be viewed as a catalyst for fiscal reforms that would be necessary anyway to ensure sustainability'.

These eight properties cover a mix of political and economic concepts. Some of them are more political than economic, whereas the reverse is true for the others. A simple way to assess the quality of SGP is to test how it fits the optimal properties listed above (for a complete discussion see Buti *et al.* 2003; Creel 2003).

Regarding the first feature, for example, the SGP appears only partially *well-defined* with respect to the policy variables subject to constraints (budget balance and gross public debt) and the institutional coverage (general government), since a new reference value, i.e. the cyclically adjusted budget balance, was added without an appropriate specification. Indeed, it is not often emphasized that such a rule would be effective to alleviate the strictness of the SGP during cyclical downturns only in *ex ante* terms, because *ex post* measures of output gap are conditioned by effective output results. The problem here is to share common and unquestionable estimations of potential output for a reasonable period (at least five years). The SGP also specifies the escape clauses (the exceptional conditions under which the 3 percent of GDP deficit ceiling can be exceeded) and the penalties to be applied in the case of persistent excessive deficits. However, elements of ambiguity remain.

The SGP medium-term target of 'close to balance or in surplus' remains vague and the exceptional conditions under which the 3 percent of GDP deficit ceiling can be exceeded are not well established, since they under-line that the medium-term target of 'close to balance or in surplus' would be related to a potential output concept, thus implying a zero debt rule for EU countries in the long run.

As to *flexibility*, different elements play differently. On the one hand, the SGP includes a tight specification of the escape clauses, thereby redu-cing the discretion of the Council and the flexibility of the rules. On the other hand, by putting more emphasis on medium-term targets and high-lighting the implications of cyclical fluctuations, it increases flexibility com-pared with a simple deficit ceiling targeted in the short run. Nevertheless, as discussed above, this flexibility derives from a lack of transparency and from a not well-defined concept of a cyclically adjusted budget balance used as a medium-term target.

It also seems quite obvious that the pact is not enforceable at all, at least until the credibility of possible sanctions will not be increased. Evid-ence shows that a country facing a proposition of early-warning mechan-ism by the European Commission does not face reputational costs under the form, say, of higher long-term interest rates. The imposition by the Ecofin council of an early-warning procedure on France had no impact, at least until mid-2003, either on long-term interest rates or on the willing-ness of the French government to reduce its deficit at a faster pace. This is heightened by the fact that the council is in charge of the final decision on the implementation of sanctions and hence a risk of a partisan application of the rules exists. It is not surprising that at the end of 2003 an early-warning procedure against France and Germany was interrupted by Ecofin: the effect was to suspend the enforceability of the SGP.

Finally, a good fiscal rule has to be internally consistent and consistent with other policies. Even though the former point is sufficiently satisfied, the latter has been seriously missed twice. First, a strong emphasis on annual targets may have created a tension between fiscal policies and structural policies. For instance, the existing rules may deter pension reforms that enhance sustainability in the long run but may involve a tem-porary rise in the deficit. During 2003, in fact, this point was strengthened by including structural reforms in the European Commission Judgement on National Stability Programs. Second, and by far the most important, the present design of SGP does not appear consistent with a single mone-tary policy set for a group of countries characterized by persistently different rates of inflation. As shown in our previous work (De Novellis and Parlato 2004) and in Creel and Le Cacheux (2003), this situation could entail divergent dynamics in the public finances of each European country, thus hindering a transition toward a steady state in which member states are economically homogeneous. As a corollary, homogeneous fiscal rules defined in the Stability and Growth Pact are ill suited and might even be counterproductive, exacerbating such diverging paths.

Such criticisms could be summarized by a couple of issues identifying the weak points of the pact, on which basis several proposals to replace or radically revise the pact are proposed.

First, the SGP reduces budgetary flexibility, since the 3 percent of GDP reference value is not such a hard ceiling to breach, and not only in exceptional circumstances and for a limited period. As the literature on currency areas (and the recent experience) has shown, higher budgetary flexibility is required to respond to country-specific shocks in the absence of national monetary independence. In order to create sufficient room for maneuver, a rapid transition to broadly balanced budgets in structural terms is required, but in a situation of subdued growth, such a transition would require pro-cyclical policies that may worsen the cyclical conditions.

Second, the pact does not curb governments' incentives to increase expenditure or cut revenue in favorable cyclical periods. Evidence of a pro-cyclical bias still affecting budgetary policies in euro area countries is provided by fiscal behaviors in 2000. In a situation of buoyant growth (3.4 percent for the euro-area as a whole) and an oil price hike that put upward pressure on inflation, countries with high deficits failed to seize the opportunity to reduce their fiscal imbalances.

Third, unlike the Maastricht convergence, sticking to the rules of the SGP may not pay politically. As argued by Buti and Giudice (2002), under the SGP, the carrot of entry has been eaten while the stick of exclusion has been replaced by the threat of uncertain and delayed sanctions. Moreover, the very success of the SGP in reducing the budget deficits would, in fact, be to rebuild the capacity of governments to pursue politically motivated fiscal actions. This temptation may prove irresistible in election years.

Furthermore, the SGP discourages public investment. Maintaining budget positions 'close to balance or in surplus' implies that capital expenditure will have to be funded from current revenues. Hence, it will no longer be possible to spread the cost of an investment project over all the generations of taxpayers who benefit from it. This may imply a disincentive to undertake projects producing deferred benefits and entailing a significant gap between current revenues and current expenditures. The disincentive is stronger during consolidation periods.

Finally, by focusing on short-term commitments, the SGP disregards structural reforms. This criticism has different nuances. First, the SGP focuses almost exclusively on short-term objectives for the budget deficit. As such, it provides incentives for creative accounting and one-off measures that blur the transparency of public accounts. Second, the stock of public debt does not enter the SGP and neither do the contingent liabilities of public pension systems. Hence, the pact treats equally countries with different medium and long-term prospects and different debt levels. This may imply that the pact is too demanding for countries in sound fiscal positions. Third, the pact may prevent countries from implementing policies – such as pension reforms – which improve sustainability over the medium and long term at the price of a short-term deficit worsening.

4.7 A new stability and growth pact for the enlarged Europe

By using the above criticisms as a starting point, several proposals were put forward to revise the fiscal rules that regulate public governance in Europe. They include procedural reforms, institutional reforms and measures aimed to enhance financial market discipline. All these issues, anyway, do not establish how to change or correct the SGP, but they indicate how to help to ameliorate fiscal policy governance by using non-numerical rules. Therefore, they are not very close to the scope of this chapter, i.e. to discuss numerical rules that well fit the public financial needs of EU enlargement.

In this spirit, proposals on how to change the focus of SGP were largely produced. They encompass rules accounting for the composition of the public finance variables or for long run sustainability. The focus on quality has been translated into two proposals for reforming the SGP: the so-called *golden rule* of deficit financing and the expenditure target/rule. Having just discussed the former it is possible to restrict the judgement to the latter.

Expenditure rules present some positive aspects as they refer to the budgetary items that governments can control and they can be easily defined and monitored. Moreover, they allow stabilizers to work on the revenue side and may prevent expenditure relaxation in upturns.

The use of expenditure rules in a multinational context, however, appears problematic, since uniform spending rules would *de facto* impose homogeneous social preferences on politically heterogeneous countries, while country-specific rules would be difficult to enforce (Buti *et al.* 2003). Furthermore, they would have to be complemented by a deficit or debt rule, since they do not say anything about the revenues behavior.

As regards long run sustainability and heterogeneity, the current EU rules do not appear to be very concerned with these issues. Two solutions have been proposed in the literature: the first is to choose a medium-term target that ensures long-term sustainability while taking on board country specificities; the second is to focus directly on the public debt ratio.

In a previous work (De Novellis and Parlato 2004) we stressed the problem of heterogeneity. The accumulation of public debt depends on the deficit and on the growth of nominal GDP. As catching up countries are characterized by higher potential growth and higher inflation (the latter due to the Balassa–Samuelson effect), they can afford to have higher deficits without endangering the long-term sustainability of public finances. Hence, the 3 percent ceiling and the close-to-balance rule are over-restrictive for these countries. Given the higher public investment needs of less mature economies (especially in an enlarged EU), the current fiscal rules could harm the catching up process.

Even if such reasons could justify a revision of the SGP, it is also true that a rule encompassing all the shortcomings could be unfeasible. Buiter and Grafe (2002), for example, propose what they call a Permanent Balance rule, which would ensure sustainability and fiscal prudence while taking into account country differences. Their rule is based on the permanent budget balance, which is given by the difference between the constant long run average future values of tax revenue and government spending. While the rule is theoretically rigorous, its applicability appears doubtful, since it requires the estimate of the permanent value of tax and spending, thus likely violating the criteria of simplicity and enforceability discussed above.

However, as pointed out above, rules that allow fiscal constraints to be relaxed during the transition phases entail non-secondary problems in the long run. For example, nominal GDP growth can be higher in catching up economies but also highly variable. This implies a potential conflict between discipline and stabilization. If a country, which maintains a high structural deficit, is hit by a shock, the automatic stabilizers may lead to very high deficits. While, in principle, these deficits are of a cyclical nature, the risk of spiraling debt and interest payments should not be disregarded. This risk is particularly high in accession countries, which still suffer from limited creditworthiness and may see capital inflows dry up quickly.

A possible solution to this drawback could be the adoption of a non-uniform ceiling across member states, under which a nominal deficit is forced to stay, whatever the shock hitting the economy. To fix such a maximum allowed deficit for each member, a measure of fiscal sustainability could be adopted. For example, the debt-to-GDP ratio could be used as a reference value. However, this type of rule, if clearly made explicit, would entail a non-homogeneous target across countries, thus heavy violating the SGP.

Since the cost of abandoning the SGP would be too high (Blanchard and Giavazzi 2004; Buti *et al.* 2003), a more complex rule would be needed. On the other hand, the enlargement implies that the more the rule must govern the more complex it will be.

Posed in these terms, the proposal that arises implies an internal revisiting of SGP, by adopting a multiple targeting criteria still in the spirit of Maastricht accession criteria. Specifically, the rule of 3 percent should still be maintained but weighted by the level of the debt-to-GDP ratio and, where available, by the cyclically adjusted primary balance. Moreover, the new SGP should be addressed towards a golden rule conditional on the debt-to-GDP ratio in order to promote public investments without putting at risk the fiscal sustainability in the long run. The rationale underlying this setting would resemble the one used in the conduction of monetary policy by the ECB. As the European Central Bank uses two pillars in conducting monetary policy in Euro 12, one simple and easily accountable (the 2 percent limit of inflation rate), the other not defined but considering (money growth), the 'enlarged' European Commission could adopt a similar strategy by declaring the 'targets' in terms of deficit and the debt-to-GDP ratio, but not revealing *ex ante* in which way it evaluates the sustainability of national public finances. Given a deficit and a debt-to-GDP ratio, sustainability would depend on judgements about GDP growth, the composition of revenues and expenditures, the launch of structural reforms, and so on.

If the ECB has been successful in conducting monetary policy without curbing inflation under 2 percent, then the European Commission could in the same way ensure fiscal stability by allowing some countries to breach the 3 percent limit!

Of course, this proposal would involve some procedural adjustment in order to make the Commission more accountable and more powerful in its role, but this would seem to be an unavoidable price to grant stability, flexibility and co-ordination to fiscal policy in an enlarged Europe.

References

Blanchard, O. J. and Giavazzi, F. (2004) 'Improving the SGP through a proper accounting of public investment', CEPR Discussion Paper 4220.

Buiter, W. H. and Grafe, C. (2002) 'Reforming EMU's fiscal policy rules. Some suggestions for enhancing fiscal sustainability and macroeconomic stability in an enlarged European Union', CEPR Discussion Paper 3496.

Buti, M. and Giudice, G. (2002) 'Maastricht's fiscal rules at ten: an assessment', *Journal of Common Market Studies*, 40: 5, 823–47.

Buti, M., Eijffinger, S. C. W. and Franco, D. (2003) 'Revisiting the stability and growth pact: grand design or internal adjustment?', CEPR Discussion Paper 3692.

Coricelli, F. and Ercolani, V. (2002) 'Cyclical and structural deficits on the road to accession: fiscal rules for an enlarged European Union', CEPR Discussion Paper 3672.

Creel, J. (2003) 'Ranking fiscal policy rules: the golden rule of public finance vs. the stability and growth pact', OFCE Working Paper 4.

Creel, J. and Le Cacheux, J. (2003) 'Inflation divergence and public deficits in a monetary union', OFCE Working Paper 5.

De Novellis, F. and Parlato, S. (2004) 'Reducing fiscal pressure under the Stability Pact', in Bernardi, L. and Profeta, P. (eds) *Tax Systems and Tax Reforms in Europe*, London: Routledge.

European Commission (2004) *Economic Forecast Spring 2004*, Brussels: EU Commission, April.

Honohan, P. and Lane, P. R. (2003) 'Divergent inflation rates in EMU', *Economic Policy*, 37, Autumn.

Issing, O. (2003) *Considerations on Monetary Policy Strategies for Accession Countries*, Budapest: National Bank of Hungary.

Kopits, G. and Symansky, S. (1998) 'Fiscal policy rules', IMF Occasional Paper 162, Washington, DC: IMF.

Padoa Schioppa, T. (2002) 'Accession countries on the way of the euro: a central banker's view', *Conference on Economic Policy Directions in the OECD Countries and Emerging Markets: Analyzing the Experiences*, Warsaw, March.

Wyplosz, C. (2003) 'Chi ha paura dell'eurizzazione?', http://www.lavoce.info.

Zogada, M. (2003) 'Fiscal aspects of the EU accession – Poland and Czech Republic', in Zukrowska, K. and Sobczak, D. (eds) 'Eastward enlargement of the eurozone. Monetary and fiscal policy related issues', Ezoneplus Working Paper 17E.

Zukrowska, K. and Sobczak, D. (2003) 'Eastward enlargement of the eurozone. Monetary and fiscal policy related issues', Ezoneplus Working Paper 17E.

5   Tax administration and the shadow economy

Viktor Trasberg

5.1 Introduction and contents

This chapter generalizes certain aspects concerning tax administration developments in the New European Union Member countries from Central Europe and the Baltic states. During the last decade, all these countries have passed radical social and economic reforms to become full members of the EU. One of the most difficult challenges in transition countries has been institutional build-up in line with general economic restructuring, privatization and stabilization activities. Nevertheless, developing a new tax system, and establishing a well-organized and fiscally capable revenue collection mechanism is not an easy task.

The tax system inherited by the former transition countries was not 'generally suitable for gradual reform' (Taxation and Transition 1994). In the command economy, resources for production of public goods were channeled primarily from state-owned enterprises to the government budget. There was no need for special revenue collection and resource allocation institutions other than central planning agencies or committees.

As companies became private, foundations for the already-existing government budget revenues declined radically. Moreover, in the situation of fast falling output and a decrease in individuals' real incomes, the transition countries' governments became fiscally trapped. Implementation of structural reforms and social protection required adequate funds for public spending but the revenue basis disappeared or was being eroded. Therefore, governments in new emerging market economies had to adopt new tax system principles and to establish efficient revenue collection institutions.

Certain criteria have been developed which an efficient tax system and administration should meet.[1] In addition, researchers have analyzed different aspects of tax reform conditions, developments and results for transition countries.[2] In particular, a new tax system in those countries must respond for the needs of an expanding market economy, guarantee the required fiscal resources for government activities and distort, as little as possible, the entrepreneurial incentives (Taxation and Transition 1994).

As a general principle, a tax administration should be organizationally effi-cient, and also transparent, understandable and logical for taxpayers.

Tax levels and administration procedures are also significant elements of an investment environment. Entrepreneurs, when planning investments, are concerned not only about the level of tax rates but also about tax-related procedures and other tax system characteristics. As has been said, 'a revenue administration, that is perceived to be arbitrary or predatory, discourages investment' (Gill 2003).

Nevertheless, the majority of the literature about the reforming tax system in transition countries is concerned more with general tax policy developments and less attention is given to how to reform the tax adminis-tration organization itself (Hôgye 2000; Mitra and Stern 2003). Developing a new tax system is a large-scale, time consuming and permanent process. For that reason, improving tax administrative capacity is still an impera-tive issue in all New EU Member countries. It includes not only adopting new laws, founding new tax structures and a radical improvement of the tax administrative process, but also changing the behavior of all involved parties – as well as taxpayers and administrators.[3] It is crucial to create and strengthen a new 'tax culture and ethics' as an important factor that sup-ports a well-organized tax administration.[4]

In particular, the tax collecting capacity is directly correlated with the scope of the shadow economy activities. For certain reasons, which will be discussed below, most of the transition economies suffered from bursts of shadow economy activities in the early period of market reforms. A high level of unofficial economic conduct limits potential budget revenues, destabilizes public morale and has various other negative impacts on economy and society. Accordingly, the progress of tax administration reforms in transition economies is widely related with gaining control of, and thereafter reducing, unofficial economic activities.

Above all, this chapter's main focus is on drawing interrelations between tax administration processes and shadow economy activities, along with analyzing those issues in certain New EU Member countries. Therefore, the chapter is structured as follows. After the introduction, the second section presents a formal scheme to analyze the tax gap as a weak-ness in the tax administration and the extent of shadow economy activities. The third section characterizes the tax administration situation and devel-opments in the transition period and last part generalizes shadow economy activities in New EU Member countries.

5.2 Shadow economy and tax administration

Tax gap reasons

The most important task of the tax administration is fiscal – to collect the planned amount of tax revenues to cover the requirement for public expenditures. In reality, tax administrators in many countries are struggling with revenue administration inefficiencies that do not allow them to collect the predicted amount of tax revenues. Therefore, the tax administration should be continuously improved or totally reshaped, as in the case of the transition economies.

A widely recognized measure of the tax revenue service effectiveness, is the size of country's tax gap – the 'difference between the tax that should be paid according to the tax laws … and the tax which is actually collected' (Silvani and Baer 1997).

There are several reasons for a tax gap or taxpayers' non-compliance. Rationally, the tax gap includes taxes not paid due to evasion; tax arrears; the shortfall in taxes due to taxpayers' misunderstanding of the tax laws and other reasons (Silvani and Baer 1997). Nevertheless, the exact size of the tax gap is difficult to calculate because it is not viable to obtain an overwhelming amount of data to estimate the precise potential tax base and predict tax subjects' compliance level. In particular, the extent of the tax gap largely depends on the country's economical, political, historical and cultural circumstances. In this chapter, we focus on two important aspects of the tax gap – inefficiencies related to the tax administration and the extent of shadow economy activities.

Figure 5.1 shows the main relations causing the tax gap as well as depicting their interrelations and rationale. The circles connect blocks whose activities are interrelated or interdependent. Later, the figure will be taken as an explanatory tool for analyzing transition countries' tax administration developments and the extent of shadow economy activities.

As mentioned, there are several reasons why potential tax revenues differ from actually collected ones. From the figure, the tax gap depends on an inadequate tax administration and shadow economy activities, which both result in tax avoidance or evasion.

The tax administration cannot be efficient without a comprehensive legislative basis, and as well as strong legal foundations for taxation, an institutional aspect is also critically important. Tax administration means establishing capable tax collecting agencies; distributing employees among tax offices; maintaining information systems between governmental agencies; calculating and levying taxes; inspection of individuals and companies; solving the contradiction between taxpayers and revenue administrators; charging penalties on non-compliant taxpayers, and many other activities.

Therefore, tax collection institutions and agencies should be well organized, properly managed and capable. For example, taxpayers' non-compliance depends directly of the possibility of control of their activities' records or incomes. As stated, 'administrators overall effectiveness will be low if auditing are not effective in discouraging evasion' (Silvani and Baer 1997). However, post-communist countries' tax administration in the early period of reforms is characterized by a clearly inadequate and unstable

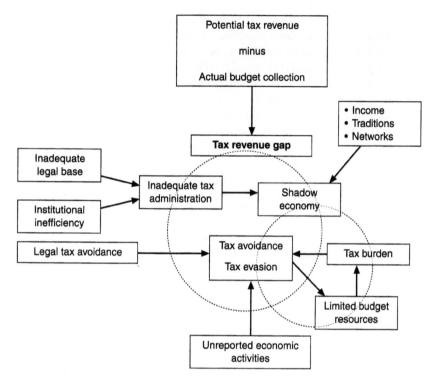

Figure 5.1 Tax administration and the shadow economy (source: see text).

legal base combined with inefficient tax administering. Technically poorly equipped tax agencies, low skilled and little motivated (or even corrupt) tax officials are some reasons for unsatisfactory tax revenue collection.

To generalize, all aspects of tax administration must be continuously monitored and analyzed to make required improvements in the case of organizational and institutional inefficiencies. In particular, it is important in the circumstances of greater than ever globalization of economic activities and widening difficult-to-tax businesses such as Internet-related commercial transactions.

Tax gap and shadow economy

There is an extensive literature that analyses the extent of the shadow economy and its impact on economy and society.[5] Researchers also have developed comprehensive taxonomies of the conception of the shadow economy.[6] Nevertheless, we are here concerned with only those shadow economy aspects that are related to tax evasion, and are not focusing on several other negative (or sometimes positive) results, which arise from unofficial economic activities. Therefore, here the term *shadow economy* is used to 'refer to the value of economic activity that would be taxable were it reported to the tax authorities' (Brooks 2001). Logically, the larger the extent of the shadow economy, the wider the gap between the potential amount of taxes and that actually collected.

What are the motives behind entrepreneurs' shadow economy activities and an individual's reasons for avoiding reporting their incomes or for cheating? In common understanding, there is a mix of several reasons for existence of shadow economy activities (see also Figure 5.1). Here we consider three aspects, which are also considered as related tax gap reasons.

First, different theoretical and empirical studies have proved that the extent of shadow economy activities is related to a high tax burden on individuals and companies.[7] Some authors extend that cause and emphasize the burden of total government regulations as a rationale for the shadow economy (Johnson and Kaufmann 2001).

By staying outside of the official economy and not reporting their incomes, individuals will save considerable amounts of money, which would otherwise be taken by governments as taxes. Similarly for companies, a possibility to not pay taxes maintains income and also gives them competitive advantage compared with law-abiding companies. For example, companies might be motivated to use unofficial labor, which allows evading of payments of social security contributions.

Second, several findings suggest that inadequate and weak tax institutions are reasons for shadow economy activities.[8] Similarly, the adequate strength and efficiency of the government institutions reduces the extent of the shadow economy. If there are poor legal foundations or law enforcement is weak and unstable, then the motivation and opportunities to avoid taxes will increase.

Making tax administration stronger does not automatically mean that the government should just add a number of tax laws and statutes, or toughen law enforcement. There is a risk that increased regulation makes the tax system more complex and enhances the power of bureaucracy. In particular, in the situation of fragile democracies in transition countries, stronger government action might lead to increased tax non-compliance, depressed entrepreneurial activities and corruption. The extent of corruption is one clear reason for limits on a government's ability to collect taxes (Tanzi and Tsibouris 2000; Johnson and Kaufmann 2001). Corruption undermines a society's trust in the tax authorities, distorts and decreases the transparency of the economic environment and therefore decreases both domestic and foreign investment. Worldwide, tax administrations constantly figure near the top of public-sector organizations that have a high level of corruption (Gill 2003).

The third group of reasons explains the shadow economy activities on the grounds of a society's historical traditions and mentality. For example, 'social networks, personal relationships and high profit from shadow economy activities' are strong motives, which keep people away from working unofficially (Schneider and Enste 2000). By some means, supportive main-set towards shadow economy demonstrates also citizen's distrust or ignorance against the state. Owing to earlier harmful experiences, former post-communist countries clearly had many reasons not to trust their governments. Therefore, the shadow economy should be considered as a 'natural wrongdoing' that always exists and cannot be replaced completely. The question should therefore be focused in another way – how to diminish scope of the shadow economy and reduce its negative consequences, particularly with respect to societies' tax collecting abilities.

Tax avoidance and evasion

Weak tax administration and underground economy activities both become visible as tax avoidance and tax evasion (see Figure 5.1). Tax avoidance is defined here as the attentive activities of businesses or individuals to minimize their tax burden. Tax avoidance includes, for example employee discounts, fringe benefits, all do-it-yourself work and neighbor help (Hôgye 2000; Schneider and Enste 2000). Usually, these activities are not illegal; however, inadequate or unclear laws implicitly support tax avoidance.

Legal tax avoidance happens if it is possible to use loopholes in tax laws. Often, this is possible due to a combination of the complexity of tax laws and inexperienced tax officials. As examples, consider the wide use of *offshore* companies in transition countries for business dealings to avoid taxes or the great difficulties in properly taxing sophisticated stock market transactions.

Paradoxically, on one hand, sophisticated and detailed tax regulations can largely cover all possible income sources and economic transactions, but on the other hand may provide additional possibilities for legal tax avoidance. For example, there is a causal link between the complexity of an income tax system and its impact on the shadow economy (Schneider and Enste 2000). Schneider and Enste (2000) conclude that a sophisticated tax system creates the possibilities for legal tax avoidance due to tax exemptions, but, positively, it decreases labor supply in a shadow economy.

In contrast, tax evasion is identified when taxes – imposed on individuals or businesses – are just not paid and thus an illegal act is committed. Tax evasion includes unreported income from self-employment or different and other business activities. Tax evasion therefore means cheating and is considered as a shadow economic activity.

Tax avoidance and evasion are directly related to a potential budget revenue shortage[9] (see Figure 5.1). Limited budget revenue cuts a government's abilities to put into practice its spending policies – the provision of public services and the implementation of welfare programs. As a short-term reaction, governments make efforts to fulfill the budget short-fall by increasing tax rates. In turn, a higher tax burden distorts tax sub-jects' economic conduct and may increase tax evasion and shadow economy activities. As the literature points out, spiral-like movements can take place in such circumstances – a decrease in tax revenue collections will force governments to increase tax rates, which again are opposed by taxpayers through attempts to evade taxes (Schneider and Enste 2000).

To some extent, closing tax loopholes by governments can reduce legal tax avoidance and illegal tax evasion. However, too strong and bureau-cratic tax administrations bring risks that the tax base will be distorted. In particular, in transition economies 'too heavy-handed approach in dealing with tax evasion could damage dynamism of small business and the infor-mal sector' (OECD 2000).

5.3 The tax administration situation and developments in the transition period

Structural changes and the decline of government

The organizational principles of command type economies are widely pre-sented in the literature concerning transitional societies. In these societies, a centralized planning system regulates resource allocation, production decisions and public spending (Tanzi and Tsibouris 2000). The majority of financial flows required for public needs are generated by the state-owned enterprises as 'surpluses' of their economic activities. These surpluses are captured by the state budget, using a mixture of taxes, such as turnover taxes on goods, 'profit taxes' and payroll taxes (Taxation and Transition 1994). These 'taxes' were mainly individualized as 'normative' by enter-prises or industries for fiscal transfers to the centralized budget. Planning bodies were able directly to control and distribute enterprises finances due to the limited number of production entities. As resources for funding social and public programs were obtained directly by the planning institu-tions, there was no need for (tax) revenue administration.

Governments' expenditure size in former communist countries was remarkably high compared with the EU average level in the early 1990s. At the beginning of reforms in 1989–91, in many countries, government expenditure covered more than 50 percent as weighted against the GDP level (see Table 5.1).

As a part of market reforms rationale in all transition countries, the economic role of the government started a remarkable downturn during the course of transition. Many of government functions just disappeared or were given to private economic agents. Along with the state role in the economy declining, its expenditure share in GDP decreased. On average, the Baltic countries' governments expenditure size in GDP was lower than that of the Central European transition countries.

Table 5.1 Consolidated government expenditure in transition countries, percentage of GDP, average level per period

	1989–91	1992–94	1995–97	1998–2000	2001–02
Czech Republic	59.6	48.2	42.4	42.2	45.4
Slovak Republic	59.6	55.8	45.9	43.9	48.1
Hungary	58.2	62.0	50.3	47.4	52.3
Poland	45.5	50.0	47.1	42.4	43.9
Slovenia	44.3	46.2	43.4	43.7	42.6
Estonia	33.8	36.5	39.9	40.7	37.7
Latvia	42.0	33.9	40.7	43.1	38.0
Lithuania	47.3	31.2	34.5	37.2	31.6

Source: Transition Reports on years 1994, 1997 and 2003 and author's calculation.

However, besides the natural process of government sector decline, other factors also limited the government's expenditure capacity. Namely, at the beginning of reforms, most of the governments in transition countries were just not able to collect as much revenue to continue with the previous expenditure level. Two reasons for this must be pointed out, the collapse of former budget revenue funding principles and the explosion of shadow economy activities.

The preceding revenue collection principles were practically paralyzed and the traditional 'tax' base disappeared in most of the transition countries. Soviet-type enterprises, previously the main taxpayers, were economically unstable and their activities declined sharply. In addition, in the early 1990s, total output fell in all transition countries. As pointed out by various studies, emerging new firms in the private sector could not immediately generate enough tax revenue (Hôgye 2000).

In addition, the legal base for tax collection was insufficient and tax law enforcement remarkably weak. As mentioned, the 'old system is largely gone, but a new system [was] far from coming into existence. Thus ... a kind of institutional vacuum has developed' (Tanzi and Tsibouris 2000, p. 3).

In present-day terms, tax-administrating institutions were missing or were in an emerging stage in most transition countries. Personal income taxation was in its infant phase and consumer taxes (VAT, excises, other) were missing in most of the transition countries.

In addition, tax administration institutions were often incapable of dealing with the unprecedented explosion of shadow economic activities. The new emerging private sector had strong incentives not to declare revenues and also had 'outstanding' inventiveness in finding and using tax law weaknesses. Success by governments in encouraging new private companies to report their incomes was insubstantial and, as a result, extensive tax evasion took place.

General government fiscal balance

Despite the fact that most governments of transition countries cut their expenditure in the period 1989–91, most of them were not able to keep the general government budget balanced.[10] The transition countries general government balance, during the transition years, is presented in Table 5.2.

There is no common level of government budget unbalance for all transition economies during the years 1989–2002. One group of reformer countries, such as Estonia, Latvia and Slovenia, were able to cut their expenditures and maintain a balanced or low deficit even in the situation of a considerable decline in output and a decrease of government revenues in the years 1989–94. Another group of countries (Hungary, Poland and Lithuania) failed, for different reasons, to radically cut government expenditures and therefore suffered from larger budget deficits.

All these countries' general government budgets, except for Estonia, were in deficit during the period 2001–02. During recent years, New European Union Members had to implement costly structural reforms to be qualified to EU and NATO requirements. Necessary structural reforms included implementation of pension and healthcare reforms, improving environment protection and infrastructure functioning, and were accomplished with military and other reforms. As Table 5.2 shows, the governments' budgets deficit during 2001–02 were even larger than a decade ago.

Tax administration reform in New EU Member countries

Tax administration reforms

Reforming or improving the tax system and administration is not only a problem for transition or developing countries. Governments in developed countries have a continuous pressure to modernize their tax systems in order to keep their economies competitive and to collect adequate resources for social programs.

Table 5.2 General government balance in transition countries (percentage of GDP), average per period

	1989–91	1992–94	1995–97	1998–2000	2001–02
Czech Republic	−1.4	−0.4	−1.8	−3.2	−5.9
Slovak Republic	−1.4	−7.3	−2.0	−7.2	−7.3
Hungary	−1.1	−6.5	−5.5	−3.9	−7.0
Poland	−3.6	−5.3	−3.2	−3.3	−6.1
Slovenia	0.9	0.2	−0.5	−1.2	−2.2
Estonia	3.4	0.1	−0.2	−1.8	1.0
Latvia	3.1	−1.0	−1.8	−2.6	−2.4
Lithuania	−4.4	−2.8	−3.6	−5.7	−1.6

Sources: Transition Report, 1994, 1997, 2003 and author's calculations.

Nevertheless, a clear difference between developed EU and transition countries was the time limit within which the new tax systems must be put into operation. Transition countries required a new tax system and institutions promptly – to replace, without delay, the old revenue system. There was no time and few possibilities for gradual improvement or for experimenting with existing tax arrangements. Building up a new and efficient tax administration system is not an easy task in the situation of a fast collapse of half a century's existing economic and social organization.

As a matter of fact, fast reforms brought essential changes to individuals' and companies' activities. Equally, at the personal and business level, in many transition countries tax obligations were an entirely new phenomenon and an additional burden during the period of radical reforms and falling living standard. Obviously, one of the reasons for individual taxpayers' high non-compliance was also a lack of experience in tax reporting. In addition, the attitude towards tax authorities was not very helpful.

As mentioned, there was an urgent need in transition economies to establish a tax system that can respond to the conditions of the market economy and ensure funding of government programs in the situation of fast decline of production. Success of the reforming tax administration and increasing tax-collecting capacity was directly related to achievements in general economic reform. Privatization, economic restructuring and stabilization activities influenced the build-up of new taxation systems and forced the continuous development of the legal foundations. At the same time, progress in tax system reform had a positive impact on attracting foreign investments, the stabilization of government finance systems and the decline of the shadow economy.

Reforming the tax administration was highly dependent on the government's political commitment and its capability to make radical and fast changes. As mentioned by the United Nation Economic Commission for Europe, the prospect of EU membership had an enormous impact on the process and nature of tax reform in these economies, especially in more recent years, before they became EU members (Secretariat of the Economic Commission For Europe 2004).

Nevertheless, while the New EU Member countries have developed modern tax policy and legislation, the institutional changes in tax administration delayed policy. This is due, 'not only to a greater focus on changes in [tax] policy rather than administration in the early years of transition, but also to the fact that demands on administration arising from changes in tax policy would usually precede development of supporting institutions' (Mitra and Stern 2003). Considering this, those shaping the frames of tax reforms should consider imminent European Union membership and therefore increase their administrative capacity and institutional efficiency.

Institutional efficiency

Tax administration inefficiency in transition countries was caused by legal, institutional and managerial weaknesses. These are interrelated components, which must be improved to increase the effectiveness of the tax procedures generally.

The legal aspects of tax administration mean that the law should adequately cover taxation-related issues. Most of the transition countries' loopholes in tax law have been obstacles for efficient revenue collection. Tax laws and regulations have changed, often due to the fast-changing economic environment. In addition, the law has not been strong enough to allow authorities successfully to pursue cases of tax evasion through the courts (OECD 2000). At the same time, driven by administrative considerations, tax legislation should be as simple as possible so as not to devastate new entrepreneurial incentives and confuse unsophisticated taxpayers.

Institutionally, an increase of tax administration efficiency has many similarities to business organizations and consists of many specific characteristics.[11] Generally, a capable institution requires a clear vision of its functions and an organizational structure; a rational allocation of employment and professional management; improvements in technology and better client service.

A tax administration institution should have appropriate autonomy and its responsibilities and organizational structure exactly defined. Studies in transition countries have revealed disorganized coordination between tax administration agencies, unclear administrative power and inadequate delegations of responsibilities and illogical distribution of employees by bureaus and departments (Hôgye 2000).

From a managerial aspect, revenue collection offices in transition economies are often poorly equipped and managed. The problems include inappropriate use of modern computer and office technology; ineffective use of available information to control non-compliance; weak collection enforcement and the existence of corrupt practices. Often, the motivation of tax authorities' employees was weak owing to low salaries and unpleasant working conditions (Hôgye 2000).

Nevertheless, tax administration has been strengthened in all New EU Members and has improved towards purpose-oriented, functional and efficient tax collection institutions.

5.4 Shadow economy and non-compliance

Explosion of the shadow economy

As economic activities moved outside the state sector, a match between government revenue and expenditure became problematic in all transition economies. In addition, as living standards generally fell, governments faced pressure to increase expenditure at the same time as the economic downturn reduced the tax base. The emerging private sector was not able to produce a suitable amount of revenue to fill the revenue gap.

Attempts to increase the existing tax burden were followed by large-scale tax avoidance and the growth of unofficial economic activities. Then taxpayers became 'subject to an ever greater tax pressure ... prompting many to withdraw from business or to opt for the underground economy' (Åslund 2002).

Therefore, radical reforms began in the early 1990s. All transition economies met the sudden increase of shadow economy activities. The shadow economy included a wide range of activities – from 'innocent' unreported labor activities to criminal actions. Many of these activities were related to tax evasion, tax fraud and corruption.

Table 5.3 shows the average level of the shadow economy in transition countries for the first half of the 1990s. To estimate the level of underground activities, different methods can be used.[12] As the table shows, countries' results are different due to the various methods used by different researchers.

The figures presented by Schneider and Enste show smaller levels of shadow economy activities than those estimated by Lacko. As the table shows, the estimated level of total underground activities varies from about 13 percent in the Czech Republic to more than 38 percent in Lithuania in period 1990–93. In the later period, the average size of the shadow economy was about the same in Central European states but increased in the Baltic states. However, the level of the shadow economies remains high in most of the transition countries, and hence had a negative impact on potential government budget revenues.

The explosion of the shadow economy in combination with falling output and the disappearing tax base immediately created problems with budget revenues. The turn to the shadow economy undermines the tax

Table 5.3 Size of the shadow economy in transition countries, as GDP level, per period

Country	1990–93	1994–95
Czech Republic	13.4 (28.7)	14.5 (23.2)
Slovak Republic	14.2 (30.6)	10.2 (30.2)
Poland	20.3 (31.8)	13.9 (25.9)
Hungary	30.7 (30.9)	28.4 (30.5)
Slovenia	– (28.5)	– (24.0)
Estonia	23.9 (35.9)	18.5 (37.0)
Latvia	24.3 (34.9)	35.3 (43.6)
Lithuania	26.0 (38.1)	25.2 (47.0)

Sources: Schneider and Enste (2000) and studies of Johnson *et al.* (1997) and Lacko (1999). Estimates are given in brackets.

base and makes it hard for the state to provide important public services, such as infrastructure development, social programs and health care.

Decrease of the shadow economy in New EU Member countries

As noted above, there are many reasons for tax avoidance and shadow economy activities. Concerning the possibilities to decrease the shadow economy in the transition economies, three general aspects are emphasized here.

First, the apparent excessive tax burden on individuals and businesses is the main reason for making tax evasion a 'sin worth committing', particularly in the situation where the government lacks the capability to enforce proper compliance, and there are emerging businesses. The experience of the Baltic states suggests that high tax rates have encouraged informal economic activities and discouraged formal employment (OECD 2000). An increase of tax and government regulations in low-income transitional societies is resisted more strongly than far richer societies.[13] Therefore, an optimal level of tax rates will keep businesses in the official economy and individuals are not so hostile to reporting their incomes.

Second, a high level of regulations, bureaucracy and corruption, generalized as a burden imposed by government, is realized to be an even stronger reason for the rise of the shadow economy than high marginal corporate or personal income rates (Johnson and Kaufmann 2001). The fast demolishing of the formerly strongly centralized political and economical system left a gap before new democratic institutions were able to govern the society efficiently. As a result, an uncertain legal environment and a lack of democratic control over institutions was followed by an increase in bureaucracy and corruption. Building up efficient administrative institutions is a relatively slow process and requires remarkable legal, administrative and behavioral activities. Nevertheless, as economic and social reforms have progressed, most of the transition countries have experienced a general shift towards formal activities (OECD 2000; Hôgye 2000).

Third, there is need to create and promote tax 'ethics' and social 'norms', which are widely recognized by the society and support law-abiding behavior. The existence of such norms suggests, that individuals will comply with tax responsibilities because they believe that it is good social behavior.[14] The tax administration should shape individuals' and entrepreneurs' behavior towards loyalty with their tax liabilities and therefore, incorporate them into official taxpayers 'society'.

Taking into consideration New EU Members' post-communist legacy, there has been a prevailing mutual mistrust between taxpayers and the tax authorities, which materialized in the absence of a tradition of voluntary compliance with tax liabilities. Enhancing trust in the fairness of the tax administration would encourage voluntary compliance (Mitra and Stern

2003). Based on this, the transition countries' tax administration reforms have been targeted to a wide recognition of voluntary compliance, self-assessment of tax obligations by taxpayers and clearly defined rights and obligations both of the tax authorities and the taxpayers. Hunting non-compliant taxpayers and punishing tax evaders are not in themselves the main objectives of the tax administration. Successful administrations make the tax-paying community realize that non-compliance will be detected and effectively punished (Silvani and Baer 1997).

In conclusion, in the course of economic reforms and strengthening of government capability, the tax administration has increased efficiency and the amount of taxes in most of the New EU Member countries. The goal of harmonizing their systems of public finance with those in the EU has provided one of the most important catalysts of the reforms (Secretariat of the Economic Commission For Europe 2004). In line with a decrease of tax burdens, taxpayer-friendly tax procedures and transparent government activities, the extent of the shadow economy activities decreased in all former transition countries.

Notes

1 Institutionally, EBRD, World Bank, International Monetary Fund, OECD and others have developed their recommendations and strategies for tax administration reforms. Relevant references are presented in the list of website sources.
2 For example, Mitra and Stern (2003); Tanzi and Tsibouris (2000); Ebrill and Havrylyshyn (1999); Silvani and Baer (1997); Hôgye (2000).
3 The general structure of activities needed for tax reform in transition countries is given in Tanzi and Tsibouris (2000), Hôgye (2000) and Mitra and Stern (2003).
4 More detailed analyses of the concept is provided in the works of Alm and Martinez-Vazquez (2000); Nerré (2001), and Tanzi and Tsibouris (2000).
5 The mentioned literature here includes the works of Schneider and Enste (2000), Johnson and Kaufmann (2001), Johnson *et al.* (1997), Lacko (1999) and Brooks (2001).
6 For example Schneider and Enste (2000).
7 All earlier mentioned authors emphasize the tax burden as a main reason for shadow economy activities.
8 For example, Tanzi and Tsibouris (2000); Schneider and Enste (2000); Johnson and Kaufmann (2001).
9 The term is used here to differentiate from term 'budget deficit', which has a more specific meaning.
10 Only Hungary and Poland had, in the period 1989–91, full control over their national budgets, all other selected countries were, in that time, parts of federal countries.
11 For example, a detailed description of activities required by tax administrative institutions is given in Hôgye (2000).
12 Methods described by Schneider and Enste (2000); Brooks (2001).
13 Johnson and Kaufmann (2001).
14 A more detailed explanation of the concept is provided by Alm and Martinez-Vazquez (2000); Tanzi and Tsibouris (2000); Brooks (2001).

References

Alm, J. and Martinez-Vazquez, J. (2000) *Institutions, Paradigms, and Tax Evasion in Developing and transition Countries*, World Bank Internet Homepage www.worldbank.org/wbi/publicfinance/publicresources/.

Åslund, A. (2002) *Building Capitalism*, London: Cambridge University Press.

Brooks, N. (2001) *Key Issues in Income Tax: Challenges of Tax Administration and Compliance*, Asian Development Bank 2001. http://www.adb.org/Documents/Events/2001/Tax_Conference/paper_brooks.pdf.

Ebrill, L. and Havrylyshyn, O. (1999) 'Tax reform in the Baltics, Russia and other countries of the former Soviet Union', IMF Occasional Paper 182. Washington.

European Bank for Reconstruction and Development (1994) *Transition Report 1994*, London: EBRD.

European Bank for Reconstruction and Development (1997) *Transition Report 1997*, London: EBRD.

European Bank for Reconstruction and Development (2003) *Transition Report 2003*, London: EBRD.

Gill, J. (2003) *The Nuts and Bolts of Revenue Administration Reform*, The World Bank Complement for presentation on Revenue Administration Reform January 2003, Washington, DC: World Bank. http://www1.worldbank.org/publicsector/tax/NutsBolts.pdf.

Johnson, S. and Kaufmann, D. (2001) 'Institutions and the underground economy', in Havrylyshyn, O. and Nsouli, S. M. (eds) *A Decade of Transition: Achievements and Challenges*, Washington, DC: IMF.

Johnson, S., Kaufmann, D. and Shleifer, A. (1997) 'The unofficial economy in transition', Brookings Papers on Economic Activity, 2, Washington, DC: The Brookings Institution.

Lacko, M. (1999) 'Hidden economy an unknown quantity? Comparative analyses of hidden economies in transition countries in 1989–95', Working Paper 9905, Department of Economics, University of Linz, Austria.

Hôgye, M. (ed.) (2000) *Local and Regional Tax Administration in Transition Countries*, Budapest: OSI Publications.

Mitra, P. and Stern, N. (2003) 'Tax systems in transition', WB Working Paper 2947, Washington, DC: The World Bank.

Nerré, B. (2001) 'The emergence of a tax culture in Russia', paper presented at The 57th Congress of the International Institute of Public Finance: The Role of Political Economy in the Theory and Practice of Public Finance, Linz, Austria, 27–30 August, 2001.

OECD (2000) *Regional Economic Assessment: The Baltic States*, Paris: OECD.

Schneider, Fr. and Enste, D. (2000) 'Shadow economies around the world: size, causes and consequences', IMF Working Paper 00/26, Washington, DC: IMF.

Secretariat of the Economic Commission For Europe (2004) 'Tax reforms in the EU acceding countries', *Economic Survey of Europe 2004*, 1, Geneva.

Silvani, C. and Baer, K. (1997) 'Designing tax administration reform strategy: experiences and guidelines', IMF Working Paper 97/30, Washington, DC: IMF.

Tanzi, V. and Tsibouris, G. (2000) 'Fiscal reform over ten years of transition', IMF Working Paper 113, Washington, DC: IMF.

Taxation and Transition (1994) *Transition Report 1994*, European Bank for Reconstruction and Development, London: EBRD.

Websites

http://www.imf.org/ – International Monetary Fund.
http://www.oecd.org/ – OECD Tax Administration.
http://www1.worldbank.org/publicsector/tax/ – World Bank Tax Policy and Administration.

6 Competition for FDI and the role of taxation

Jeffrey Owens

6.1 FDI and the role of taxation[1]

Foreign direct investment (FDI) flows to the 'transition' economies of Central and Eastern Europe (CEE)[2] have risen dramatically over the past decade. The region's share of the global total has increased from 0.2 percent in 1988–90, to 2.3 percent in 1998–2000. Total inward FDI for the region amounted to US$26.5 billion in 2000, an increase of roughly 5 percent over the preceding year, close to double the amount received in 1996, and nearly 90 times the figure for 1990. FDI flows to CEE countries increased further to $27.2 billion in 2001, a year in which global FDI flows declined by half. The bulk of the total (over 75 percent) has gone to four countries – the Czech Republic, Hungary, Poland and the Russian Federation.

FDI flows to the SEE Member countries of the Stability Pact for South Eastern Europe (SEE)[3] also rose substantially over the last decade, with the year 2001 volume reaching almost 50 times that for 1991. However, after a sharp initial rise, the annual inflow remained largely static over the period 1998–2000, at just under $4 billion a year, although rising to $4.5 billion in 2001. Romania, by far the largest country in the region, accounts for more than one-quarter of the total, with Bulgaria and Croatia the other principal recipients.

To what extent does taxation have an impact upon FDI decisions? This question has been the subject of many studies over the past 30 years, and answers provided and opinions on the subject continue to differ widely. Some studies have considered the effects of tax systems generally, some have examined specific taxes (especially the corporate income tax), while others have concentrated on tax incentives.

In principle, taxation ought to be important, since it influences after-tax profitability. Investors that are able to achieve reduced tax exposure in one project would be expected to choose it over an identical project that has the same level of risk and return. This much seems self-evident. However, econometric studies, which seek to establish the relationship (if any) between tax burdens and FDI levels in a particular country, have been mostly inconclusive, largely due to difficulties in modeling and measuring variables thought to influence FDI flows, and in measuring consistent FDI series over time and across countries. Survey studies, based upon questionnaires addressed to MNE managers, tend to show taxation as ranking relatively low compared with other factors, while in some cases taxation is singled out as an important consideration (depending largely on how and to whom questions are posed).

It is evident that certain tax considerations are more likely than others to affect FDI decisions. The overall level of taxation in a country, as measured, for example, by its tax-to-GDP ratio, does not appear to directly influence inward or outward FDI. Among OECD member states, Japan has a relatively low level of taxation and receives very little FDI, whilst Belgium and Sweden are comparatively high-tax countries yet have substantial FDI inflows. This suggests that, to the extent that tax is relevant, it is the tax mix and design features that are more important, possibly to a varying extent depending on the type of investment in question. Tax administration (and transparency) would also be expected to be important.

Not surprisingly, corporate income tax (CIT) has received the greatest attention from analysts, since it most closely affects the amount of profit of a MNE that is available for distribution to shareholders. Several recent studies have found a significant relationship between effective host country CIT rates and levels of FDI.[4]

However, as noted above, a number of difficult modeling and data measurement problems continue to pose challenges to researchers (while survey findings raise difficulties of their own). A key problem in estimating the sensitivity of FDI to host country taxation stems from difficulties in measuring host country tax burdens. A host country average effective tax rate is measured, in principle, by dividing host country CIT revenues (plus possibly other host country taxes) by true host country profit measured on an arm's length basis. However, true host country profits are difficult (if not impossible) to measure given the existence of tax-motivated profit stripping to low-tax jurisdictions (in principle, profits booked in low-tax jurisdictions should be taken into account). But this requires (confidential) firm-level data on cross-border transactions, as well as estimates of the tax-motivated elements of inter-affiliate cross-border payments.

Individual income tax and employee and employer social security contributions are generally less important considerations, except where they have an unusually large impact on labor costs. Consumption taxes, such as the value added tax, would also typically have relatively little relevance to market-oriented FDI decisions. Such taxes tend to be passed on to consumers rather than borne by producing enterprises, and apply equally to competing domestic products and to imports.[5]

By contrast, import taxes and customs duties may be quite important in two ways. High import taxes and duties constitute a tariff wall, which may encourage MNEs to invest in a country rather than export to it. Once they are there, such duties provide protection against imports from competitors: in that way high import duties may actually constitute an incentive to some types of market-oriented investment. But at the same time, high duties and taxes on the import of machinery and other capital goods increase the initial cost of investment and the cost of imported goods used in production, and may constitute a substantial disincentive to FDI.[6]

It is widely held that export-oriented FDI is more sensitive to the host country tax burden than is market-oriented investment. Taxes that directly affect the cost of production and corporate income tax are typically reflected in the price of exported products or services, tending to make demand for those products (and therefore investor interest in a given export site) sensitive to host country tax considerations. Tax considerations seem to be of the greatest importance to firms exporting services,[7] followed by those manufacturing for export, and seem to be less important to firms in the natural resource sector. These differences reflect the relative mobility of the investment and the range of choice of possible locations.

By contrast, market-oriented FDI tends to be relatively little affected by considerations of taxation unless the host country tax is unusually burdensome – that is, unless the tax system (policies and/or administration) imposes compliance and possibly other costs that cannot be shifted onto others. Taxes that affect the cost of production, to the extent that they are borne by domestic and other MNE competitors and can be passed on to consumers, may not be problematic (depending on the degree of competition in output and factor markets), while taxes on profits may, to some extent, be passed on to consumers. Finally, MNEs with global operations (or more limited operations but with finance affiliates located in tax havens) may have considerable scope to 'manage' (reduce or largely eliminate) host country tax burdens, implying that statutory provisions may have little bearing on actual tax burdens and investment decisions.

Apart from tax rates and tax base considerations, two other tax-related factors are likely to be taken into consideration. First, MNEs will prefer to invest in countries that have concluded tax treaties with their home country in order to avoid potential double taxation, although the existence of a treaty may not be a decisive factor, particularly if an investor can invest through a third country that has a treaty with both the home and target (host) country (i.e. opportunities exist for 'treaty shopping') and to have available dispute resolution procedures. Second, the quality of the potential host country's tax administration is often a major consideration. Uncertainty, ambiguity, too frequent changes in the legislation, inconsistency in its interpretation and application, corrupt officials, excessive penalties and related administrative factors can constitute a severe disincentive to investment.[8]

A further factor, and one that is often overlooked, is that a large proportion of FDI is in the form of reinvestment, or of additions to existing investments. Taxation may not have played a major part in the initial decision to invest in a particular country but it may have an important influence on decisions to reinvest or to expand. Among the reasons commonly given for dissatisfaction with host country conditions are inconsistent tax laws and erratic tax administrations. This 'never again' factor inevitably has a substantial effect on future investment plans.

Most of the studies undertaken before 1990 found that taxation was a relatively minor consideration in most FDI decisions. More recent studies have tended to suggest otherwise: taxation is becoming an increasingly important factor. For this development, there may be a number of explanations.

- As other barriers to FDI are eliminated, the remaining obstacles assume an increased importance. Taxation has always been recognized as being a factor in FDI decisions, other considerations being equal. Today, many of those other considerations have become more or less equal.
- The process of globalization is characterized by greatly increased international production: the components that go to make a finished automobile may come from five or six different countries. Sales are no longer made principally in the country of production and investment is no longer oriented to a single market.
- The creation of common markets, customs unions and free trade areas has had a similar effect, making it easier to supply a number of national markets from a single location unimpeded by tariff barriers, and also sometimes reducing other differences between the Member countries. Thus, the distinction between market-oriented and export-oriented investment has become less clear.

These latter two points seem especially important. The fact that export-oriented investment is more likely than market-oriented investment to be influenced by tax considerations has been recognized for many years. However, the growth of international production and the coming into existence of free trade areas or common markets has changed the picture radically. When goods and services are allowed to move freely within a single multinational market, it is possible for FDI to be both market-oriented and export-oriented. A single location may be selected within that market to supply all of the countries composing the market. The market potential of the actual country where production is located becomes relatively unimportant, the cost of production becomes more important, as do other factors such as central location, communications, availability of labor – and taxation.

6.2 Tax considerations in SEE countries

FDI decisions in the SEE region are typically based on expectations of above-normal rates of return, but accompanied by a high perceived level of risk (including political, economic, governance and other risks). Difficulties in predicting macroeconomic developments tied to political and economic instabilities in the region, difficulties in predicting the application (or not) of host country laws, and difficulties in predicting costs tied to dealings with host country bureaucracy, on top of other market-related uncertainties, imply significant project risk. These difficulties in predicting project outcomes tend to render questions over the exact level of the effective host-country tax rate as relatively unimportant, provided that the effective tax rate is not viewed as excessively high. This is particularly true where significant scope exists for multinationals to effectively set the effective host country tax burden that they are willing to bear, through the use of careful tax planning.

This view was confirmed in a survey of SEE investors by Emerging Market Economics Ltd, which found that special tax incentives, rather than encouraging FDI, either were not taken into account (were judged to be unimportant), or operated to *discourage* investment. Tax incentives were discouraging to investment where the provisions were difficult to track, understand or comply with and/or invited corrupt behavior on the part of tax officials, tending to increase project costs and uncertainty. Particularly discouraging were non-transparent incentive regimes, including those subject to frequent change and involving excessive administrative discretion. Investors exhibited a strong preference for stable and sound tax systems that did not deviate significantly from international norms.

The following conclusions are relevant to addressing tax impediments to FDI in SEE countries.

- Unstable and non-transparent tax policies, combined with non-transparent and corrupt administrative practices, have contributed to project costs and heightened perceptions of project risk in many SEE countries, tending to discourage investment. Tax incentives have tended to contribute to uncertainty and project risk, particularly where administered in a discretionary fashion.
- The 'enabling environment' should include a relatively simple tax system offering competitive host country tax treatment, with basic corporate tax rules that generally follow international practice.
- Statutory Corporate Income Tax (CIT) rates currently in force in the SEE countries, in the range of 15 percent to 25 percent are already moderate or low by international standards. Efforts to improve competitiveness of tax systems should concentrate on removing impediments, streamlining and relaxing certain basic features of tax systems,

improving transparency and predictability, while imposing a reasonable tax burden on host country profits. Such changes should operate to lower project costs, lessen the scope for corruption, and reduce actual and perceived levels of risk, which taken together should operate to encourage additional greenfield FDI.

- Countries relying on book income, as a basis for measuring taxable income, should aim to ensure that national (and, where relevant, international) standards for proper, transparent financial accounting are established, understood and followed by taxpayers and adhered to by public (auditing) officials.
- Progressive and regressive corporate tax rate structures should be reconsidered, given the benefits of a flat (single) corporate tax rate structure.
- The classical tax variant with final withholding tax on dividends paid to resident shareholders, which most SEE countries have opted for, offers a number of advantages, including simplicity, relative ease of administration, and reduced scope for evasion. SEE countries relying on alternative mechanisms to integrate corporate and shareholder-level taxation should reconsider the benefits of this approach.
- Double, or possibly multiple, taxation of profit distributed along a chain of related corporations should be avoided, for example by providing dividend exemptions on inter-corporate dividends between related companies, with final withholding on dividends paid outside a corporate group. Dividend gross-up and credit provisions at the corporate shareholder level should be avoided if found to add to complexity.

A substantial portion of the study focuses on targeted corporate tax incentives, which have been widely used by SEE countries to promote investment. A key finding of the study is the coexistence in SEE countries of generous and largely inefficient tax incentive provisions alongside core corporate income tax provisions that, in certain areas, are at odds with international norms.

- Business loss carry-forward provisions have been found to be restrictive in certain SEE countries (e.g. three-year loss carry-forward), relative to international norms (five-to-seven year or more). Where tax is a factor in business location choice, restrictive loss carry-forward provisions could be a discouraging factor. Countries with restrictive loss carry-forward rules are therefore encouraged to relax those rules as quickly as possible.
- Depreciation rules, another key component of corporate income tax systems, are found in a number of SEE countries to be overly complex and/or restrictive in the amount of tax relief provided. Certain changes (e.g. greater use of the declining-balance method, a reduction in the

number of depreciable asset classes) would streamline tax calculations while providing considerable scope for encouraging investment, while limiting revenue losses. Where depreciation claims continue to be mandatory (i.e. unclaimed capital costs cannot be carried over), greater importance should be placed on relaxing loss carryover provisions (as noted above).

As regards the international aspects of corporate tax systems, and to the operation of other domestic taxes, certain policies are recommended (e.g. introduction or strengthening of base protection measures) but it is recognized that different approaches and variants may be chosen at the 'domestic' level.

- Where tax treaties do not currently exist with major capital exporting nations, and the conclusion of such treaties is expected to be a number of years off, countries should consider reducing statutory (non-treaty) rates to levels closer to treaty norms.
- Countries without thin-capitalization rules, or with variants that have been found to be weak, should consider introducing or strengthening those rules.
- Countries without transfer pricing rules should consider their introduction, while those with such rules are encouraged to examine their application in practice to ensure enforcement of arm's length prices in international transactions.
- Countries with relatively high employer social security contribution rates should consider lowering those rates to international norms as quickly as possible. Where such reductions are not possible currently due to budgetary pressures, labor market conditions should be examined to determine if institutional changes are possible to enable a partial shifting of such contributions onto employees.
- Where special customs duty exemptions are provided on imports of machinery and equipment for certain investors, consideration should be given to a general reduction or elimination of import duties on most types of machinery and equipment. Where revenue requirements make immediate implementation impossible, consideration might be given to an announced gradual reduction.

A critical issue is the continued existence in many SEE countries of profit-based incentives, including tax holidays and partial profit exemptions, which are particularly prone to aggressive tax planning. The review and analysis of incentive regimes underscores the need of policy-makers to recognize the various avenues by which domestic and foreign investors can artificially characterize non-qualifying profits as profits qualifying for tax relief. Revenue losses to unintended investments obviously erode the ability of a given incentive to meet a cost-benefit test.

These concerns are compounded by the fact that protecting the host country tax base from aggressive tax-planning opportunities created by certain tax incentives requires *effective* defensive tax measures and tax administration to counter the 'stripping' of host country profits to offshore financing subsidiaries. Unfortunately, SEE countries generally do not have such measures and practices, owing to the relatively limited experience of SEE tax officials in the international tax area.

The following conclusions emerge regarding the use of tax incentives in SEE countries.

- Tax holidays are an especially inefficient form of tax incentive, being the most open to tax planning. Unlike incentives earned as a percentage of investment (which cap revenue losses to some fraction of qualifying expenditures), tax holiday relief is not limited in this way to the desired activity. Instead, all returns over the holiday period on investment – including returns covering initial investment costs as well as normal and 'super-normal' profits – are earned tax-free. Providing this level of tax relief on targeted profits – as well as on profits of related non-qualifying firms, transferred to tax holiday firms using non-arm's length pricing and financing arrangements – should be seen as excessive. In addition, contrary to certain views, tax holidays offer limited 'simplification' opportunities (e.g. where taxpayers must maintain taxpayer accounts to support tax calculations over the post-holiday period).

- For similar reasons, partial profit exemptions are viewed as an inefficient form of incentive, as they provide tax-planning opportunities and tax relief not tied to investment (albeit possibly on a reduced scale, proportionate to the percentage relief offered). Like tax holidays, partial profit exemptions are unlikely to create an efficient result, with opportunities for tax planning and corresponding revenue losses outstripping any benefits.

- Reinvestment allowances, providing a tax deduction equal to some percentage of (pre-tax) reinvested profit, are of questionable use. If incentives tied directly to investment are desired, it would seem preferable to rely on provisions that provide relief in respect of investment expenditures without regard to the specific sources of finance.

- Accelerated depreciation may be an attractive option, but likely of limited interest to investors if the basic capital cost allowance system is restrictive (e.g. mandatory depreciation claims combined with limited loss carry-forward rules). However, general accelerated depreciation applied to a streamlined system of capital cost allowance categories, when combined with five to seven year loss carry-forward rules, offers a relatively simple and efficient means to encourage investment (as elaborated earlier).

While unconditionally promoting the use of accelerated depreciation is not suggested, it is recognized that policy-makers have to respond to political pressures to introduce incentives to promote FDI. Given this, there may be relative advantages with this form of tax incentive. Some support can also be found for investment tax credits (largely to the limits such incentives place on revenue losses, compared to profit-based incentives). However, such incentives, while offering certain advantages, raise some concerns in the SEE context.

- Investment tax credits and investment tax allowances provide a relatively flexible mechanism for targeting additional tax relief (beyond that provided through depreciation) to qualifying investment expenditures. Unlike tax holidays, they provide a means to curb tax revenue loss by limiting the amount of relief earned to some fraction of qualifying investment; by possibly limiting the amount of credit to some fraction of (pre-credit) tax payable (or limiting the amount of allowance to some fraction of (pre-allowance) taxable income). However, such measures may be abused by taxpayers (e.g. 'churning' of qualifying assets to enable multiple access to tax relief), require separate special accounts to track unclaimed balances, and may distort investor choice towards short-lived assets.

  Certain other observations are made as regards tax incentive use, including problems with multiple 'stacking' of incentives, scope for zones to exacerbate rather than control rent seeking, and the need for 'automatic' triggering mechanisms and a 'workable' set of rules for investors and tax administrators.

- Countries should avoid excessive 'stacking' of corporate tax and other incentives. Offering multiple incentives tends to be counterproductive, as it increases complexity contributing to compliance and administrative costs. It also leads to unintended patterns of tax relief across different taxpayers and asset types, leading to inefficiencies in resource allocation. Furthermore, it can create an impression to investors that the country does not have basic 'enabling conditions' necessary for profit-making in the host country, and is attempting to rely on an 'easy fix'. It can also cast doubt over the fiscal position of the country, and contribute to concerns over sovereign risk.

- Special 'zones' giving relief from profit-based taxes tend to attract highly mobile labor-intensive activities (as opposed to long-term capital intensive activities). Incremental investment will be low where zones largely cause capital to be diverted from elsewhere in the country. Where rights to operate from a special zone are granted by officials on a discretionary basis, they invite rent-seeking behavior and weaken efforts aimed at routing out corruption.

- The triggering mechanism for tax incentive relief (whatever its form) should be as 'automatic' as possible, with qualifying criteria stipulated clearly in accessible laws and regulations, in an effort to minimize the

scope for corruption and rent seeking (which tends to escalate with the degree of discretion given to tax officials in granting relief).
- When considering alternative incentive mechanisms, a fundamentally important requirement is a 'workable' set of rules and regulations that are understandable not just to taxpayers, but also to tax administrators. Tax incentive design should avoid overly complicated provisions to the extent that the tax administration is inexperienced, or otherwise weak.

Perhaps the most effective investment 'incentives' are realized by addressing impediments in the basic tax system (i.e. simplifying tax calculations and lowering tax rates on business where possible, taking into account overall fiscal requirements and the incidence of alternative tax bases). Examples could include the use of a single (rather than multiple) corporate tax rate structure; streamlining complex capital cost allowance systems; liberalizing restrictive loss carry-forward rules; increased reliance on (withholding) taxation at source; lowering employer social security contribution rates (offset possibly by increased Value Added Tax (VAT) or Personal Income Tax (PIT) rates). In addition, providing a stable regime that is applied in a transparent and non-arbitrary fashion is essential to attract and retain investment.

Lastly, there are a number of issues raised with the targeting that arises with incentives which, by definition, provide targeted rather than generally available tax relief. A number of general conclusions may be drawn.

- Targeting incentives specifically to foreign investors creates distortions to the extent that foreign investors favor certain sectors or business activities over others. Such targeting is also open to tax planning (with domestic companies disguising themselves as foreign by investing through offshore holding companies), and can foster taxpayer resentment of foreign capital and apathy towards the tax system (discouraging voluntary compliance and feeding the underground economy). Targeting foreign investors may also run counter to national treatment obligations (e.g. WTO and/or EU law).
- Targeting incentives to new investment projects attempts to limit tax relief to new capital. However, qualifying new investment may not be incremental (i.e. would occur in the absence of tax relief). Windfall losses are also imposed on existing capital (reduced share values), raising equity concerns. Tax planning is also encouraged, with investors characterizing 'old' (existing) capital as 'new' (e.g. through selling a company to an offshore holding company, which then reinvests the funds into the host country).
- Targeting by size of investment creates distortions over the choice of firm size and the organization of business activities, resulting in inefficiencies. An exception may be drawn if market failure results in an

under-investment in small firms. However, it is important that one assess whether small firms are being denied capital for reasons of market failure, or as a result of the normal and proper functioning of credit and equity markets. If instances of true market failure tend to be the exception rather than the rule, such targeting should be discouraged, given the inability of government to target incentives properly. Where small firms are targeted, rules should be introduced to discourage large firms from dividing assets across new companies so as to qualify for relief.

- Targeting by business activity, in general, should be discouraged, in particular where it is unclear that government has better information than the private sector in determining which activities/sectors are likely to be more profitable (picking 'winners'). Exceptions may apply where market failure can be identified, for example in the case of R&D and environmental protection, where the private sector tends to ignore social 'spillover' benefits and under-invests. However, even in these areas, it remains necessary to administer certain 'grey' areas (e.g. subsidizing pure research versus other forms of research versus development). Difficulties in assessing the degree of market failure suggest that incentive relief should be moderate.

- Targeting incentives to underdeveloped regions may be called for to address market failures curbing investment. However, regional-based incentives have rarely been efficient in encouraging FDI. Where programs have failed, it is normally because of a lack of 'enabling conditions', and an inability of incentives to create a critical mass of activity that would help generate these conditions. Where regional incentives are used to promote activity, despite efficiency concerns, the incentives should be carefully targeted to investment in well-specified areas, and monitored on a frequent basis to assess results. Sunset provisions in general should apply (see below), and the continuation of incentives should depend on results.

- Targeting by type of finance (e.g. retained earnings) creates distortions in capital markets and should be avoided. If the objective is to encourage investment, it would be more efficient to target investment expenditures directly (without regard to how they are financed). If the tax system is creating distortions towards excessive levels of debt finance, consideration should be given to introducing/strengthening thin-capitalization rules.

- Targeting incentives to apply for a fixed period to temporarily boost economic growth runs a risk of mistiming (aggravating rather attenuating cycle effects). However, announcing and immediately implementing targeted incentives to apply for a short period (e.g. one to two years) may shift forward investment that would have otherwise been delayed. Furthermore, in general, all incentives should be introduced with a sunset clause stipulating that a given incentive will expire at a certain date (which may then be extended, conditional on a positive evaluation of past effects).

- For SEE countries working towards membership of the EU, in the longer term their tax incentives will have to be consistent with the state aid rules and, consequently, it seems advisable to avoid incentives of such a duration or type that they will have to be dismantled on eventual accession.

- Whatever the form of targeting, the benefits in terms of avoiding tax relief to unintended recipients must be weighed against the additional administrative costs in monitoring the program, defending boundaries under pressure, and implementing measures to address tax abuse.

- Finally, excessive discretion in the targeting of incentives, by contributing to a lack of transparency, invites corruption and increases perceived risks, thereby discouraging investment across all (targeted and non-targeted) activities. Thus, as with the provision of incentives themselves, the process of identifying qualifying activities should be as 'automatic' as possible, through careful drafting of the applicable tax laws and regulations.

On balance, there may be merit in policy change in the direction of a relatively simple tax system offering a competitive statutory corporate income tax rate, accelerated depreciation with flexible loss carry forward rules, and possibly carefully targeted investment tax credits (or allowances) with anti-abuse rules. At the same time, SEE countries need to implement base protection rules (e.g. transfer pricing rules, thin-capitalization rules) to guard against aggressive tax planning and enable collection of a fair and reasonable share of tax on host country profits that can be easily managed by MNEs. A number of tax policy changes recently introduced by SEE countries move in the direction of the arguments elaborated in this chapter.

Given that a simple corporate tax system can deliver a low effective host country tax burden – while avoiding compliance and administration costs associated with complex and possibly redundant incentive provisions – SEE countries may wish to resist the use or introduction of 'add-on' fiscal incentives to enrich the tax pot, given their poor track-record in encouraging incremental FDI. This view recognizes that the ability to use the tax system to attract investment depends critically on the state of the 'enabling environment' in a host country. Special tax incentives are unlikely to attract investment where political instability, economic instability, and/or governance problems remain a serious issue. In such cases, efforts to administer a tax incentive may heighten uncertainty and perceived risks and *discourage* investment. Having said that, it is unchallenged that there is pressure on SEE countries to offer a list of special incentives given the fierce competition for FDI within the region and the availability of a wide range of tax incentives in competing jurisdictions. However, SEE countries are advised to reflect seriously on the merits of adhering to a structurally sound system capable of generating tax revenues to help finance public expenditures (e.g. infrastructure development in support of an 'enabling environment'), taking into account country experiences and the various considerations raised in the report.

Annex: tax systems, rates and incentives in SEE countries

This section reviews host country tax systems, tax rates and incentives in SEE countries, with a focus on direct taxation and corporate income tax in particular.

The corporate income tax systems in all of the countries are fairly conventional, adopting essentially the 'classical' model, and in most cases applying final withholding tax on dividends paid to domestic individuals.[9] Exceptions apply in FYR Macedonia and Serbia, which impose tax at the personal shareholder level. Under Macedonia's system, personal tax is levied on dividends received, with a personal tax credit for tax withheld at source. Serbia's partial inclusion approach is somewhat unique. Tax is first withheld at source on 50 percent of distributed profit (giving an effective withholding tax rate of 10 percent), and rather than providing a credit for this tax, shareholders are taxed on half of dividends received. This results in a slightly higher effective personal tax rate than if dividends received were taxed in full, with credit for withholding tax.

All of the SEE countries adopt a broadly similar approach to the computation of taxable income, although the rules on deductible expenditures may be seen as somewhat restrictive in Albania, FYR Macedonia and Serbia and Montenegro.

Over the past decade there has been a fairly steady reduction in CIT rates throughout the SEE region, mirroring worldwide trends, and perhaps evidencing an element of tax competition. Figure 6.1 shows where basic corporate income tax rates stood on 2001. None of the countries have what would be considered high statutory corporate tax rates. Of course, the statutory rates, while relevant to tax-planning incentives, do not tell the full story in determining effective tax rates: the determinants of the tax base, and special tax incentives must also be factored in.

The depreciation systems appear to differ considerably across SEE countries in terms of their level of complexity (although it is unclear from certain questionnaire responses whether full detail was provided). In certain cases, most notably perhaps in the case of Serbia and Montenegro, scope would appear to exist for simplification of depreciation frameworks, perhaps in combination with more generous depreciation provisions.

Most of the countries permit losses to be carried forward for five years. However, Albania and FYR Macedonia permit only a three-year loss carry-forward, and Moldova appears to provide no loss relief at all. Provisions denying loss carry-forwards beyond three years may be seen as

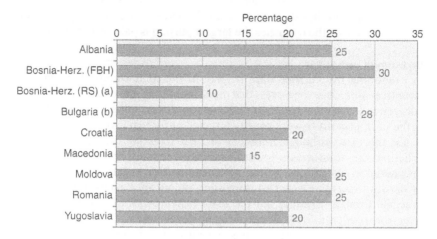

Figure 6.1 Statutory CIT rates in the SEE countries, 2001.

Notes
The CIT rates shown are those applicable to retained earnings (as opposed to distributions).
FBH denotes Federation of Bosnia Herzegovina; RS denotes Republic of Srpksa. (a) The
rate shown is the top CIT rate (under a regressive schedule). (b) The rate shown is the top
CIT rate (under a progressive schedule).

impeding investment, particularly when judged against international
norms. The rules are particularly onerous where depreciation claims are
mandatory, as they are in most SEE and other transition economies.
There are also important considerations as regards the interaction of loss
provisions and investment incentives, particularly investment allowances
(addressed below).

   Certain differences are found in the treatment of intercorporate dividends. Bulgaria and Macedonia (FYR) waive such dividends from withholding tax at source, imposing withholding tax only when profits are
ultimately distributed to individual shareholders. Albania limits the
exemption to distributions to related companies as a means of eliminating
multiple-taxation of profits distributed along a (related) corporate chain.
Distributions to unrelated companies are subject to withholding tax (at 15
percent, versus 10 percent on distributions to resident individuals), which
is creditable at the intermediary level. Romania levies withholding tax on
intercorporate dividends without relieving measures, tending to discourage vertical corporate structures. Serbia also levies withholding tax on
intercorporate dividends, but relies on a gross-up and credit system at the
corporate level to relieve withholding and (notional) corporate tax paid at
source.

   Personal income taxes are generally fairly low: the top rate varies from
a low of 18 percent (FYR Macedonia) to a high of 40 percent (Romania),
although the thresholds for the highest rate, being related to local income

levels, are relatively low. By contrast, payroll taxes and social security contributions are significant, and vary from 32 percent to about 53 percent of wages. In most of the countries the largest portion is paid by the employer.

Investment incentives

In examining the current state of play in the SEE countries in the tax incentive area, one observes that most countries have moved towards adherence to national treatment, and in some cases full adherence. While, in the past, incentives were overtly targeted at foreign investors, today this is not the case, although instances of such targeting can still be found. Whether the adjustments toward national treatment were motivated by international obligations, or out of concerns over negative consequences of denying incentive relief to domestics, or out of a recognition that, in practice, foreign investors are the main beneficiaries of direct tax incentives, this reorientation is an encouraging development.

The review of current and past incentive use in recent years is also illuminating. All SEE countries have tested a variety of tax incentives in the past, often with seriously disappointing results, and have moved to eliminate or replace them. A number of countries have changed their tax incentive provisions significantly over recent years: Bulgaria and Romania, in particular, have followed rather erratic courses, removing incentives and replacing them with others at regular intervals. At the same time, SEE officials have recognized the importance of establishing credibility in the tax policy area to investors, and the corresponding need to provide 'grandfathering' provisions, despite the ensuing revenue losses (see Table 6.1).

Currently, one observes widespread reliance on VAT and customs duty exemptions and zone incentives. Outside its zone legislation, Albania limits its VAT and customs duty relief to a three-year deferral for purchases, or in-kind share contributions, of machinery and equipment. Raw materials are exempt for customs duty, but only for inward processing for ultimate export.

All SEE countries currently have zone legislation, with varying degrees of incentive relief and take-up activity. In Albania, while zone legislation has been drafted, no such zones have been established. This may be at least in part explained by the fact that corporate tax relief (e.g. tax holidays, profit exemptions) are not on offer, whereas they are in zones in other SEE countries.

Investment expenditure-based incentives are currently used in all SEE countries, in some countries more faithfully than others. While examples of an investment tax credit and investment allowances can be found, one observes a preference for the investment allowance variety. This is clearly the case in FYR Macedonia, which currently employs no fewer than three variants – one targeted at environmental protection, another targeted at regional activities, and a third that is more general in application. In each case, the full amount (100 percent) of expenditure on qualifying assets

Table 6.1 Investment tax incentives in SEE countries

	Albania	Bosnia and Herzegovina	Bulgaria	Croatia	Macedonia	Moldova	Romania	Yugoslavia (FR)
Tax holidays		X		X	X	X		X
Partial profit exemption		X			X			
Preferential CIT rate				X			X	
Accelerated depreciation			X	X	X		X	X
Investment allowance		X			X			
Reinvestment allowance							X	
Investment tax credit			X					X
Customs duty exemption		X		X	X	X	X	X
Customs duty deferral	X						X	
VAT exemption	X							
VAT deferral	X						X	
Special zones offering								
Customs duty exemption	X	X	X	X	X	X	X	X
VAT exemption		X	X		X	X	X	
Tax holiday (CIT exemption)		X		X	X	X	X	
Other tax exemptions		X			X		X	

Notes
These provisions apply as of 2001. This table reports incentives available for new investment (ignores 'grandfathering' provisions).

may be set off against taxable income. This is also the case for investment allowances provided in Bosnia and Herzegovina.

However certain overall limits may apply. FYR Macedonia caps its regional allowance at 50 percent of taxable profit, for example, whereas its general allowance is subject to a 25 percent cap. Similarly, the Republic of Srpksa caps its allowance at 15 percent. On the other hand, the environmental allowance in Macedonia is not subject to a cap, nor is the investment allowance in the Federation of Bosnia and Herzegovina.[10] Unrestricted investment allowances may be problematic to the extent that they enable the conversion of unutilized tax allowances into tax losses, which can then be carried forward subject to loss carry-forward restrictions. Even where the allowances are capped, their interaction with other provisions (e.g. accelerated depreciation) may have a similar effect.

Another interesting variant is the approach taken by Romania, where the allowance appears to be strictly targeted at investment financed by retentions, rather than debt-financed investment or investment financed by new share issue. The general reinvestment allowance also differs from those noted above in that half rather than the full amount of expenditures on qualifying assets may be deducted from taxable profit, while the SME reinvestment allowance permits the full amount to be deducted. The reinvestment allowance for large investment projects is earned at a 20 percent rate, which is supplemented with accelerated depreciation provisions that boost the first year deduction to 70 percent of qualifying investment expenditures.

Reliance on a reinvestment allowance may be motivated by an effort to encourage foreign direct investors to reinvest profits in Romania, rather than distribute those earnings to parent or holding companies abroad. But given the aim of encouraging domestic investment, it is not clear why investment financed by new share issue would be denied relief. If a concern exists over highly-leveraged firms, given the base-eroding effects of interest deductions, attention to other policy areas might be preferable to a source of funds restriction. Such areas could include introducing thin-capitalization rules (currently Romania does not have such rules), and revisiting policies towards the setting of non-resident withholding tax rates on interest paid to treaty partners that do not tax interest income.

The only SEE country relying on the investment tax credit variant was Serbia. The credit follows very closely international norms in the use of this measure, with credits earned on qualifying capital at a 10 percent rate, and with total claimed credits capped to not exceed 50 percent of tax otherwise payable. A richer variant is targeted at SMEs, with the credit rate increased to 30 percent and the cap lifted to 70 percent.

Croatia, FYR Macedonia, Romania and Serbia all promote their corporate systems as offering accelerated depreciation. However, while the relevant provisions for Croatia and Macedonia do provide for depreciation of qualifying assets at a faster rate (25 percent higher) than would otherwise apply, it is unclear whether these higher rates are actually higher relative to true economic depreciation. Accelerated depreciation appears more likely in Croatia, which doubles its depreciation rates for targeted capital, and Romania which, as noted above, provides a first-year deduction of 50 percent of qualifying depreciable capital costs as part of its 'large project' incentive program.

Despite the disappointing results associated with profit-based incentives – those offering tax relief as a percentage of profits of qualifying firms – it is unfortunate that a number of SEE countries continue to use them. In some cases, tax holiday and partial profit exemption incentives are available without regional restriction. In others, their application is targeted at profits derived from zone activities. Wherever used, however, it is highly unlikely that such incentives would be found to be efficient given the tax-minimization opportunities created, unless qualifying firms are audited on a regular and professional (arm's length) basis.

Targeting such relief to zones may help limit incentive abuse – in particular, related-party transactions and financial structures aimed at artificially characterizing non-targeted profits as profits from zone activities. The use of zones would tend to limit the number of firms eligible for profit exemptions, and increase prospects for auditing of tax accounts to establish if profits are determined on an arm's length basis. However, in practice it is unclear whether this potential is realized. Without safeguards ensuring transparent and arm's length relationships between zone companies and tax officials administering incentives, a zone program – by bringing together tax officials and select companies to negotiate an agreement on zone activities – may contribute to, and institutionalize, a setting that is ripe for corruption. In other words, zone programs providing for profit exemptions may feed rather than lessen scope for abuse and corruption.

As noted, the use of profit-based incentives is widespread in the SEE region. Indeed, all of the countries considered resort to these incentives, with the exception of Albania and Bulgaria. Bosnia and Herzegovina, FYR Macedonia and Moldova all offer tax holidays targeted explicitly at FDI. Firms that are entirely foreign-owned enjoy a five-year tax holiday in Bosnia and Herzegovina, compared with a three-year holiday in Macedonia. Firms satisfying a minimum foreign participation threshold (20 percent) enjoy a partial profit exemption in both countries, with the exempt proportion in FYR Macedonia tied to the proportion to foreign participation, and in Bosnia and Herzegovina, set at fixed, descending amounts (100 percent, 75 percent, 30 percent) over a three-year period. Foreign participation of at least 30 percent (or investment of at least $250,000) triggers a tax holiday of one to six years in Moldova, subject to turnover restrictions. Tax holidays in Croatia at ten years, standing out as the most generous of those examined, may be seen as implicitly targeted at FDI, given the requirement of a minimum of $7 million invested (or alternatively 75 new jobs created).

Regionally-targeted tax holidays and other variants are also observed. In the Republic of Srpksa, a three-year tax holiday is provided to new firms operating in regions designated as underdeveloped. In Serbia, profits on activities in underdeveloped regions may be fully exempt for two years. Special tax holidays of up to five years are also available in Serbia for profits derived from concession contracts. Other variants also exist, including the 50 percent profit exemption for listed-companies in FYR Macedonia.

While Albania and Bulgaria stand out from the rest in not providing a 'carte blanche' to MNEs in setting their own effective corporate tax rate, it is noteworthy that this vision has been learned the hard way. Prior to 1999, Albania gave a four-year tax holiday to domestic and foreign-owned enterprises engaged in manufacturing activities. Following the holiday, manufacturing firms were provided with a 60 percent profit exemption. This program was found to be inefficient, and difficult to administer. Particularly difficult to administer was the requirement that tax be paid *ex post* on profits exempted over the holiday period in the event that firms terminate their activities following the holiday. The Albanian rules contained a provision requiring that the manufacturing activities, qualifying for the holiday, continue for six years (for a total of ten beyond the holiday period). Such provisions, typical under most tax holiday programs, are notoriously difficult to enforce. The Albanian tax holiday was also found to be open to corruption, given discretion over the selection of qualifying firms, and the overall prevalence of non-arm's length relationships between officials and those firms.

Similarly, Bulgaria provided a three-year tax holiday to foreign-controlled firms (satisfying a 50 percent foreign ownership requirement), followed up with a 50 percent profit exemption for two years. For priority investment projects (in excess of $5 million), the 50 percent profit exemption was available for ten years. Again, the program was found to be inefficient, open to taxpayer manipulation, and prone to rent-seeking behavior on the part of tax officials.

A particularly striking and important finding is that one currently observes a perplexing combination of generous tax incentives in a number of SEE countries, alongside restrictive rules governing basic tax treatment (e.g. treatment of losses). Other tax impediments to investment are also observed, including complex and cumbersome depreciation rules.

Notes

1 This chapter and the accompanying annex are based upon a study undertaken in the context of the Investment Compact for South East Europe, a key component of the Stability Pact. The study was led by W. Steven Clark, Head of the Tax Policy and Statistics Unit at the OECD Centre for Tax Policy and Administration, and Professor Alex Easson, at Queen's University, Canada, in cooperation with the Investment Compact team. A full version of the study can be found in the publication *Tax Policy Assessment and Design in Support of*

Direct Investment: A Study of Countries in South East Europe. Luca Gandullia intensively cooperated with a careful revision to this chapter. I am indebted to him.

2 Albania, Belarus, Bosnia and Herzegovina, Bulgaria, Croatia, Czech Republic, Estonia, Hungary, Latvia, Lithuania, former Yugoslav Republic of Macedonia, Moldova, Poland, Romania, Russian Federation, Slovakia, Slovenia, Ukraine, Serbia and Montenegro.

3 The Member countries are Albania, Bosnia and Herzegovina, Bulgaria, Croatia, former Yugoslav Republic of Macedonia, Moldova (since 2001), Romania, and Serbia and Montenegro.

4 A survey conducted for the Ruding Committee, for example, found that 57 percent of MNE managers within the EU always regarded the (statutory) corporate tax rate on business profits to be a relevant consideration in deciding in which country to locate business activity. The proportion rises to 80 percent when MNEs who usually take statutory CIT rates into account are included. Next in importance after CIT rates were withholding tax rates (40 percent), depreciation rules (36 percent) and loss relief (35 percent). The survey, however, was not concerned with other types of tax.

5 Note that consumption taxes, if sufficiently high, may lower domestic consumption demand but would not be expected to have any significant influence over export-oriented investment.

6 Halvorsen, in a study of FDI in Thailand, found customs duties and import taxes to be an important factor.

7 According to the Ruding Committee report, financial service centers are the most sensitive to taxation; co-ordination centers and R&D centers somewhat less so. The survey conducted for the Committee found that tax was always or usually a major factor in the location of 70 percent of co-ordination centers and of almost 80 percent of financial centers.

8 This especially seems to be the case in some of the countries of Eastern Europe and Southeast Europe.

9 The present Croatian corporate tax system came into effect in 2001. The previous system was unique, being described by some as a business consumption-type tax, or a form of cash-flow tax. By allowing a deduction for 'interest' imputed to corporate equity, the tax base was substantially narrower than under more conventional systems.

10 An investment allowance may be restricted to some percentage (under 100 percent) of qualifying investment expenditures – but the amount of allowance earned may or may not be capped to some percentage (under 100 percent) of taxable profit (measured before the allowance). Without such a cap, the allowance may eliminate taxable profit, or if large enough relative to profit, create a tax loss (i.e. a loss that can be carried forward for tax purposes).

Part II

Country studies of tax systems and tax reforms in New EU Members

7 The Czech Republic

Simone Pellegrino[1]

7.1 Introduction and executive summary

Before the 1993 splitting of the previous Czechoslovakia unitary state, the Czech economy had been in transition from a planned economy system to a market-oriented economy. The three main goals of economic reforms were: the privatization process of both enterprises and the bank system; the liberalization of prices and of foreign trade; fiscal reform. All of these goals have almost been completed. During the 1990s, the Czech Republic made progress in restructuring and modernizing its economy, but difficulties arose from both the political and the economic side.

In the early 1990s about 80 percent of all national enterprises were privatized and today only a small proportion of the strategic industries is still in public hands. The 1990s' reforms induced a revolution in the country, so it was important to maintain social cohesion during the transition to the market model economy and balance the sacrifices of new tax system with the benefits of public expenditures (Šujan and Šujanová 1994).

The Czech Republic is a traditional industrial country and today its plants and equipment are rather obsolete. Its economy mainly depends on foreign trade, but this was in imbalance during most of the 1990s. In the early 1990s, the government debt was very small; however, in 1996 it reached just about 13 percent of GDP. During the last few years it rapidly increased because expenditures have grown more than revenues, despite the large privatization receipts of the last few years. Until 1995, the government budget continued to have a moderate surplus, while the budget of the following years had an increasing deficit. It is important to notice that an increase in poverty levels and in income inequality took place during the transition. The Czech income per capita Gini coefficient increased from 0.20 in 1988, to 0.23 in 1992 and to 0.26 in 1996, and probably it has been still increasing over the last few years. The Czech per capita GDP is not more than about 40 percent of the EU-15 average (unweighted PPP values), but is the highest in comparison with EU New Members' ones.

The fiscal reform started in 1993 and the new tax system is close to the

EU model. Mainly, it comprises the personal and corporate income taxes, the value added tax, the excise duties, the real estate tax, the road tax, the inheritance and gift tax and other minor taxes. During the following years the system was repeatedly amended, but no great improvements were made in the areas of direct taxation and in value added tax. In fact, one of the main current problems concerns VAT harmonization according to the EU standards, in particular with respect to tax rates and tax exemptions; important changes are planned for the next few years. The structure of revenues is somewhat different from EU standards. The main share of total revenues (44 percent in 1998 and not different until recently) is still given by social contributions, which thus stay as the most important levy imposed on individuals and corporations. The Czech Republic social contributions are among the highest around the world. By adding social security contributions to personal income tax, the negative consequence arises of a very high taxation of labor. This can create distortions in the labor market, open opportunities to the shadow economy and induce a loss of competitiveness, compared with other countries (especially EU New Members).

VAT constitutes the second most important tax. In 1998, its revenue amounted to 6.6 percent of GDP and to 17 percent of total revenues, and it is about 50 percent of indirect taxes. There are two rates, 22 and 5 percent, but the list of goods taxed at 5 percent was reduced at the beginning of 2004.

The personal income tax has a progressive structure, which is given by four tax brackets and some allowances. The rates range from 15 to 32 percent, but more than one half of the taxpayers fall into the lower bracket and the average effective tax rate is not higher than 10 percent. Although inflation was very high during the last decade, the income tax structure has not been fully compensated for fiscal drag. Corporation income tax revenue amounted to 3.7 percent of GDP and to 17 percent of total tax revenue in 1998; it was introduced in 1993 and its structure is close to the EU model. Starting from the year 2000, it has been applied at a flat rate of 31 percent, but up to 1999 it was at 35 percent; a rate reduction down to 28 percent is planned for 2004 (it will be 24 percent in 2006), to compete better with other new EU members, which have introduced lower tax rates during the last few years.

The Czech fiscal government structure was made up of only two tiers, but since 2001 there have been three tiers: the central government, regions and the municipalities. These number more than six thousands and their average size is very small. However, the Constitution also makes provision for some larger regions, but before 2001 these regions were not realized. Their functions were performed by 77 district offices that were merely non-autonomous arms of the central government. From 2002, 14 regions were started, but they were totally funded by the central government until 2003. This structure will be completed during the next few years, because today there is insufficient monitoring of the local government debt and expenditures and there are no adequate fiscal equalization transfers. The main aim of local budget reform is to increase the share of local sources of revenues and the municipalities' own taxes.

By considering now the 1998 distribution of fiscal burden on specific factors, it can be noticed that employed labor was the factor most heavily taxed, at an implicit tax rate of 38.6 percent, while the implicit tax rate on consumption was just 15.6 percent, a value very low in comparison with the standard VAT rate of 22 percent. From 1993 to 1998, the taxation on employed labor steadily grew, from 16.9 GDP points to 18.5, while the share of revenues of the other factors decreased: that on consumption from 13.2 GDP points in 1993 to 11.1 in 1998; that on self-employed labor from 4 GDP points to 2.9 and that on capital and business from 8.9 GDP points to 5.7 (a decrease due to the need of reducing corporate incomes tax rates from their initial levels).

The current parliament debate mainly focuses on reducing the budget deficit, to avoid an expected steep increase of public debt during the next few years. Since 1997, in fact, public debt has continued to rise, because the increasing budget deficit has been financed through the issuance of government bonds purchased by the private sector, despite large privatization receipts. Czech governments, however, are very reluctant to adopt the necessary reforms, to make expenditure cuts, industrial restructuring and to reform the legislation system and financial market transparency; instead, bank privatizations have been completed in 2001.

The deterioration of the budget balance has been due both to an increase in spending and to a decline (or a lesser increase) in tax revenue. According to new data, fiscal revenue has been steady in the last few years: in 2000 the Czech total fiscal revenue was 39.3 percent of GDP, 39.1 percent in 2001 and 39.8 percent in 2002. However, the level of public expenditure (excluded net lending) was 42.1 percent of GDP in 1998, 43.7 percent in 2000, 44.2 percent in 2001, 46.6 percent in 2002; levels that are too high to achieve the Maastricht rule of a 3 percent budget deficit. Some reforms could not be postponed, in order to stop the primary unbalance increase. A recurrent proposal is to reform the social security system, to take better account of demographic development: retirement ages should rise, as required in almost any other EU country. The pension system, in fact, operates as a pay-as-you-go system and absorbs about 9 percent of GDP and 24 percent of public expenditures.

So the most important issue of fiscal policy would be the sustainability of public finances in the medium run. No basic steps have been made during the last years, but finally a reform was approved by the government and parliament in summer and autumn 2003. At present, the equilibrium of the public finances is not under control. The reduction of the budget deficit will have to become the highest priority of the Czech government in the next few years. Its institutional framework and its low public debt, mixed with the new market power economy starting in the 1990s, were negative ingredients (from the political point of view) to create a good environment for economic growth and institutional stability over the last decade (Bronchi and Burns 2000).

7.2 The structure of the system at the end of the 1990s and its development after the collapse of the communist regime

A broad view of the current structure of taxes and social security contributions

In 1998, the Czech Republic's total fiscal revenues were 38.3 percent of GDP. Total tax revenues amounted to 56 percent of total fiscal revenues and to 21.4 percent of GDP, while the remaining 44 percent was given by social contributions that were the main source of revenue with a share on GDP of 17 percent. This share became high and exaggerated if compared with the EU average level. Still, in 1998, the net rate of employee contributions was 7.5 percent and the net rate of employer contributions was 22.75 percent of labor income. Then, social security contributions' composition was also unbalanced because of the higher value of those contributions imposed on employers than on the employees, and because of the low charge on the self employed (about 2 percent of GDP) – see Figure 7.1.

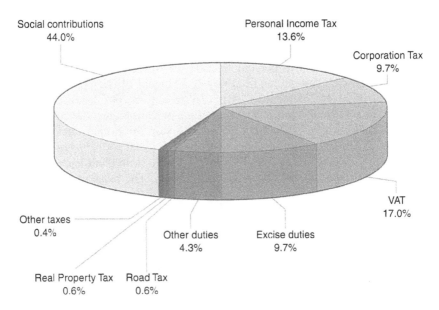

Figure 7.1 Structure of the Czech Republic total revenue in 1998 (source: see text).

Direct taxes were lower than the indirect ones and this was due to the low level of personal income tax, which amounted to only 5.2 percent of GDP and to 13.6 percent of total revenue. Corporation income tax revenue amounted to 3.7 percent of GDP and to 9.7 percent of total revenue. The second most important tax was VAT and its revenue amounted to 6.6 percent of GDP and to 17.1 percent of total revenues. Its standard rate and share of total taxation as well as its share of indirect taxes equaled about the EU average. The share of excise duties was 9.7 percent of total revenue and 3.7 percent of GDP.

The development of the system from the early to the late 1990s

During the ten years from 1993 to 2003, the Czech Republic fiscal system did not basically change because, already in the early 1990s, it was scheduled as the EU model. Despite this, the transition process and the EU harmonization required some changes. As shown in Table 7.1, the Czech total fiscal revenue decreased by 10 percent, and this was made by cutting total tax revenue from 26.3 percent of GDP in 1993 to 21.4 percent in 1998, while the social contributions' level has been relatively stable during this period (see Figure 7.2). In the same years, expenditures have been cut by only 4 percent and this gap is the origin of the net borrowing increase during the last few years.

The most relevant changes in total tax revenue composition have been the reduction of both direct and indirect taxes. The direct ones decreased by two GDP points from 10.9 percent in 1993 to 9 percent in 1998 and this difference can be split into a reduction by 50 percent of corporation tax revenue and an increase from 3.8 percent of GDP to 5.2 percent of personal income tax revenue. The cut has been more evident with respect to indirect taxes, which decreased from 15.4 percent of GDP in 1993 to 12.4 percent in 1998. This relevant decline was due not only to the VAT rate reduction from 23 to 22 percent but also to the increasing list of goods taxed at the reduced rate. VAT reduction is one third of the total cut in indirect taxes, while excise duties have been steady and the other indirect taxes have been cut by 1.9 GDP points.

At the beginning of the 1990s, it was necessary for the Czech tax system

Table 7.1 The share of tax revenues accounted for by the Czech government and local budgets

	1993	1994	1995	1996	1997	1998
Government budget	85.4	80.5	78.3	79.6	79.1	78.6
Local budgets	14.6	19.5	21.7	20.4	20.9	21.4

Source: Government Final Account of the Czech Republic for 1998, Czech Republic Ministry of Finance.

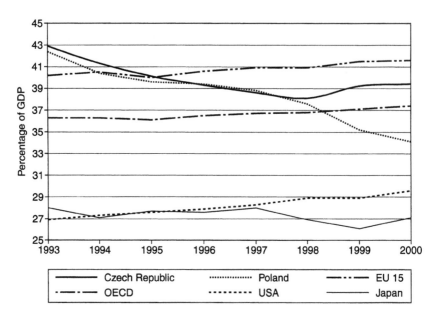

Figure 7.2 Total tax revenue in the Czech Republic from 1993 to 2000 as a percentage of GDP (source: see text).

to decrease the rate and the share of corporation tax (16.5 percent of total
revenues in 1993), because the level was one of the highest in the world
and it would not have been consistent with a market system. These cuts
were very big and fast: the tax rate was 75 percent in 1986, 55 percent in
1991, 45 percent in 1993, 39 percent in 1996, 35 percent in 1998 and now
(2003) 31 percent. The profits taxation as a percent of GDP was 7.1
percent in 1993, 5.6 percent in 1994, 4.0 percent in 1996 and 3.7 percent in
1998, but still today stays high compared with both the EU average and
EU selected New Members' level (7 percent of total revenues in the EU
area, 9.7 percent in the Czech Republic and 6.4 percent in the other EU
New Members).

Although social security contributions remained relatively stable from
1993 to 1998 as a share of GDP, their share of total revenues has increased
from 38.6 to 44 percent, but this is due to the decrease of total tax revenue.
It is important to notice that, in this period, social contribution revenues
have exceeded the social expenditures, but this surplus will be necessary in
the future because health and pension expenditures are increasing, as can
be observed in other EU countries.

The apportioning of revenue among government tiers and fiscal federalism

The Czech fiscal government structure was made up of just two tiers until 2001: the central government and the municipalities, which number more than 6000 and have a very small average size (80 percent of municipalities have less than 1000 people and 90 percent less than 2000 people). Their number grew by 50 percent from 1990 to 1992 because, at that time, a 'Municipality Act' established the liberalization of municipalities' rights and their 'absolute' independence. So, because of this breaking up of the country, one of the most important problems of fiscal and administrative structure is the efficiency level of such small bodies.

However, the Constitution also makes a provision for larger regions, but before 2001 these regions were not realized and their functions were performed by 77 district offices that were arms of the central government without any autonomy. From 2002, there are 14 regions at work but they are totally funded by the central government. This structure will be completed during the next few years, because today there is insufficient monitoring on the local governments' debt and expenditures and there are no adequate fiscal equalization transfers.

The law, in fact, provides that the debt of local governments may not exceed 15 percent of the previous year's revenues but the local governors want to increase more local spending. Today, 65 percent of municipalities are carrying some form of debt.

Although local revenues are mainly distributed among municipalities according to the number of inhabitants, the gap in economic growth and GDP per capita among the regions has been growing over time because a share of revenues was distributed according to the locations of the business activities; the concentration of enterprises and businessmen in the big cities is an important fiscal disadvantage for poor areas under the current tax sharing system. This gap can affect the opportunity to create an effective system of fiscal equalization transfers, to prevent lower tiers' financial crises and to give to local governments an adequate ability to predict their revenues in the medium run. Furthermore, the current structure of distribution of tax revenue among government tiers increases the competition among municipalities for the permanent residence of inhabitants. Finally, an important obstacle to further decentralization is the already mentioned size structure of the Czech municipalities.

In 1998, the share of total revenues accruing to central government was 73 percent of total revenues (44 percent, excluding social contributions for pensions), while that to local governments was 12 percent and that to health funds was 15 percent. From the early to the late 1990s, these shares of total revenue did not change in a relevant way. The share of central government decreased only by 4.3 percent (8 percent, excluding social contributions for pensions), while the share of local governments increased by three percentage points and that of health funds increased by 1.4 percent (Kamenìckovà 1999) – see Table 7.2.

The Czech total revenue share of sub-national level can be split in 47.7 percent of tax revenues (of which 90 percent is from income tax and 5.6 from property tax), 36.3 percent of non-tax revenues and 16 percent of grants (1999 data). This share is lower than both that existing in the EU area (27 percent) and that in selected EU New Members (19 percent). During the 1990s, grants became less important than in the previous system and other kinds of revenues have been increased, like revenue sharing of the personal income tax and of the corporate income tax. However, the most popular local tax, i.e. the property tax, has a small role in municipalities' revenues and in income redistribution; its share on total revenues is very low. This tax is collected by central government and its revenue is transferred to municipalities, and this is not an efficient system to provide for the political independency of this tier of government. Besides, the cadastral system should be modernized in the future.

In conclusion, the Czech Republic local governments have limited tax autonomy compared with the size of their spending responsibilities and local needs; this is a problem, especially for the smaller municipalities that have a bigger gap between tax capacity and expenditure needs than other municipalities. At present, central government regulates the public services under local government competence and finances a high share of spending. In fact, only a share of municipalities' revenues derives from own taxes and a consistent share derives in the form of grants from the state level. This structure cannot be efficient in allocating competencies among tiers and can tempt local governments to increase spending. In fact, some small local governments have been bankrupted in the last few years. However, the Czech system is just emerging from the centralist era that characterized the communist regime, and the fiscal reform of the early 1990s has already incorporated some important elements of decentralization that will be completed in the future (OECD 2002).

A comparison with other main New Members and the EU average

At the end of the 1990s, the Czech Republic's total fiscal revenue was similar to that observed for the other selected EU New Members, but more than four percentage points lower than the EU average. This difference is very important for fiscal planning because the expenditure level was four GDP points higher than the total revenue.

Fiscal revenue was six GDP points lower than the EU average (27.6 percent) while social contributions were two GDP points more than the EU average and three GDP points more than the EU New Members' mean level. In comparison with the other New Members, the same level of total revenues was characterized by a different tax mix: the Czech Republic

Table 7.2 Structure and development of fiscal revenue in the Czech Republic, New Members and EU 15 as a percentage of GDP, 1992–98

	1992			1994			1996			1998		
	Czech Republic	New members	EU	Czech Republic	New members	EU	Czech Republic	New members	EU	Czech Republic	New members	EU
Direct taxes, of which	10.9	10.1	13.5	10.3	10.0	13.5	9.2	9.6	13.4	9.0	9.2	13.7
Personal income	3.8	6.4	9.6	4.6	7.0	9.6	5.1	7.1	9.3	5.2	6.7	9.3
Corporation income	7.1	3.6	2.3	5.6	2.9	2.3	4.0	2.5	2.7	3.7	2.5	3.0
Indirect taxes, of which	15.4	15.6	13.4	14.4	16.5	13.4	13.5	16.9	13.7	12.4	15.5	13.9
VAT	7.6	5.1	6.7	7.3	7.4	6.7	7.0	7.4	6.9	6.6	7.9	7.0
Excise duties	4.0	3.4	3.4	4.0	4.2	3.4	3.9	4.1	3.4	3.7	4.1	3.5
Others	3.9	9.3	3.3	3.2	5.0	3.3	2.6	4.9	3.4	2.1	3.6	3.5
Total tax revenue	26.3	25.7	26.9	24.7	26.4	26.9	22.7	26.5	27.1	21.4	24.7	27.6
Social contributions	16.5	16.1	14.5	16.6	15.7	14.5	16.5	14.3	15.3	16.9	14.2	15.0
Employers	10.2	10.0	8.1	10.7	9.0	8.1	10.9	8.0	8.3	11.0	7.9	8.2
Employees	3.8	5.3	4.8	3.9	5.1	4.8	3.8	4.8	5.1	3.9	4.8	5.0
Self employed	2.5	1.8	1.6	2.0	1.6	1.6	1.8	1.5	1.9	2.0	1.6	1.9
Total fiscal revenue	42.8	41.8	41.4	41.3	42.2	41.4	39.2	40.8	42.4	38.3	38.9	42.6
Administrative level												
Central government	33.2	25.9	22.8	31.1	25.8	22.8	29.1	25.4	22.4	28.0	23.9	22.9
Local government	3.9	3.0	3.0	4.9	3.5	3.0	4.7	3.4	4.0	4.6	3.7	4.0
Social Security	5.8	12.9	14.5	5.4	12.9	14.5	5.4	11.5	15.2	5.7	11.4	14.9

Sources: EU Commission (2000a) for Czech Republic and New Members (unweighted average); Eurostat (2000) for EU-15 (1997 unweighted average).

Notes

Czech data start in 1993 and Social security is only health.

total tax revenue was three GDP points lower than in other New Members, whereas social contributions were three GDP points higher. As for the share of total tax revenue, the Czech Republic had the same level of VAT and excise duties, a lower level of personal income tax and a higher level of corporation tax.

The splitting of taxes into direct and indirect ones was different from the EU standard, which is characterized by a share of 50 percent for both the indirect and the direct ones. This disparity is due to the level of personal income tax that is four GDP points lower than the EU average. Both revenue and rate of corporate income tax are, instead, close to the EU mean levels.

Indirect taxes show a total amount which is 1.5 GDP points lower than the EU average and three points lower in comparison with New Members' mean value. However, the share of total fiscal revenue is similar to the EU average and not very different from EU New Members' mean level. Both VAT and excise duties levels are similar to the EU's. However, other indirect taxes give a low yield, including real property tax, real property transfer tax, gift and inheritance tax, road tax, local levies.

The Czech total social contributions as a share of GDP are well above both the EU (15 percent) and the New Member average values (14.2 percent). The gap can also be due to the particularly high level of employer contributions. Anyway, as a share of total fiscal revenue, Czech contributions were 9 percent higher than the EU average and 8 percent higher than EU New Members' mean value.

7.3 Some quantitative and institutional features of main taxes

Personal income tax – PIT (Daň z příjmu fyzických osob)

The personal income tax was introduced in 1993, when the Czech Republic was founded. At the time of the communist regime, this tax did not exist because the redistribution of income was pursued by subsidies to consumption goods, as in the other planned economies. Before the 1990s, different sources of income were taxed at different rates and the whole system was only slightly progressive. Wage earnings were also taxed at a flat rate, but the level of the rate changed according to the taxpayer's age, sex, marital status and number of dependants. The current personal income tax is similar to that observed in many European countries.

However, the aggregate income is not all-embracing, because many sources of income are taxed under a separate regime. The taxing unity is the individual and the tax is paid by both residents and non-residents: the worldwide income principle is put on the residents, whereas the non-residents are taxed on their Czech source income.

Income from different categories is aggregated to form the tax base and, after excluding the deductions allowed by law, a progressive rates schedule is applied. This comprises four brackets with increasing marginal rates: the lower rate is 15 percent and the highest is 32 percent. From 1993 to 1999 there were five brackets and the highest rate was at 40 percent. The subsequent reduction of the brackets was due mainly to two reasons. First, few taxpayers were taxed at the highest bracket and, second, there was the accepted fundamental paradigm to broaden the taxable base and to reduce the number and the level of the rates. The top rate of 32 percent is low compared with that mainly existing in the EU countries but it is similar to the rate in force in the other EU New Members.

There are several categories of taxable income:

a   income from wages and salaries;
b   income from business activity and independent services;
c   income from leasing or rents;
d   income from capital assets;
e   other incomes.

Social security contributions paid by employees are deductible in full while, according to the tax code, donations for purposes of science, education, culture, medicine, ecology, sports and religion are deductible up to 10 percent of the taxable base.

There are other tax allowances to promote horizontal and vertical equity. If the allowances exceed the taxable income, the taxpayer simply pays no tax because there is not a negative income tax system, but losses (only for business activities) can be carried forward for seven years. At the time of writing (2003), the basic personal allowance per year is €1188.75 (Kč38,040), and the others depend on the family's status. If the taxpayer's spouse has an annual income lower than the basic allowance, an additional allowance of €678.75 (Kč21,720) is granted to the taxpayer; there is also an allowance of €734.40 (Kč23,520) for each dependent child living in the taxpayer's household (see Table 7.3).

The taxable base from business activity and intellectual rights is determined with similar rules in force for the corporate income tax but is taxed

Table 7.3 Structure of income tax in the Czech Republic
Dan z prìjmu fyzickych osob 2003 – Values in euro

Brackets	Marginal rates	Basic allowance	Allowance spouse	Allowance for a son
Up to 3230.20	15	1188.75	678.75	743.40
3230.20–6460.40	20	1188.75	678.75	743.40
6460.40–9880.61	25	1188.75	678.75	743.40
Over 9880.61	32	1188.75	678.75	743.40

Source: see text.

with the progressive rate schedule of the personal income tax. The general rule provides that the expenses are deductible in detail from the income, but the taxpayer may determine the taxable base from all business activity by a lump sum deduction applied to these sources of income. The amount of deduction differs according to the type of business. Income from leasing or rent is taxed according to general rules.

Income from dividends and interest paid to individuals is not aggregate to the taxable base of the income tax but is taxed under a separate regime: it provides a 25 percent final withholding tax on dividends and a 15 percent final withholding tax on interest from saving accounts and from dividends and interest paid by pension funds. The capital gains basis is the difference between the selling and the purchasing price but almost all capital gains realized outside corporation income are tax exempt.

The beneficiary is both the central and local governments: 44.2 percent of the revenue from the income tax on self-employed (42.35 percent to municipalities, 1.86 percent to regions) and 25.19 percent (3.1 percent regions, 22.09 percent municipalities) of the revenue from withholding tax on wages and salaries of employees accrue to local governments and they are distributed among municipalities according to the number of inhabitants. The 23.69 percent from withholding tax on wages and salaries of the employee and the revenue from taxes withheld on interest and dividend accrue to municipalities (20.59 percent) and regions (3.1 percent). The rest accrues to central government.

Corporate income tax – CIT (Daň z příjmu právnických osob)

Corporation tax was also introduced in 1993. During the communist regime, the state gave the production plans to enterprises, showing what they had to make; prices were state-controlled and enterprises had a poor role in the allocation process. Taxes on enterprise surpluses were subject to negotiation and set with respect to national industrial policy objectives. They yielded more than 10 percent of GDP and the tax rate was far higher than those rates applied in EU countries. It was 75 percent in 1988 and 55 percent in 1991. Then, the state appropriated a high share of enterprise profits. The new corporation tax is similar to that applied in EU countries. Both public and private companies, and non-commercial bodies, are taxed on their worldwide income and the base is given by the net profits of each company because no group taxation is granted. There are also specific regulations on transfer pricing and thin capitalization. Losses can be carried forward for seven years. Non-resident companies are taxed on their Czech source income but permanent establishments of foreign companies are taxed like domestic companies.

Interests and dividends are included in the recipient's taxable income and royalties and capital gains are included in enterprise gross income. Dividends are taxed both at the company and at the shareholder level.

The double taxation is alleviated by means of a 50 percent lump-sum tax credit against the enterprise tax liability of the withholding tax on the dividends paid out. For holding companies there is a system of tax exemption for distributed profits and the tax rate is specified in the respective international double tax avoidance treaty.

Expenses that are allowed as a deduction are those incurred in obtaining the gross income. Tangible assets with a useful life less than one year are fully deductible in the year of acquisition and those with a useful life of more than one year are deductible at a rate ranging from 0.33 percent to 25 percent, according to the depreciation category. Both linear and accelerated depreciation is allowed. Inventories may not be depreciated. Intangible assets are deductible for a period ranging from four to 12 years but only if their initial price exceeds €1266.75; other intangible assets are fully deductible in the year of acquisition.

Royalties, interest, donations (in the limit of 2 percent of taxable income), paid real estate tax, social security contributions, road tax and lease expenses (if the leasing period is above 20 percent of the useful life of assets and at least three years) are deductible from the Corporate income tax.

At the time of the communist regime, there were tax incentives for direct investments; today, these incentives have been abolished and replaced with many activity-specific allowances, tax credits or relief on new assets, temporary exemptions from corporate income tax for new investment and subsidies for education of employees. Starting from 2000, a flat rate of 31 percent is applied, but it was 35 percent up to 1999. Investment companies, investment funds and pension funds are taxed at 15 percent, but this treatment will be abolished from 2004. Four-fifths of revenue from corporate income tax accrue to central government and one fifth to local government (on the basis of population).

Value added tax – VAT (Daň z přidané hodnoty)

The main difficulty of transition for the Czech fiscal system has been the shift from the turnover tax applied before 1993 to the value added tax according to EU standards. The turnover tax was applied to all goods and it was very complex, both for the number of rates, ranging from −0.74 to 733 percent, and for that of the commodities groups (1506 percent). A lot of necessary goods were subsidized.

Now, Czech VAT is similar to the EU model but there are some differences that will have to be overcome. The basis of assessment is the price of the taxable supply excluding the VAT, and the tax is also payable on imports. The beneficiaries are the central government, regions and municipalities. Only individuals and entities with a turnover above €15,834.31 must be registered for value added tax.

According to the EU directive that provides only two rates (a standard rate higher or equal to 15 percent and a reduced one between 5 and

15 percent on some goods), the Czech Republic adopted a standard rate of 22 percent, and a reduced rate of 5 percent on water, agricultural, food and pharmaceutical products, constructions and restaurant services. However, the list of goods taxed at the 5 percent rate must be reduced according to EU harmonization because the changes planned for the 2004 are not sufficient. Exports, financial services and many public services are tax exempt.

Excise duties (Spotřební daň)

The Czech Republic has several excise duties that were introduced during the tax reform of 1991 and 1992. The main items are as follows.

a   *Hydrocarbon fuels and lubricants* – The tax is charged on petroleum products and oils that are produced or imported. The beneficiary is the central government and state fund of transport infrastructure. Rates range from €258.10 per one thousand liters of motor oils to €343.29 per one thousand liters of motor car and aircraft petrol. There are many exemptions: for example, the duty on light heating oil is refunded if it is used for heating purposes.

b   *Alcohol* – The basis of assessment is the number of liters of ethyl alcohol and the rate is €7.41 per liter of ethyl alcohol and €3.00 for fruit spirits distilled by fruit growers. The tax is paid by producers, importers and processors of alcohol and liquors. The beneficiary is central government.

c   *Beer* – The basis is the hectoliters and the rate depends on annual production: €0.76 per hectoliter if the annual production is more than 200,000 hectoliters and there are five rates ranging from €0.38 per hectoliter to €0.68 applied to five brackets if the production is less than 200,000 hectoliters. The beneficiary is central government and the tax is paid by producers and importers of beer.

d   *Wine* – The rates range from €0.076 per liter to €0.74 per liter according to the wine qualities. The tax is paid by producers and importers of selected products and the beneficiary is the central government.

e   *Tobacco* – The basis is the kilogram of tobacco for production of cigarettes, tobacco refuse for smoking and pipe tobacco and the unit for cigarettes. The rates range from €0.021 (for filter cigarettes) to €27.07 (for tobacco refuse for smoking). The taxpayers are the producers and importers of tobacco products and the beneficiary is the central government.

Local taxes

a   *Real Property Tax (Daň z nemovitostí)* – An annual tax is imposed on buildings and land. Taxpayers are the owners of buildings and land and all revenue accrues to local government. The basis for buildings is the area of the ground plan of the overhead part of the structure in squares meters, and rates range from €0.032 per square meter to €0.127. For the land the bases are average prices in the cadastre areas and rates range from 0.25 percent to 0.75 percent of average price for cultivated lands. The rate for a built-up area is €0.0032 per square meter and that on developed land is €0.032 per square meter multiplied by coefficients according to the size of the municipality.

b   *Levy on Withdrawal of Land from Agriculture and Forestry* – A lump sum levy calculated depending on the environment, climate and other factors is payable by subjects who ask for permanent withdrawal of land. Forty percent of revenue accrues to municipality and 60 percent to the central fund of environment.

c   *Other taxes* – Infrastructure tax, Resort and recreation fees on visitors, Waste tax, Dog tax, Recreational unit tax, Entry tickets tax, Tax on operating slot machines, Tax on operating gambling machines and Tax on use of public space are paid to municipality.

Social security contributions

Social security contributions, applied to labor and self-employed income, were introduced in 1993. They are fully deductible from the personal and corporate income tax bases. The base of both social and health insurance of employees is the gross wage and the total rate is 47.5 percent, of which 12.5 percent is paid by the employee and 35 percent by the employer. The base of the self-employed is 35 percent of net income but there is a minimum of €579.54 (€1368.84 for health insurance) and a maximum of €15,390.95 tax base. The minimum health insurance tax base for employees is 12 times the minimum wage. The beneficiary for social insurance taxes is the central government and the taxes enter the general budget. Health insurance taxes are earmarked and health insurance funds maintain an individual account for each insured person.

Other minor taxes

a   *Road Tax (Silnicnì dan)* – Commercial cars used for an entrepreneurial activity in the Czech territory are taxed by the Road Tax. For passengers cars the tax rate ranges from €38.00 to €133.01 and the basis is the cylinder capacity in cubic centimeters; other vehicles are taxed from €57.00 to €1596.098 and the basis is the total weight in tons and number of axles. The beneficiary is the central government.

b   *Inheritance Tax (Dan dedickà)* – The heir of a property is taxed on the value of the property. Spouses and relatives in direct line are tax exempt. Relatives in collateral line are taxed with rates ranging from 3 percent to 12 percent, while all other persons are taxed from 7 percent to 40 percent. The beneficiary is the central government.

c   *Gift Tax (Dan darovacì)* – The acquirer of donated property is also
    taxed. There are three categories, as with the Inheritance tax: spouses
    and relatives in direct line are taxed on donated property from 1
    percent to 5 percent, relatives in collateral line from 3 to 12 percent
    and other persons from 7 to 40 percent. There are some exemptions
    according to the value of the donated property. The beneficiary is the
    central government.
d   *Real Property Transfer Tax (Dan z prevodu nemovitostì)* – Sellers of
    real property must pay to central government 5 percent of the con-
    tracted price of transferred real property.
e   *Customs Duties (Cla)* – The importers of goods are taxed on the
    custom value of imported goods according to the Customs tariff. All
    revenue accrues to the central government.
f   *Highway Fee (Poplatek za uzìvànì dalnice a rychlostnì silnice)* – All
    drivers of motor vehicles using a highway pay this fee to central
    government (state fund of transport infrastructure) on the basis of
    tonnage of vehicles.

7.4 The fiscal burden

The distribution of tax change: taxation by economic functions and implicit tax rates

Table 7.4 depicts the distribution of fiscal burden by economic function
and by the implicit tax rates from the early to the late 1990s. Looking at
the classification according to economic function (which shows the ratios
between the overall tax burden on different factors and a common large
basis, given by GDP), it can be seen that, in 1998, the most important contribution to the total fiscal revenues originated from employed labor, and
amounted to 48.4 percent of total revenues and to 18.5 GDP points (of
which 60 percent was paid by employers), while 2.9 GDP points (7.6
percent of total revenues) arose from self-employed labor, 11.1 GDP
points (30 percent of total revenues) from consumption and 5.7 (15
percent) from capital and business (of which 65 percent from profits, 10.5
from real estate and 12.3 from shares and saving) – see Figure 7.3.

From 1993 to 1998, only the taxation on employed labor steadily grew,
from 16.9 GDP points to 18.5, with an increase by 9.5 percent. Its total
increase can be split into 12.5 percent on employers and 87.5 percent on
employees. The share of revenues from the other factors of production
decreased: that of consumption from 13.2 GDP points in 1993 to 11.1 in
1998 (with a decrease of 16 percent), that of self-employed labor from 4
GDP points to 2.9 (with a decrease of 2.8 percent) and capital and business from 8.9 to 5.7 (with a decrease of 36 percent, which was necessary to
reduce the rates on corporate incomes from their initial non-market
levels). Thus, the 4.5 GDP point reduction of total fiscal revenue, which

Table 7.4 Structure and development of taxation by function and by implicit rates in the Czech Republic, New Members and EU 15, 1992–98

	1992			1994			1996			1998		
	Czech Republic	New members	EU	Czech Republic	New members	EU	Czech Republic	New members	EU	Czech Republic	New members	EU
Economic functions												
Consumption	13.2	13.6	10.9	12.8	14.5	11.2	12.2	14.7	11.3	11.1	13.5	11.4
Labor employed	16.9	19.7	20.6	17.6	19.4	20.7	18.1	19.0	21.4	18.5	17.9	21.2
Labor self-employed	4.0	2.9	2.4	3.1	2.8	2.4	2.8	2.6	2.4	2.9	2.6	2.3
Capital and business	8.9	4.3	7.2	7.8	5.0	6.8	6.0	4.3	7.1	5.7	4.5	7.5
Implicit tax rates												
Consumption	18.4	16.3	16.2	17.5	17.4	16.5	17.1	17.8	16.7	15.6	16.6	16.8
Labor employed	37.0	37.1	39.0	37.8	38.3	40.2	37.2	37.4	42.0	38.6	38.0	41.9
Capital and business	–	–	32.2	–	–	30.3	–	–	30.5	–	–	31.1

Sources: EU Commission (2000a) for Czech Republic and New Members (unweighted average); Eurostat (2000) for EU 15 (1997 unweighted average).

Notes

Taxation according to economic function is as a percentage of GDP. Total may stay over Total fiscal revenue in Table 7.2, because of double counting. Estonia's 1992 implicit rates and all Czech rates refer to 1993. Implicit rates for capital and business are available only for Estonia and Slovenia.

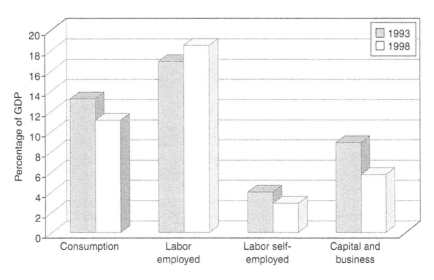

Figure 7.3 Taxation by economic function in the Czech Republic in 1993 and 1998 (source: EU Commission (2000a)).

took place in the 1990s, was obtained by cutting both consumption and capital and business revenues and increasing taxation on the labor factor.

Looking now at the implicit tax rates (Figure 7.4), which show the ratio between the total tax revenue on each factor and the total tax base of the same factor (including all taxes), we can see that, in 1998, employed labor was the most heavily taxed, at an implicit tax rate of 38.6 percent, while the implicit tax rate on consumption was only 15.6 percent, a value very low in comparison with the standard value added tax rate set at 22 percent (EU Commission 2000a).

Data for capital and business are available just for 1995 and 1996 and were, respectively, 41.7 and 38.4 percent. The dynamic of the employed labor's implicit tax rate from the early to the late 1990s was slightly growing, with an increase of 4.3 percent (from a value of 37 percent in 1993). The implicit tax rate on consumption, instead, was constantly decreasing, with a reduction of 15 percent from 1993 to 1998.

Other indicators of fiscal burden

Czech Republic social contributions are among the highest in the world; thus, the summing of contributions to personal income tax has the negative consequence of a high taxation of labor, which can create distortions in the labor market, open opportunities for the shadow economy and originate a loss of competitiveness, especially in comparison with other New EU Member Countries.

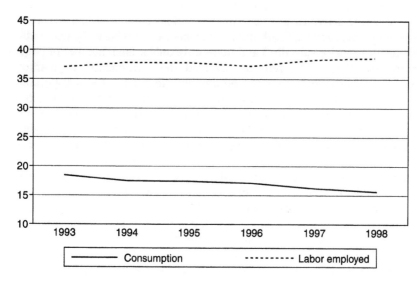

Figure 7.4 Implicit tax rates in the Czech Republic from 1993 to 1998 (source: EU Commission (2000a)).

In 1998, the labor cost was 135 percent of net wage, a value that cannot be compatible with an economy in transition and is high in comparison with the value of other countries at the time they were at the current Czech level of development. In the near future, the tax wedge on labor is planned to decrease but politicians will have to solve the problem (as in almost all developed countries) of reducing the existing generous pension schemes in the context of an aging population.

The cut of the corporation tax rate has gone in the right direction, but now further steps (such as changes of the taxable base and an increase of the effectiveness of the system, above all for foreign investors) should be carried out because a low statutory rate is important, but only effective average rates can affect the Czech capacity to attract foreign investment, and only effective marginal rates can be decisive in the choice of how many investments to do. As to capital incomes, we notice that they are taxed at very different rates: marginal tax rates on personal income and rates on interest are substantially lower than the corporation income tax rate, interests are fully deductible from corporation tax base and the 'all-in' tax rate on corporation income is different according to the firms' decisions concerning dividend distribution: these differences affect firms' financing decisions and have given rise to a preference for the debt. Thus, there are significant differences in marginal effective forward rates, according to the sources of financing (debt financing or financing with new equities) and to the specific type of assets (Holeckovà *et al.* 2002).

At the time of the communist regime, the share of GDP coming from private sector activities was very small; earnings and social benefits were extremely equalized; redistribution of income came up basically with indirect taxation (price subsidies) and there were only a small number of large enterprises. The 1990s reforms involved the introduction of market competition, large privatization and liberalization: then, it was important to maintain the social cohesion during the transition to the market economy and balance the sacrifices of new tax system with the benefits from public expenditures. For these reasons, a real evaluation of the political and economical changes of the transition period can be done only by considering taxation and expenditures and the income redistribution.

On the road to a market society, during the 1990s income inequality has risen considerably (mostly because of the fast advance of the top decile share) and the incomes structure has undergone important changes. In the meantime, both pension schemes and the social transfers were reformed; and unemployment benefits and guaranteed minimum wage were introduced. The communist countries had a lower value of Gini coefficient (0.2) in comparison with the market-driven countries, and the Czech Republic was not an exception: Czech income per capita Gini coefficient increased from 0.20 in 1988, 0.23 in 1992 and 0.26 in 1996 and probably it has been still increasing during the last few years (Vecernik and Stepankova 2002) – see Table 7.5.

From the late 1980s to the first half of the 1990s, the fiscal system became more progressive, then after-tax incomes became much greater even than before-tax incomes, while during the communist regime the tax-induced reduction of income inequality was insignificant. In 1988, the last quintile paid 39.7 percent of revenues and in 1996 it paid 53.6 percent. In 1988, 67 percent of total transfers come up to the first three quintiles, while in 1996 it increased up to 77 percent (Table 7.6).

However, it is important to underline that more than half of the total population is taxed inside the two lowest brackets of income tax, while very few taxpayers are taxed within the highest one. Then, the most relevant limit of the existent fiscal system as to income redistribution is the lack of a negative income tax: some equitable effects could be obtained at the advantage of the lowest income taxpayers if personal income allowances were replaced by tax credits. This change could induce an

Table 7.5 Gini Index on Czech household income

Per household			Per capita		
1988	*1992*	*1996*	*1988*	*1992*	*1996*
0.29	0.32	0.33	0.20	0.23	0.26

Sources: Microcensus 1988, 1992 and 1996.

Table 7.6 Distribution of taxes and transfers according to quintile shares in the Czech Republic

Quintiles	1	2	3	4	5
Taxes					
1988	1.7	11.1	20.2	27.3	39.7
1996	1.8	5.4	14.1	25.1	53.6
Transfers					
1988	27.5	23.4	17.1	15.8	16.2
1996	27.5	30.6	20.4	12.7	8.8

Sources: Microcensus 1988, 1992 and 1996.

increasing loss of revenues. It could be compensated for by an increase of the share of real property tax, which in the Czech Republic stays at a very low level (about 0.6 percent of total revenues in 1998) – see Table 7.7.

A comparison with other New Members and the EU 15 countries

In 1998, the Czech structure of revenue according to economic function was close to both the EU and EU new member average, but we can observe same differences in the 1990s dynamic and in 1998 values. In 1998, the share of consumption was the same as the EU average and two GDP points lower than that of New Members, while the share on employed labor was the 87 percent of the EU average (21.2 percent of GDP) and two GDP points more than that of New Members. The share of self-employed labor was higher than both EU and new member averages, while that of capital and business was three-quarters of the EU average and it was 1.2 GDP points more than that in New Members.

Table 7.7 Distribution of Czech household income according to decile shares

	Per household			Per capita		
	1988	*1992*	*1996*	*1988*	*1992*	*1996*
1	2.5	2.9	2.8	5.3	4.9	4.3
2	4.1	4.1	3.9	6.6	6.4	5.9
3	5.9	5.8	5.6	7.4	7.3	6.8
4	7.6	6.9	6.7	8.1	7.9	7.6
5	9.3	8.1	7.9	8.8	8.6	8.3
6	10.7	6.9	9.4	9.6	9.2	9.1
7	12.0	11.1	10.9	10.6	10.1	10.1
8	13.2	12.8	12.7	11.8	11.3	11.5
9	15.1	15.2	15.4	13.6	13.1	13.7
10	19.6	23.5	24.7	18.2	21.1	22.6

Sources: Microcensus 1988, 1992 and 1996.

During the 1990s, it can be seen that the trend of consumption revenues has been decreasing in the Czech Republic while it was basically steady in both EU and New Members. The opposite happened for employed labor: it was basically steady in EU countries, from 1992 to 1996, decreased from 1997 to 1998 in New Members and rose quite significantly in the Czech Republic. Both the EU and New Members self-employed average has been steady in this period, while it was decreasing by more than one GDP point in the Czech Republic; the same has happened for capital and business average.

In 1998, the Czech implicit tax rate on consumption was 1.2 GDP points lower than the EU average and one point lower than the New Members' one. During the 1990s, it was decreasing in the Czech Republic and steady in the other countries, while the implicit tax rate on employed labor has been increasing in both the EU and New Members as well as in the Czech Republic – but the increase has been more evident in EU countries (three GDP points) than in New Members (1.6 points in the Czech Republic and only one point in the other countries).

7.5 Tax reforms and further steps to get closer to the EU

Macroeconomic and budget outlook

Over the last decade the macroeconomic situation in the Czech Republic has changed considerably mainly because of two factors: the split of the previous Czechoslovakia Republic and the transition, starting in 1991, from the communist regime to a market-based economy. The radical economic reform wanted to obtain macroeconomic stability, low inflation and balanced state budget, and also because, during the 1980s, the average Czechoslovakian real GDP growth rate declined dramatically from 4.8 percent to 1.5 percent. Then, prices and enterprises were liberalized, the private sector was promoted, an adequate welfare state was launched, both domestic and foreign demands were stimulated, and effective monetary and fiscal policies were implemented.

However, in the early 1990s, the demand for consumer goods and investments was very low and the Czech GDP growth rate was negative (also because of a restrictive budget policy targeted to obtaining a low deficit), while price liberalization and VAT introduction determined a drastic increase in the inflation rate. However, the consequent devaluation of the national currency resulted in an increase of exports. In 1992, unemployment rate was still very low, near to full employment, but it increased during the following years. The economic recession stopped only in 1994 but the inflation dynamic was decreasing, albeit in a swinging way, for the rest of the decade. Both public debt and the state budget deficit were very low.

In the second half of the 1990s, further economic and political difficulties arose: a new recession started in 1997 as a consequence of a currency crisis: the GDP growth rate was then −0.8 percent. The recession ended only in 2000, when the growth rate recovered to 2.9 percent (3.6 percent in 2001). During this period, the unemployed rate rapidly increased from 3.5 percent in 1996 to 9.4 percent in 2000 and to 8.9 percent in 2001, while the inflation rate continued its decreasing trend from 8.8 percent in 1996, 10.7 percent in 1998, 2.1 percent in 1999 and 4.7 percent in 2001. The macroeconomic stabilization policy, aimed at restructuring the economy, facilitated the inflation decrease. As a result, the total domestic demand increased by 3.9 percent in 2000, sustained by an increase in productivity growth of the industrial sector (OECD 2001).

However, these results have been initially obtained with an expansive fiscal policy that became a structural feature of budget policy after the end of the economic recession: the general government budget deficit was 1.7 percent of GDP in 1996, 2.7 percent in 1997, 3.8 percent in 1998, 4.0 percent in 1999, 4.2 percent in 2000, to increase further to 7.5 percent in 2001 and to 9 percent in 2002.

According to new data, fiscal revenue has been steady in the last few years: in 2000 Czech total fiscal revenue was 39.3 percent of GDP, 39.1 percent in 2001 and 39.8 percent in 2002. Instead, the level of public expenditure (excluded net lending) was 42.1 percent of GDP in 1998, 43.7 percent in 2000, 44.2 percent in 2001, 46.6 percent in 2002; levels that are too high to achieve the Maastricht rule of 3 percent budget deficit. This is also due to the very low level of public debt (which was about 24 percent of GDP in 2001 but only 12.9 percent in 1997) in comparison with the Maastricht 60 percent level. This can be an advantage or, contrarily, a problem for admission into the EU area, because politicians can undervaluate the necessity of radical tax and expenditure reforms and go on with a further accumulation of the debt. Today, on the expenditure side, 'general government deficits are not of cyclical character' and 'expenses are only partially allocated in areas that would generate positive multiplication effects in the long run' (Ministry of Finance 2003).

During the last few years public expenditure has raised more than revenue and, from a political point of view, this has been possible because of the just-mentioned level of public debt and the large privatization receipts that have contributed to control the debt increase. However, more attention will be carried out in the next few years according to the EU accession requirements: without reforms the debt is expected to grow to 40–45 percent of GDP in the next few years. If this happens, the Czech Republic will see a rapid increase of interest expenditure that will make it more difficult to stay within EU budget deficit limits, through the reduction of other budget items (Jurajda 2001).

Despite the stop and go movements of the 1990s, the Czech economy is at the top among the EU New Members: its economic level was, and is, very high in comparison with all the other post-communist countries for both the GDP per capita level and unemployment rate. It was the first post-communist country to receive an investment-grade rating by international credit institutions. However, without structural reforms it will be difficult to continue with a strong GDP growth and a rapid fall of the unemployment rate, because Czech industrial plants and equipment are rather obsolete. The only way is to promote a more competitive industry and a well-functioning capital market and to continue in bank and telecommunication privatization (Matalìk and Slavìk 2002; Mitra and Stern 2003).

In this way it could be possible to improve the current low level of private investment, which negatively affects the profitability of enterprises, and then to revitalize the industrial sector and increase foreign investment. As a result, a higher GDP growth rate could facilitate the reduction of the budget deficit, if these policies mix with a greater effectiveness in the control of public expenditure. In fact, a fast growth is forecast for the period 2003–06, sustained by private consumption and investment; in particular, 2.3 percent in 2003, 3 percent in 2004, 3.5 percent in 2005 and 4 percent in 2006 (Ministry of Finance 2003). However, the needs of a tight fiscal policy targeted to budget consolidation can affect the effective growth under the Czech potential rate.

Last years' and planned tax reforms

A decade after radical changes in the fiscal system, the Czech Republic has now to consolidate the obtained results. However, as we have seen, during the last five years the consolidation of the fiscal system proceeded slowly. Only in 2001 did parliament adopt a number of amendments to the previous tax legislation.

The personal income tax bracket were reduced from five to four and tax allowances were increased; no changes in tax rates are expected for the next few years, but a lower tax progression is planned, through an increase of child allowances to €109.01 per month. It has been calculated that this measure could increase the share of taxpayers exempt from tax from the current 1.7 percent to 4.3 percent in the case of a households with an employed head and to 19.7 percent in the case that the tax allowance is allowed for every dependent child. However, this measure could cost about 30 percent of income tax current revenue (1.7 percent of GDP). However, to make this reform budget compatible, tax rates will probably be increased. In the period 2003–06 no important changes are forecast; only the allowance for children will be raised.

As to corporate income tax, some adjustments were adopted with respect to the tax base (intangible assets and their depreciation) and the tax treatment of foreign enterprises. From 2000, the tax rate was reduced from 35 percent to 31 percent and, from 2004, a new reduction to 28 percent is foreseen, because other EU New Members have introduced lower tax rates during the last few years. Also in 2000 (and amended in 2001), a new law was passed on investment incentives for domestic and foreign investors. For the next few years a reduction is foreseen to 26 percent in 2005 and to 24 percent in 2006; in addition there will be changes in the tax base.

The VAT domain shows the main difficulties. According to the EU directives, the Czech Republic adopted a standard rate of 22 percent and a reduced rate of 5 percent, but the list of goods taxed with this latter rate must be reduced because of the EU VAT harmonization. The new government has planned to start this change by 2004 when many goods and services will shift to the standard rate. Only food, medicines, books and newspapers will not be affected by the new law. In addition, the turnover limit for mandatory registration to VAT was reduced from €93,750 (three million Kč) to €62,500 (two million Kč) starting in October 2003 and it will be reduced to €31,250 (one million Kč) in 2004. Other increases are planned for tobacco products, alcohol, fuels and other excise duties. However, all these changes must be implemented gradually, in order not to provide negative consequences on economic growth.

Due to tax evasion and to the government decision to slow the VAT harmonization and to subsidize the consumption of a lot of goods, we can see that VAT productivity (the ratio of VAT revenue on GDP and the statutory standard VAT rate) is very low in comparison with other countries. Less than half of the goods and services consumed in each year was taxed at the standard rate. However, in 2003 the share was 40 percent. In fact, VAT productivity decreased during the 1990s: it was 60 percent in 1993, 57.4 in 1997 and 50 percent in 1998. In the future, it will be possible to broaden the consumption taxable base and to reduce the standard rate that today is high in comparison with other countries.

At the legislation level, although an equal treatment for foreign and domestic investors has been introduced in these years, a new bankrupt norm according to the EU model, restrictions on special investment incentives and new holding company structure taxation will be introduced, in particular to allow the intra-group compensation of the losses.

After the 2002 elections, the new minister committed the government to reducing the budget deficit before 2006 to the range of 4.9–5.4 percent of GDP, through a mix of tax increases and expenditure cuts. However, the increase of fiscal revenue on incomes and consumption, as proposed, in meeting political opposition. Instead, according to the Economic Forecasts for the Candidate Countries of European Commission (April 2003), the level of public budget is 5.5 percent of GDP in 2001, 6.5 percent in 2002, and 5.9 percent in 2004 (provisional data). Without reforms, the budget deficit forecast is around 8 percent of GDP and the debt around 47 percent (Ministry of Finance 2003, Passive scenario).

According to the proposal, tax revenue will increase as a consequence of excise duties' increases and changes to value added tax. Expenditures should be cut through reducing the number of public employees, modifying the system for the calculus of the pensions, and reducing some state contributions. However, the adjustment process will be inevitably slow and it is unlikely that the Czech budget deficit will be less than 3 percent of GDP in the year of EU admission.

Therefore, the most important issue of fiscal policy would be the sustainability of public finances in the medium run. No basic steps have been made in the last few years but this reform was finally approved by government and parliament in summer and autumn 2003. This is the right direction, also because one of the most important objectives of the Czech Republic in the next few years is to maintain a modern social state. A radical reform could affect the economic performance at least, in the short run, but it is important for the credibility in the long run. In addition, there are other problems to be considered for an appropriate tax policy in the Czech Republic: the rate of taxation is above that in other development countries and it is lower than that in the EU countries. This situation is not positive for the potential growth of this country and for the 'tax competition' after EU accession. On the other hand, a radical change is not possible because of the budget constraints.

The need for further steps

Because of the increase in net borrowing in the last few years, it will be important for the Czech government to slow the decline of total revenue: this happened from 1998 to 2001 but government diligence in 2002 has not been sufficient because many revenues came from the privatization receipts that have financed the shortfall of revenues of the last two years.

An expenditure control and a reduction of tax evasion (Hanousek and Palda 2002) are both essential because a further increase in Czech revenues and net borrowing could have negative consequences on a country's economy, its competitiveness and its future growth rates.

An intervention that can sustain a domestic industry should be helpful, albeit without affecting government spending. On the other hand, there is the need to implement a new structure of the mandatory expenditures and subsidies to enterprises, to reduce expenditure level, to favor the sectors with the highest development potentials, and to increase public investment in less developed areas.

At the moment, problems arise both with reference to the total tax burden and to public expenditure. A quite high tax burden can reduce both the attractiveness for foreign investments in the country and the profitability for existing ones, and then undermine the potential economic growth of the Czech Republic. Besides this, during the last few years, some budget items, such as health and pensions expenditures, had a growth faster than national income. Then, in the near future, the present decoupling between expenditures and revenue has to be attentively kept under control (IMF 2002).

The government will have to increase the decentralization to local governments so as to control the expenditures growth, to make local governments more responsible, and to allow more flexibility in determining tax rates and fiscal independency. This requires an increase of local own taxes, such as the property tax, that today gives only a small revenue to the municipalities in comparison with other countries. Greater coordination among regional, municipal and central levels of government will be the required to reach a well-coordinated economic policy's aims, to make the budget process more effective and to reduce growth and employment differentials across regions.

In addition tax expenditures and public pensions need reforming: the first to make it more targeted and to harmonize it with the general social policy; the second to decelerate the expansion trend of this budget item that is now 24 percent of government expenditures, to 9 percent of GDP (it is expected to grow to 6 percent of GDP in 2030 without reforms).

To sum up, by imposing market discipline on the enterprise sector, establishing a good climate for foreign investments and security of property rights, simplifying regulatory procedures, from 1993 to 1998, the private sector share on GDP increased with the number of firms (from 1993 to 1997 more than two million business licenses for physical persons were issued) but their average size is very small. The share of employment in small enterprises increased from 24 percent in 1993 to 56 percent in 1998 and consequently the share of value added in small enterprises also increased. This created difficulties in Tax administration and, to minimize the room for tax evasion, the law's complexity was increased. It is impossible to have an efficient tax collection when the number of taxpayers increases so rapidly, also because it is difficult to distinguish clearly the private consumption income from the business profit (Vitek *et al.* 2003a) – see Table 7.8.

Instead, costs to collect taxes are around 1.5 percent of total revenues, a value similar to that of the other countries, while the number of Tax administrative employees is around 15,000 people. During the transformation process the collection costs increased but the efficiency of tax administration is low and there are a lot of small tax offices. The major

Table 7.8 Number of taxpayers in the Czech Republic

Taxpayers	2001	2002
Personal income tax	2,685,938	2,877,730
Corporate income tax	305,517	321,487
Road tax	921,492	970,825
VAT	432,282	433,837
Excises	4824	4858

Source: Czech Ministry of Finance and Annual Reports.

costs are for the collection of the small property taxes, road tax and VAT (Vitek *et al.* 2003b, 2003c).

Total revenue must be increased to obtain a deficit reduction, the ratio with respect to the GDP of the indirect taxation should be increased, a more rapid harmonization of the VAT close to the EU model should take place, and the effectiveness of tax administration must be improved, in order to reduce tax evasion through more effective controls and enforcement and create better tax collection.

Note

1 A preliminary version of this chapter was carefully revised by Jan Pavel of University College, Prague, and by Leos Vitek, University of Economics, Prague, to whom I express my warmest thanks.

References

Bronchi, C. and Burns, A. (2000) 'The tax system in the Czech Republic', OECD Economics Department Working Papers 245, Paris: OECD.

Czech Government Council for Social and Economic Strategy (2002) *Social and Economic Consequences of the Czech Republic's Integration into the European Union*, May.

EU Commission (2000a) *Structure of the Tax Systems in Estonia, Poland, Hungary, the Czech Republic and Slovenia*, Brussels: EU Commission.

EU Commission (2000b) 'Recent fiscal developments in the candidate countries', Enlargement Papers 2, Brussels: EU Commission, Directorate General for Economic and Financial Affairs.

Eurostat (2000) *Structures of the Taxation Systems in the European Union, 1970–1997*, Brussels: EU Commission.

Eurostat (2002) *Statistical Yearbook on Candidate and South-east European Countries*, Brussels: EU Commission.

Hanousek, J. and Palda, F. (2002) 'The evolution of tax evasion in the Czech Republic: a Markov chain analysis', CERGE-EI.

Holeckovà, J., Vitek, L. and Pubal, K. (2002) 'Distorting effects of taxation on assets and sources of finance: effective tax rates in the central and eastern European countries during transition', *Proceeding from the International Conference 'Tax Policy in EU Candidate Countries'*, Riga: Eurofaculty, September.

IMF (2002) *Czech Republic – November 2002 IMF Staff Visit*, Concluding Statement, November.

Jurajda, S. (2001) 'The Czech Republic: awaiting elections and a fiscal reform', *The Stockholm Report on Transition*, 11, 3.

Kamenìckovà, V. (1999) *Fiscal Decentralization in the Czech Republic*, Praha: Ministry for Local Development, May.

Matalìk, I. and Slavìk, M. (2002) 'Fiscal issues and central bank policy in the Czech Republic', paper presented at meeting 'Fiscal Issues and Central Banking in Emerging Economies', Bank for International Settlements, Basel, December.

Ministry of Finance (2003) *Budgetary Outlook 2003–2006*, Ref. No. 10/46716/2003, Praha: Ministry of Finance.

Ministry of Finance – Department of Financial Policies (2003) *Czech Republic Macroeconomic Forecast*, Praha: Ministry of Finance.

Mitra, P. and Stern, N. (2003) 'Tax systems in transition', WB Working Paper 2947, Washington, DC: The World Bank.

OECD (2001) *Economic Survey of Czech Republic*, Policy Brief, Paris: OECD.

OECD (2002) *Fiscal Decentralization in EU Applicant States and Selected EU Member States*, Paris: OECD.

Šujan, I. and Šujanová, M. (1994) 'The macroeconomic situation in the Czech Republic', CERGE-EI, Working Paper 46.

Tanzi, V. and Tsibouris, G. (2000) 'Fiscal reform over ten years of transition', IMF Working Paper 113, Washington, DC: IMF.

Vecernik, J. and Stepankova, P. (2002) 'Redistribution of income through taxes and benefits in the Czech Republic between 1989 and 2000 and beyond: observation and simulation', paper prepared for the 27th General Conference of The international Association for Research in Income and Wealth, Stockholm, August.

Vitek, L., Pavel, J. and Krbovà, J. (2003a) 'How ineffective is the Czech tax system case study of the Czech administrative and compliance costs', *Proceeding from the International Conference 'Tax Policy in EU Candidate Countries'*, Riga: Eurofaculty, September.

Vitek, L., Pavel, J. and Pubal, K. (2003b) 'Effectiveness of Czech tax system – administrative and compliance costs measurement', paper presented to IIPF 59th Congress, Prague, August.

Vitek, L., Pubal, K. and Pudil, P. (2003c) 'Tax policy and tax administration in Czech and Slovak Republics: developments during transitions', *IASIA Annual Conference: 'Public Administration: Challenges of Inequality and Exclusion'*, Miami, September.

Websites

http://www.czso.cz – Czech Statistical Office.
http://www.mfcr.cz – Czech Ministry of Finance.

8 Estonia and the other Baltic states

Evelin Ahermaa and Luigi Bernardi[1]

8.1 Introduction and executive summary

This chapter is mainly concerned with the fiscal system of Estonia. This is neither the widest nor the most populated among the Baltic New Members (Estonia, Latvia and Lithuania). However, enough fiscal data are available for this country. As all the Baltic states are quite similar, a final short section will be devoted to Latvia and Lithuania.

Estonia is a small country, of 45,227 square km and 1358 million inhabitants. It became an independent republic in 1918, and remained so up to the beginning (1940) of the Second World War, when it was incorporated into the USSR. Independence was gained again in 1991 and a new parliamentary Constitution was adopted in 1992. Estonia entered de facto into the EU in 2004. The local currency is the Estonian Kroon (EEK1 = €0.063911), GDP is about €5150 million, nearly €3760 per capita, somewhat less than 20 percent of the EU average.[2] After a 1999–2000 slowdown, the economy is at present growing fast, at rates of more than 5 percent per year, but unemployment is still over 10 percent. Inflation runs around 2–3 percent, as does the government deficit. Public debt is not more than 5 percent of GDP.

Current total fiscal pressure in Estonia reaches about 37–38 percent of GDP. This level has been criticized as being too high, compared with the need not to interfere with the development process, but it is somewhat lower with respect to other New Members. Direct taxes are below indirect taxes which will be increased (especially excises) as a consequence of access to the EU.

Labor income has been heavily hit, preventing job-intensive growth while inducing the development of the underground economy, albeit that during the last few years the problem of the so-called 'envelope salaries' is decreasing, as is the problems of illegal goods and smuggling. This raises an equity problem, due to the fact that inequality in income distribution is increased greatly from the end of the Russian regime. As in any former communist country, the level of local government activities is low compared with Western European standards. Financing is raised mainly by taxes, which are mostly given by shares of National (income) taxes.

The fiscal reform, adopted after the collapse of the USSR and independence, went quickly during the first years of the new Republic: unlike in many other transition countries, no revenue fall occurred. As a consequence, during the 1990s, the quantitative structure of the system did not radically change. In the late 1990s and the early years of this century, a general revision of tax laws was performed. Furthermore, the efforts to implement a modern tax administration were fairly successful. The main problem concerns the enforcement of tax collection. However, corruption has not been perceived as being very high, and firms' bribing behavior is comparatively lower than in other transition economies.

At present the broad features of Estonian main taxes are not very different from the corresponding EU models, albeit they are generally simpler and show some distinctive features. Income tax exempts almost all capital incomes and its structure is rather similar to a linear income tax at a marginal rate of 26 percent. The same rate is charged on corporate profits but only distributed profits are taxed, while all retained earnings are not taxed at all. This mild fiscal treatment of corporations is a common feature in the Baltic states. VAT is the usual tax-to-tax European model: the standard rate is set at 18 percent, some essential commodities are taxed at 5 percent and welfare and other public services benefit from a zero rate scheme. A complex structure of excise duties and stamp duties are the remaining main state sources of revenue. The local taxes may be levied on the same bases as state taxes or on different ones (in particular on land). Quite high rates must be paid for social contributions on labor income: 20 percent for pensions and 13 percent for health.

Concerning the distribution of fiscal burden, the main contributions to total revenues come from labor-employed income and, to a lower extent, from consumption. Notice that in a low income setting, where wages are mostly the main component of both total income and the consumption of total expenditure, the two kinds of taxation may overlap. Regarding the fiscal burden on specific factors, implicit rates show that labor employed income suffers from a burden (about 40 percent) almost twice that charged on capital and business income.

Estonia's government budget roughly balanced during the 1990s. This was due also to the lack of the monetary financing of the Central Bank (prevented by law). In 1999, the deficit jumped to nearly 5 percent, in the wake of Russian crisis, but during following years a buoyant economic growth and fiscal discipline contribute to gradually reaching a budget surplus of 1.3 points of GDP in 2002. It is expected to turn to deficit in 2004, but for no more than half a point of GDP.

Recent tax reforms were intended, in particular, to harmonize the existing tax system with EU requirements, particularly in the field of VAT and excise duties. A relevant change, as mentioned before, was adopted for corporation tax: only distributed profits are now subject to tax, while the retained ones' are exempt. The new incentive seems particularly intended to attract foreign capital, in competition with other transition economies. Anyway, it will be right to continue to have a mild taxation on corporations and productive activity. Simplified tax regimes will have to be envisaged for small business and this could also alleviate tax administration activity.

Progress toward the EU (and then EMU) requires further harmonization efforts and keeping a low taxation of enterprises. This in turn requires a strict monitoring of expenditure, since the budget must continue to be balanced, even if the population is declining and aging.

The fiscal situations of Latvia and Lithuania are not very different, but present some peculiarities. Regarding total taxation, Latvia and, in particular, Lithuania tax less than Estonia. Social contributions are particularly low in Lithuania, while both income tax and VAT in each country are under the Estonian levels. From the early to the late 1990s, total fiscal pressure did not change too much in Latvia and the same occurred in the composition of the tax mix among different taxes. On the contrary, fiscal pressure decreased in Lithuania: the market-oriented cut of corporations' tax rates was not substituted by an adequate increase of other taxes. The high degree of centralization of both revenues and expenditures in Lithuania is similar to the Estonian figure, while Latvia shows some more decentralization in both revenues and expenditures. The main taxes (Income tax, Corporation tax, VAT, Social contributions) do not show strong structural differences from their Estonian counterparts. In particular, income tax replicates the linear flat tax model and corporation tax tries to be mild with earnings and with reinvested profits. Economic growth is running at a high level in both Latvia and Lithuania from the end of the 1990s. Latvia adopted a policy mix which favored a higher growth (6–8 percent) coupled with an inflation rate at about 2–3 percent and a government deficit on the upper bound of the Stability Pact. Lithuania's preference was in favor of a fiscal discipline that allowed the rate of inflation to decrease to around 1 percent and the government deficit not to be greater than 2 percent. Thus, both countries are substantially in line with EU and EMU financial requirements.

8.2 The structure of the system at the end of the 1990s and its development after the collapse of the USSR

A broad view of the current structure of taxes and social security contributions

At the end of the 1990s, Estonia's total fiscal pressure (37.5 percent) was not far from the New Members' average (38.9 percent), but was some points under the EU mean level. The Estonian broad fiscal structure (see Table 8.1) can be split almost exactly into two thirds taxes and the remaining third social contributions.

Table 8.1 Structure and development of fiscal revenue in Estonia, New Members and EU 15 as a percentage of GDP, 1992–98

	1992			1994			1996			1998		
	Estonia	New members	EU	Estonia	New members	EU	Estonia	New members	EU	Estonia	New members	EU
Direct taxes, of which	13.3	10.1	13.5	11.6	10.0	12.9	10.0	9.6	13.4	11.1	9.2	13.7
Personal income	8.5	6.4	9.6	8.1	7.0	9.3	8.3	7.1	9.3	8.5	6.7	9.3
Corporation income	4.8	3.6	2.3	3.5	2.9	2.4	1.7	2.5	2.7	2.6	2.5	3.0
Indirect taxes, of which	12.3	15.6	13.4	14.9	16.5	13.7	15.5	16.9	13.7	14.3	15.5	13.9
VAT	9.2	5.1	6.7	11.2	7.4	6.8	10.0	7.4	6.9	8.8	7.9	7.0
Excise duties	1.9	3.4	3.4	2.1	4.2	3.5	3.3	4.1	3.4	3.8	4.1	3.5
Others	1.2	9.3	3.3	1.7	5.0	3.4	2.1	4.9	3.4	1.8	3.6	3.5
Total tax revenue	25.5	25.7	26.9	26.5	26.4	26.6	25.5	26.5	27.1	25.4	24.7	27.6
Social contributions	12.1	16.1	14.5	13.1	15.7	14.9	12.2	14.3	15.3	12.1	14.2	15.0
Employers	11.9	10.0	8.1	12.9	9.0	7.9	12.0	8.0	8.3	11.9	7.9	8.2
Employees	0.0	5.3	4.8	0.0	5.1	5.2	0.0	4.8	5.1	0.0	4.8	5.0
Self employed	0.2	1.8	1.6	0.2	1.6	1.8	0.2	1.5	1.9	0.2	1.6	1.9
Total fiscal revenue	37.7	41.8	41.4	39.6	42.2	41.5	37.7	40.8	42.4	37.5	38.9	42.6
Administrative level												
Central government	16.6	25.9	22.8	22.0	25.8	22.4	20.3	25.4	22.4	20.1	23.9	22.9
Local government	9.0	3.0	3.0	4.5	3.5	3.2	5.2	3.4	4.0	5.3	3.7	4.0
Social Security	12.1	12.9	14.5	13.1	12.9	14.9	12.2	11.5	15.2	12.1	11.4	14.9

Sources: EU Commission (2000a) for Estonia and New Members (unweighted average); Eurostat (2000) for EU-15 (1997 unweighted average).

Notes
Czech data start in 1993 and Social security is only health.

Direct taxes are still lower than indirect ones, but far less than in the average of the New Members. The yield of personal income tax is not low, although it is limited by the narrow base as well as by the flat rate of income tax (see section 8.3).

The total amount of indirect taxes looks comparatively higher. This is not due to the existence of a complex structure of excise duties, but rather to the narrow coverage of the VAT's reduced rate and to the small number of operations that benefit from a zero-rate scheme.

Social contributions on employed work are slightly lower than the average of both New Members and the EU, and are paid by the employers. However, do not forget that the theory of fiscal incidence firmly states that attributing by law the tax charge to employers or employees does not much matter as to its final incidence.

Finally notice that this structure is close to the 'optimal' case, as has been proposed by Mitra and Stern (2003) for the whole set of transition countries of Eastern Europe and the former Soviet Union.[3]

The development of the system from the early to the late 1990s

The Estonian new Constitution was adopted in 1992 and the fundamental laws of the fiscal reform were passed during the early 1990s. Then, the transition from the previous (USSR) regime moved quite fast and thereafter no dramatic changes occurred in the basic structure of the fiscal system. Some small changes did occur in the relative share of corporation tax and excise duties.

Corporation tax progressively decreased (from 4.8 percent of GDP in 1993 to 2.6 percent in 1998) as it assumed the features of a proper market-oriented corporation tax. Excise duties doubled, during the 1990s, from 1.9 percent in 1993 to 3.8 percent in 1998.

One must have well in mind that the transition to a market-oriented tax system raised tremendous institutional, administrative and behavioral changes, besides quantitative developments (Tanzi and Tsibouris 2000; Ebrill and Havrylyshyn 1999). A completely new set of administrative bodies and laws had to be created. Previous hidden levies became transparent to taxpayers. Estonia and the other Baltic states were performing comparatively well with this process (e.g. Aghion and Blanchard 1994; Coricelli 1997). The early introduction of new taxes[4] was not followed by any significant fall in total government revenues. Previous discretional tax practices gave no rise to the perception of a widespread and deep corruption.[5] Consequently, firms' bribing behavior was comparatively lower than in other transition economies.

The apportioning of revenue among government layers

The share of total revenues accruing to central government (20.1 percent of GDP in 1998) is nearly twice that which goes to Social Security bodies (pensions and health: 12.1 percent). The room for autonomous financing of local government is relatively wide, at least when compared with both New Members' and the EU's average.[6] These shares did not change much during the 1990s, except for an exceptional increase in the share of central government, balanced by a reduction in that of local governments.

However, according to the institutional setting inherited from the USSR structure, expenditure functions and taxing powers are strongly centralized. Local governments' expenditure in 1999 reached not much more than 7 percent of GDP (OECD 2002 for this and subsequent data). Having the local budgets to balance, local governments' total revenues equal total expenditures at about 7 percent of GDP, and are close to 22 percent of total general government revenues. This figure can in turn be split into about 68 percent taxes, 9 percent non-tax revenues, and 22 percent grants from central government. Notice that, again, just a small portion of taxes (about 10 percent, property taxes) is effectively local governments' own resources, while the remaining 90 percent (income taxes) being merely a non-autonomous revenue sharing of central taxes.

A comparison with other main New Members and the EU average[7]

Total fiscal pressure (37.5 percent) is about 1.5 points under the average of the New Members, 38.9 percent), but more than five points below the EU average (42.6 percent). Notice, however, that the share of taxes on total fiscal revenues is somewhat higher with respect with both the New Members' and the EU's cases. The root of this spread can be mainly found in the absence of social contributions directly charged on employees and in the low burden of such taxes paid by the self-employed. The splitting of taxes into direct and indirect taxes seems to characterize the Estonian system as being more advanced with respect to New Members and less in comparison with EU 15. Estonian direct taxes are high when compared with those of selected New Members but low with respect to EU countries. The opposite is the case of indirect taxes. See Table 8.1.

The Estonian level of local expenditure (7.1 percent) is very close to the European and Baltic New Members' average (7.2 percent), but is less than half the mean value of EU unitary countries (16.2 percent). The share of local taxes on total revenues (69 percent) is comparatively high against both the other New Members (56 percent) and EU countries (43 percent). The financing by means of central government grants is consequently lower (22.5 percent), particularly in comparison with EU members (46 percent). Recall however that the Estonian local tax revenue mainly comprises shares of national taxes.

8.3 Some quantitative and institutional features of main taxes[8]

National tax on individual income – PIT (Üksikisiku Tulumaks)

Estonian personal income tax was introduced in 1993[9] and further amended in 1999. It is close to the PIT standard model, but its features are somewhat simpler and country-specific. The yield from resident persons accrues at 44 percent into the state budget and at 56 percent into local governments. Some items of the potential base are exempt by law, the main ones' being as follows.

Capital incomes: Domestic dividends, interest received from credit institutions, inheritances and gifts. Dividends are subject to distribution tax (see below), while all other types of interest are included in the taxable income:

a   capital gains, from the sale of taxpayer's own domestic dwelling and coming from the restitution of expropriated property and privatization of the economy;
b   premium and expenses paid to qualified pension schemes;
c   almost all insurance proceeds. However, pensions from qualified schemes are taxed at a lower rate of 10 percent by way of a final withholding.

The taxing unity is the individual, including children with own income, but resident spouses may submit a joint tax-return. The tax structure is very close to the linear income tax scheme. There is a flat rate at 26 percent, but a basic allowance of about €770 (EEK 12,000) allowed per tax year. The same amount holds for any child until 17 years old, starting from the third child. Other main allowances concern interest paid to buy a house, educational expenses, alimony payments, various social merit donations and social contributions.

Corporate income tax – CIT (Ettevõtte Tulumaks)

This tax was adopted in 1993 and amended in 1999 and 2000. The tax is payable to the benefit of central government, not only by limited liability companies but also by resident partnerships, cooperatives, associations, foundations, public-law legal persons as well as by Estonian branches or permanent establishments of non-resident similar entities insofar as they derive Estonian-source income.

The base is made up of worldwide net income, including financial items. From 2000, the tax has not yet been levied on any retained earning but only on distributed profits, gifts and capital gains. The rate is set at 26/74 of the net amount of the distribution (26 percent of the gross amount).

Value added tax – VAT (Käibemaks)

VAT was introduced in 1993; it was further amended in 1999 and benefits the central government. Persons (individuals, legal entities and public bodies) liable to taxation are those making supplies in the course of their business or importing goods and services into Estonia.

The structure is given by the standard European VAT and exemptions follow the general rules: education, health and public services, credit and financing institutions services, individual letting of housing and so forth.

The standard rate is set at 18 percent, but it is scaled down to zero (input tax being deductible) in the following main cases: exports, scholarly textbooks and Estonian subscribed periodicals. A reduced rate of 5 percent applies to certain books, medicines and medical equipment, treatment of hazardous waste, funeral requisites and services, theatrical performances and concerts, heat and solid fuels sold to natural persons.

Excise duties (aktsiis)

Estonia maintains a wide system of excise duties, which has been largely updated during the 1990s. The main items are:

a   *alcohol* – The beneficiary is the state, but peculiarly 3.5 percent of the revenue is transferred to the Cultural Endowment of Estonia. Curiously enough, rates are increasing not only from beer to other fermented more alcoholic beverages, but also from these to sparkling wines;

b   *tobacco* – The beneficiaries are the same as in the case of alcohol's excise. The tax is paid through revenue stamps, which can be bought by the producers and the importers of manufactured tobacco. The stamps' value is around €0.50 per package of cigarettes. This value will be increased each year until 2010 (roughly EEK1–2 per year);

c   *fuel* – All the revenue accrues to central government. The tax is imposed (albeit with some exemptions) on any kind of motor fuel both manufactured in Estonia and imported. Rates range from about €0.02 per liter of fuel oil to about €0.25 per liter of gasoline. These excises will also be harmonized with the EU, beginning in 2004 there will be an increase;

d   additionally, there is the excise duty on packaging. The tax is paid by the importer of packages, by the user of packages, i.e. who fills the packages with goods, or by the re-importer of the packaging.

Heavy goods vehicle tax (Raskeveokimaks)

There will be a heavy goods vehicle tax from the beginning of 2004. A heavy goods vehicle tax is paid on the following classes of vehicles that are intended for the carriage of goods: (1) lorries with a maximum authorized weight or gross laden weight of not less than 12 tons; (2) road trains comprising trucks and trailers with a maximum authorized weight or gross laden weight of not less than 12 tons. Heavy goods vehicles belonging to the fire and rescue service agencies of the Defence Forces, National Defence League, Border Guard, police authorities, and also state and local government agencies of the fire and rescue services, are exempt from the heavy goods vehicle tax.

Local taxes

The autonomous sources of financing of local authorities (fully or with sharing by central government) are basically the following:

a   *local taxes (Kohalikud Maksud)* – They may be imposed on bases already taxed or not by central government. In particular: sales tax (maximum rate at 1 percent), boat tax on owners of boats, advertisement tax, tax for closing roads and streets (for demonstrations, processions and so on), local tax on motor vehicles, tax on keeping animals, entertainment tax on recreational activities and parking charge;

b   *land tax (Maamaks)* – The tax is due from the owners or users of land to the benefit of local authorities. The tax is assessed on the value of owned land and the rates range from 0.5 to 2 percent.

Social security contributions (Sotsiaalmaks)

Social security contributions were adopted by law as late as 1998 to the benefit of Social Security and Health Insurance, as a part of the move of the welfare system to a Bismarkian model (Oksanen 2001). The total rate for all workers is quite high, being set at 33 percent, of which 20 percent is for social insurance and 13 percent is for health insurance. In addition, unemployment insurance contributions must be paid on employees' income. The employer's contribution is levied at a rate of 0.5 percent and the employee's contribution at 1 percent.

Other minor taxes

Stamp duties (*Riigilõiv*) accrue to the state budget, and are imposed on legal acts and the release of administrative documents. A gambling tax is levied on income gained from operating games of skill and betting, to the benefit of both the state and local governments. Finally, a first faint move toward environmental taxation has been done, by introducing in 1999 a pollution fee (*Saastetasu*) payable to central government by the owner of an immovable property who releases pollutants or wastes into the environment.

8.4 The fiscal burden

The distribution of tax charge: taxation by economic functions and implicit tax rates

The value of taxation according to economic function is given by the ratio of the total tax revenue assigned to some factor, divided by a general measure of economic activity, i.e. in practice GDP. The resulting values come from combining tax rates with the size of any factor and thus enable us to evaluate how any factor contributes to the total value of revenues.

Keeping this in mind, we can see from Table 8.2 that the overall structure of Estonian taxation according to economic function, broadly speaking, is not at all unusual. Labor employed was the main source of tax revenues in Estonia in 1998 (19.8 percent). The next highest contribution came from consumption (12.7 percent), whereas the shares of self-employed labor as well as capital and business[10] were quite small. Profits are the main components of capital and business taxation. Revenues from real estate and financial activities (shares and savings) are still quite low. Finally taxes on environment totaled 2.3 percent in 1998, but 1.7 percent of this was given by taxes on energy.[11]

From the early to the late 1990s, the functional structure of Estonian taxation stayed almost unchanged. However taxation of consumption increased by a little more than one point from 1992 to 1998, as a consequence of the increase of excise duties, as we have already seen. Taxation of employed labor increased by about two points, while that of self-employed labor remained constant at a very low level. That on capital and business practically did not go over the zero level.

Implicit rates are defined as the ratios of the total tax revenues assigned to an economic factor, divided by total National accounts income or cost of this factor.[12] Therefore, they show the weight of the fiscal burden suffered by any factor, for any dimension of the base. Consider again Table 8.2. In 1998, employed labor appears to be the factor more heavily taxed, at an implicit rate of near 40 percent. This however means that average rates of income tax are low, given the total value of social contributions (33 percent, as we saw earlier). Furthermore, it is not surprising that the implicit rate on consumption (15.5 percent) does not differ very much from the incidence of consumption tax measured by economic category. Obviously, when income per capita is as low as it is in Estonia (about 20 percent of the EU average), consumption exploits almost the total amount of internal allocation of resources. The current implicit rate on capital and business looks as gentle as one could expect just looking at taxation by function. This can be easily explained by considering the small share of these incomes on total incomes (Figure 8.1).

Looking back at the early 1990s, both the consumption and labor rates show an overall increasing trend, particularly during the first half of the

Table 8.2 Structure and development of taxation by function and by implicit rates in Estonia, New Members and EU 15, 1992–98

	1992			1994			1996			1998		
	Estonia	New members	EU	Estonia	New members	EU	Estonia	New members	EU	Estonia	New members	EU
Economic function												
Consumption	11.4	13.6	10.9	13.5	14.5	11.2	13.5	14.7	11.3	12.7	13.5	11.4
Labor employed	19.7	19.7	20.6	20.4	19.4	20.7	19.7	19.0	21.4	19.8	17.9	21.2
Labor self-employed	1.3	2.9	2.4	1.2	2.8	2.4	1.2	2.6	2.4	1.3	2.6	2.3
Capital and business	0.3	4.3	7.2	0.3	5.0	6.8	0.3	4.3	7.1	0.3	4.5	7.5
Implicit tax rates												
Consumption	14.4	16.3	16.2	15.9	17.4	16.5	15.9	17.8	16.7	15.5	16.6	16.8
Labor employed	37.5	37.1	39.0	35.6	38.3	40.2	37.1	37.4	42.0	39.4	38.0	41.9
Capital and business	29.4	–	32.2	33.9	–	30.3	20.2	–	30.5	21.5	–	31.1

Sources: EU Commission (2000a) for Estonia and New Members (unweighted average); Eurostat (2000) for EU 15 (1997 unweighted average). 1992 implicit rates and all Czech rates refer to 1993. Implicit rates for capital and business are available only for Estonia and Slovenia.

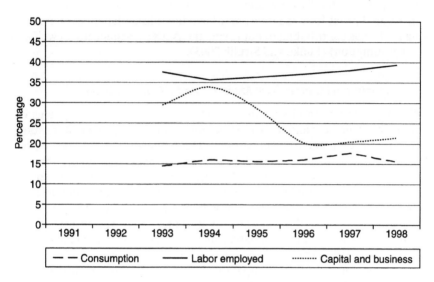

Figure 8.1 Implicit tax rates in Estonia (source: EU Commission (2000a)).

decade, albeit with some recurring ups and downs. The trend was needed to compensate for the slump of capital and business rate which occurred from 1994 to 1996. It was simply given by a wide cut in transfers due to the state by (publicly held) corporations during the Soviet regime.

The ability to attract foreign direct investment

During the 1990s, more than US$100 billion in foreign direct investment flowed to the central and Eastern European former communist countries and to the new CIS states. Indeed, the FDI was highly correlated with cumulative privatization process but was also influenced by an investment friendly climate. Estonia performed quite well (Mitra and Stern 2003). Foreign direct investment reached 3.9 percent of GDP in 1992–95, when the average values were 0.5 percent for the central and Eastern European and 1 percent for the CIS countries. The Estonian score was better still in 1996–99, when FDI reached 5.2 percent of GDP. During these years, however, the performance of the European (3.3 percent) and the CIS (2.5 percent) countries also improved. Contrary to the common trend, Estonian FDI was not very correlated with the diffusion of small enterprises, but instead was induced by a good interaction between tax and non-tax incentives. Tax-incentives (see section 8.5) first took the form of generous allowances and ad hoc tax-regimes. Subsequently, it was realized that a more general mild tax environment would be preferable, according to the suggestions of the recent literature (Holland and Owens 1997). It has been estimated that the Tax Reform Act of 2000 (which made exempt non-distributed profit from taxation) may have the substantial effect of attracting FDI, thus contributing to improving the Act's consequences on welfare (= consumption) (Funke and Strulik 2003).

A comparison with other New Members and EU 15 countries

We may compare the Estonian tax system in 1998 with those systems of both New Members and the EU 15 countries, by looking again at taxation both by function and by implicit rates. The Estonian share of taxation on consumption is slightly lower than in New Members and higher than in EU countries. However, this rank changes when considering the corresponding figures of implicit rates: the burden of Estonian taxes imposed on consumption is about one point below the level of both New Members and EU countries. These three clusters do not much differ with respect to the share of taxation on labor employed and the corresponding implicit rates. Taxation spreads increase when comparing the burden on capital and business. Estonian figures are comparatively lower from both points of view (i.e. by economic function and by implicit rates). A tentative conclusion, at least for consumption and labor, is that the shares of burden are determined more by the relative wideness of the bases than by the specific statutory rates.

8.5 Tax reforms and further steps to get closer to the EU

Macroeconomic and budget outlook

During the 1990s, the Estonian general government budget roughly balanced,[13] also because the Central Bank is prevented by law from money financing. The economic slowdown of 1999 in the wake of the Russian crisis increased, however, the deficit up to 4.7 percent of GDP. VAT and excises went down, particularly on imports. Higher unemployment gave rise to a contraction of social contributions and income tax yields. During the following years, up to 2002, the economic recovery was particularly buoyant (at about 5 percent of yearly GDP increase) (EU Commission 2000b). A fast growth characterized 2003 and is forecast to continue in 2004, notwithstanding the risks from external environment. Growth performance and fiscal discipline gradually changed the late 1990s' government deficit in a budget surplus that reached 1.3 percent of GDP in 2002. The forecast decreasing revenues coming from incentive-inducing tax cuts and additional expenditures due to EU and NATO membership will somewhat deteriorate the budget balance, which is expected to turn negative, but only to some half point of GDP in 2004, a figure well inside the boundaries of Stability Pact. Inflation could go on to be the main Estonian departure from European financial requirements. However, the inflation rate, which reached 7.1 percent in mid-2001, decreased to 3.5 percent in 2002–03 and is forecast to be stable at this level for 2004 (EU Commission 2003).

The last few years' reforms and planned tax reforms

The Estonian tax system has been subject to some changes during the last few years and some others are planned for the near future (EU Commission 2000a; IBDF 2002b). A common aim is to make the system closer to the EU 15 standards. This target informed the reform (and increase) of excise duties (2001–02) and a significant change in VAT. The regime was made consistent with the EU 'VI Directive' and a reduced rate (5 percent) was adopted for medicines, books and other minor items. International tax treaties were signed with some EU 15 countries. Importantly, only distributed (in any form) corporations' profits are now taxed, while those retained and invested have been made exempt. This is a relevant point (not exclusive of Estonia) which deserves a short digression.

The change has been justified as a general measure devoted to promote investments and growth. The true reason is somewhat subtler (Easson 1998). Recall that the main source of state financing was state-owned enterprises transfers, under the USSR regime. By transforming transfers into a corporation tax, very high rates emerged (around 60 percent). This level would have discouraged any foreign investments in Estonia (and in any other former communist country). A preferential tax treatment was then accorded to foreign investors. As the corporation tax rate fell, there were no reasons for the survival of the specific regime.

Beginning from about 1996–98, tax competition to attract (Western) direct investments begun to increase among Eastern and Central Europe transition countries, and various kinds of tax incentives were introduced in the corporation tax. Estonia has also competed by the allowance for retained profits. By means of a dynamic AGE model, this allowance has been estimated to be able to increase substantially investments and capital accumulation. However, some crowding out of consumption is likely to occur, leaving welfare unimproved, at least in the short-to-medium run (Funke and Strulik 2003).

The need for further steps

Summing up, the Estonian tax system seems relatively close to the EU 15 ones. The main rates are in line with the EU 15 average. Regarding the shares of broad aggregates of taxes, the Estonian main deviation concerns a wider room for social contributions and indirect taxes. Directly or indirectly employed labor is thus heavily hit. Consequently, a double problem of both efficiency and equity arises. On the grounds of efficiency, a reduction of employed labor tax burden is recommended, to allow a more job-intensive growth, taking in account that the unemployment rate was still at 12 percent in 2000 (European Commission 2002). The equity side of the problem comes (Tanzi and Tsibouris 2000) from the transition process having raised inequality in incomes per capita from a before-tax Gini of 0.23 in 1987 to a figure of 0.35 in 1995. The tax system should correct this fall of welfare, but it is difficult to envisage how it could do it. Since most incomes are highly concentrated around a low mean figure, the income tax redistributive effect is necessarily poor.

There will be further changes in tax rates in the field of indirect taxation. Estonia has got the transition periods for harmonizing excise duties of cigarettes and smoking tobacco until 2010, and VAT on heat and solid fuels sold to natural persons until 2007 (from 0 percent to 18 percent). Additionally, other changes in tax rates will take place after joining the EU on 1 May 2004; for example, excise duties on fuels will be increased, VAT will be levied at 5 percent on subscribed periodicals and scholarly textbooks etc. The transition period of tobacco products was applied for because it allows a step by step increase in excise duty, otherwise the sharp increase in the tax rate would not be administrated effectively (the prices of cigarettes should be roughly double), there would be a tax revenue loss (due to the spread of illegal trade generated by price differences between Estonia and its neighboring countries) and it would not correlate with the growth of the standard of living. Further recommended actions (EU Commission 2000b) suggest a stronger harmonization of tax policy with EU requirements, while preserving a simple and transparent tax policy of lower rates for enterprises. A strict control of expenditure is then needed, especially taking into account the trends of a declining and aging population. In fact, we have already seen that in 1997 the government reformed the pension system, by introducing a three-pillar scheme: this however had some additional costs for the public budget. To stimulate further growth, it would be helpful to devise a simplified tax regime for small businesses, which constitute the most dynamic sector of the economy. For the same aim, the remaining tax exemptions and tax reliefs should be eliminated. Along these lines, the operating difficulties of the tax administration could be alleviated (Mitra and Stern 2003).

8.6 Some information about Latvia and Lithuania

Both Latvia and Lithuania are similar to Estonia, with respect to location, size and, broadly speaking, the number of inhabitants and per capita income. The history of the three countries has been largely common, particularly during the last decades. Therefore, it is usual to refer to these countries as the 'Baltic states', a community of about 6.5 million people, whose economy grew fast during the last few years. For both Latvia and Lithuania we give brief fiscal data in National account format, as estimated by IMF-WB staff.

The story they tell shows few departures from the Estonian case. Regarding current taxation, both Latvia and, even more, Lithuania tax less than Estonia. Social contributions are particularly low in Lithuania, while both income tax and VAT in each country are under the Estonian figure. This might be explained by the lower level of per-capita income of Latvia and Lithuania (around $3500), compared with that of Estonia (about $4300).

From the early to the late 1990s, the total fiscal pressure did not change much in Latvia, and did not change the main taxes' basic features. However, fiscal pressure fell in Lithuania: the market-oriented cut in corporation tax rates was not adequately substituted. The high degree of centralization of both revenues and expenditures in Lithuania is similar to the Estonian figure, while Latvia shows more decentralization of both revenues (11 percent of GDP) and expenditures (9.5 percent) (OECD 2002 for about 1999). Both Latvian and Lithuanian local governments do not have their own tax. They are financed almost exclusively (Lithuania) or largely (together with grants and non-tax revenues) by sharing National taxes.

In Latvia (IBDF 2002a), individuals are subject to individual income tax. This is levied on all income received by the taxpayer, albeit with some standard exemptions, particularly with respect to capital incomes. As in Estonia, the rate is flat, at 25 percent. A personal credit (about €450) is allowed for employment income; a credit (€230) is allowed for each dependent. Corporations are subject to 'enterprise income tax' which hits once for all corporate income in the hands of the corporation, without any further levy on distributed dividends. The tax rate has been decreasing from 2001 (25 percent) and reached 15 percent by January 2004, but more than one favorable regime has been retained. Land and buildings are taxed by local authorities at a rate of 1.5 percent of cadastral value. VAT is due when the total yearly value of the supply or import of goods and services exceeds about €18,000 for each taxable person. The standard rate is set at 18 percent, but – as at 2001 – a reduced rate of 9 percent is applied to some essentials. The National Insurance Fund provides benefits for almost all kinds of social risk. The rate of contributions given by employers is 26 percent, that from employees is 9 percent, and that from the self-employed is 32.3 percent.

Lithuanian taxes are not very different (Ministry of Finance of Lithuania). The standard flat rate of personal income tax is set at 33 percent. A reduced rate of 15 percent is applied however to certain income sources as distributed profit, interest, pensions and insurance payments, royalties and properties' rents. Corporation tax has a standard rate on both retained and distributed profits of 15 percent. The present structure of VAT is quite close to the EU's model. The standard rate is 18 percent. In addition, reduced rates of 5 percent and of 9 percent are applied. The law on VAT envisages cases when the supply is exempt and there are special VAT schemes for farmers, tourism services and so forth.

During the late 1990s, growth was very fast in Latvia (at rates of 5–8 percent). This trend is projected (EU Commission 2003) to continue in 2004, driven by private consumption and fixed investments. The budget balance has benefitted slightly from economic expansion. This has been due to the already mentioned cuts in corporation tax, which were only partially compensated for by VAT increases. Thus, at the time of writing, the general government deficit runs at about two-to-three points of GDP on the upper bound of the Stability Pact. The inflation rate is somewhat lower than in Estonia in the range of 2-to-3 percent. The picture is not very different for Lithuania. Paradoxically, GDP growth is somewhat lower, while both inflation rate (0.3 percent in 2002) and government budget (-1.9 percent in 2002) seem to perform better. This is a result of a persistent strict fiscal discipline adopted from 1999, when the government deficit reached 5.6 percent of GDP.

Notes

1 Respectively, Estonian Institute of Economic Research, Tallinn, Estonia, e-mail: evelin@ki.ee, and Department of Public and Environmental Economics, University of Pavia, Italy, e-mail: luigi.bernardi@unipv.it. Thanks are due for suggestions in a number of areas to C. Bronchi, M. Chandler, M. Galizzi and L. Pench. A preliminary version was presented at the Congress 'Tax Policy in EU Candidate Countries', Riga, 12–14 September 2003.
2 All UN 2002 data, not weighted in PPP terms.
3 Total taxes (37.5 percent of GDP) are higher than the upper bound suggested by Mitra and Stern (31 percent). Income tax (8.5 percent) stays near the proper level (9 percent). VAT (8.8 percent) is high compared with the proper level (7 percent) as are excise duties (3.8 percent compared with 3 percent). Most of all, social contributions (12.1 percent) are over the recommended level (10 percent). The conclusion should be that the Estonian economy could gain efficiency by a substantial cut of taxes, especially indirect taxes and social contributions. Notice, however, that Mitra's and Stern's suggested rates are 'optimal' only in the sense that they have been extrapolated from the most common trends resulting from a cross-section of developing and high income countries. On the same topic, see Gupta *et al.* (2001).
4 All Baltic states got the maximum score regarding the progress in tax policy reform, among both Central and Eastern European as well as CIS countries (Ebrill and Havrylyshyn 1999).
5 Data reported in Tanzi and Tsibouris (2000) show for 1997 a level of the index near three times that of Russia and twice that of China.
6 Notice that the ESA95 National Accounting System does not include sharing national taxes in this figure.
7 A detailed discussion may be found in Mitra and Stern (2003).
8 This section owes much to EU Commission (2000a) and IBDF (2002a, b).
9 1993 is a crucial year for tax reforms in Eastern and Central Europe transition countries. Not only Estonia, but also the (then) Czech–Slovak Republic, Hungary and Poland introduced entirely new tax codes, under the clear influence of bodies such as IMF and OECD, after the 1989 initial reforms (Easson 1998).
10 Capital and business here are substantially given by National accounts operating surplus, less self-employed income. The main items are thus given by incomes and capital gains from the various kinds of wealth.
11 Data not reported here. See EU Commission (2000a).

12 Notice that, in this case, self-employed labor income is included in operating surplus, i.e. capital and business.
13 General government budget was in surplus by 2.2 percent of GDP in 1997, and in deficit by 0.3 percent in 1998.

References

Aghion, P. and Blanchard, O. (1994) 'On the speed of transition in central Europe', NBER Macroeconomics Annual, pp. 283–320.

Blejer, M. I. and Ter-Minassian, T. (eds) (1997) *Fiscal Policy and Economic Reform: Essays in Honor of Vito Tanzi*, London and New York: Routledge.

Coricelli, F. (1997) 'Restructuring, phases of transition and the budget', in CEPR, *Fiscal Policy in Transition, Economic Policy Initiative*, 3.

Easson, A. (1998) 'Tax competition heats up in Central Europe', *Bulletin of International Bureau of Fiscal Documentation*, May, 192–97.

Ebrill, L. and Havrylyshyn, O. (1999) 'Tax reform in the Baltic, Russia, and other countries of the former Soviet Union', O.P. 182, Washington, DC: IMF.

EU Commission (2000a) *Structure of the Tax Systems in Estonia, Poland, Hungary, the Czech Republic and Slovenia*, Brussels: EU Commission.

EU Commission (2000b) 'Recent fiscal developments in the candidate countries', Enlargement Papers 2, Brussels: EU Commission, Directorate General for Economic and Financial Affairs.

EU Commission (2002) *European Economy*, 3, V, pp. 131–54, Brussels: EU Commission, Directorate General for Economic and Financial Affairs.

EU Commission (2003) 'Economic forecasts for the candidate countries. Spring 2003', Enlargement Papers 15, Brussels: EU Commission, Directorate General for Economic and Financial Affairs.

Eurostat (2000) *Structures of the Taxation Systems in the European Union, 1970–1997*, Brussels: EU Commission.

Eurostat (2002) *Statistical Yearbook on Candidate and South-east European Countries*, Brussels: EU Commission.

Funke, M. and Strulik, H. (2003) 'Taxation, growth and welfare: dynamic effects of Estonia's 2000 income tax act', Discussion Paper 2003/10, Helsinki: Bank of Finland, Institute for Economies in Transition.

Gupta, S., Leruth, L., de Mello, L. and Chakrawarti, S. (2001) 'Transition economies: how appropriate is the size of government?', IMF Working Paper 55, Washington, DC: IMF.

Holland, D. and Owens, J. (1997) 'Taxation and direct foreign investment: the experience of the economies in transition', in Blejer, M. I. and Ter-Minassian, T. (eds) *Fiscal Policy and Economic Reform: Essays in Honor of Vito Tanzi*, London and New York: Routledge.

IBDF – International Bureau of Fiscal Documentation (2002a) *European Tax Handbook 2002*, Amsterdam: IBDF.

IBDF – International Bureau of Fiscal Documentation (2002b) *Annual Report, 2001–2002*, Amsterdam: IBDF.

IMF (2002) 'The Baltics: Medium-term fiscal issues related to EU and NATO accession', CR 02/07, Washington, DC: IMF.

Mitra, P. and Stern, N. (2003) 'Tax systems in transition', WB Working Paper 2947, Washington, DC: The World Bank.

OECD (2002) *Fiscal Decentralization in EU Applicant States and Selected EU Member States*, Paris: OECD.

Oksanen, H. (2001) 'A case for partial funding of pensions with an application to the EU candidate countries', E.P. 149, Brussels: EU Commission.

Tanzi, V. and Tsibouris, G. (2000) 'Fiscal reform over ten years of transition', IMF Working Paper 113, Washington, DC: IMF.

Websites

http://www.stat.ee – Statistical Office of Estonia.
http://www.fin.ee – Ministry of Finance of Estonia.
http://www.csb.lv – Central statistical Bureau of Latvia.
http://www.fm.gov.lv – Ministry of Finance of Latvia.
http://www.sdt.lt – Lithuanian Department of Statistics.
http://www.finmin.lt – Ministry of Finance of Lithuania.

9 Hungary

Francesca Sala[1]

9.1 Introduction and executive summary

Hungary is a landlocked country in Central Europe, with a population of 10.1 million inhabitants and an area of 93,036 km². After the Second World War, Hungary experienced a communist regime until the region's collapse in 1989. In 1990, free, multi-party parliamentary elections were held for the first time in 43 years. In 1994, Hungary was the first country of the region to apply formally for EU membership and, in 1998, the accession negotiations were finally launched. After joining NATO in 1999, Hungary *de facto* entered into the EU in 2004, as the Nice Treaty established it in 2001. Local currency is the forint (HUF1 = €0.0039).[2]

Growth in Hungary has averaged 4.5 percent since 1997, and was well maintained at close to 4 percent in 2001, when GDP was about 61 billion euro (per capita, PPP unweighted: about €6150); in the same period unemployment fell below 6 percent. The economy outperformed most of the other countries during the 2001–03 international slowdown largely owing to a strong fiscal impulse and to a consequent increase in private consumption. The highly expansionary fiscal policy caused a worsening of the general government deficit, which reached 5.2 percent of GDP in 2001 and 9.2 percent in 2002. Inflation was below 5 percent in 2002.

Total fiscal pressure in Hungary, after a declining trend during the first half of the 1990s, reached 39 percent in 1999 and has been rather stable since then. This level is considered too high and harmful for potential growth. Furthermore, as in other New Members, tax revenue continues to depend much more on indirect taxes while the shares of revenue generated by income taxes on capital and labor as well as property taxes remain relatively low. Social security contributions, making up one third of total revenue, are by law levied predominantly as the employers' share, thus generating a high tax burden on labor to the detriment of labor market participation and employment. As in any former communist country, the share of local governments' revenues on GDP, generally used as an indicator of the size of local governments, appears rather low if compared with the EU countries' levels. The revenue autonomy too is still very low, with only one third of local government financing coming from own revenues, but major changes have occurred since the beginning of the transition period.[3]

The time development of the tax structure since the beginning of the transition period in 1991 was dominated by the structural changes that have been achieved in order to move to the fiscal systems prevailing in the EU. In the earlier period, from 1991 to 1996, one can see the effects of the economic transition in marked changes of the level of total taxation, which was decisively lowered from 47 percent of GDP to 41 percent between 1991 and 1996 and has remained around 39 percent since then. This trend is explained by a substantial reduction in the direct taxes to GDP ratio and also by a decrease in the social contributions to GDP ratio, whereas the indirect taxes share of GDP lowered to a less extent.

The tax system in Hungary seems relatively close to the EU 15 ones, although some distinctive features are still present and further adjustments of rates and procedures are needed for accession to the EU. A progressive personal income tax with three brackets is applied on aggregate individual income, with the exclusion of income from capital and capital gains, which are taxed separately; a number of tax allowances in the form of tax credits are granted. The taxation of corporate profits is based on a partial integration system: corporate profits are taxed at a flat rate of 16 percent[4] and dividends are taxed by way of a flat rate withholding tax of 20 percent; beside the standard regime, a number of tax incentives is envisaged for large-scale investment or offshore companies.

The VAT system is very similar to that applied within the EU, although transitional measures regarding rate levels and exemptions have been required by the EU; the VAT standard rate is 25 percent, the highest among the New Members, but reduced rates of 15 percent and 5 percent are applied on some basic products and services.[5] As stated by EU legislation, excise duties are levied on alcoholic beverages, tobacco and hydrocarbon fuels. Among local taxes, a major role is played by the local business tax, which accounts for some 85 percent of all local governments tax revenues. Finally, relatively high social security contributions and payroll taxes must be paid by employers on gross wages, thus augmenting the direct cost of labor.

As to the distribution of fiscal burden according to economic function, the main source of tax revenues as a percentage of GDP comes from employed labor and, to a lower extent, from consumption. If compared with EU 15 countries, Hungarian taxation shows a higher role of taxes on consumption, while taxes on employed labor do not differ significantly from the EU average. Implicit tax rates confirm the overall picture.

Considering the macroeconomic and budgetary outlook for 2003 and 2004, growth is projected to accelerate slightly and new inflation targets have been established in accordance with the Central bank; fiscal policy is required to return to the announced consolidation path, with a stabilization of the deficit at around 5 percent in 2003 and a further reduction to below 4 percent in 2004.

Tax reforms in recent years appear to have been driven by the commitment gradually to harmonize with the EU and by the aim to improve further the environment for the business sector. The former objective has informed mainly the VAT and excise duties systems, whereas the latter has been translated into a favorable corporate tax regime and into a wide range of tax incentives, especially for offshore companies. At present, Hungary's taxation system is, to a large extent, aligned with the EU's requirements, although further harmonization efforts are needed, notably regarding rates of VAT and excise duties. Another recommended action concerns the progressive reduction of social security contributions, in order to reduce the tax burden on labor and hence stimulate employment. The corporate taxation regime should also be reconsidered in light of the risk of a harmful tax competition within the EU and a possible EU action against specific incentives.

9.2 The structure of the system at the end of the 1990s

A broad view at the current structure of taxes and social security contributions

In 1999, the level of aggregate taxation in Hungary was 39 percent of GDP, roughly two percentage points below the EU average. The distribution of fiscal revenues, which can be split into two third of taxes and one third of social contributions, shows some striking differences with the EU average. As in the other New Members (with the only exception being the Czech Republic) indirect taxes play a larger role than in the EU, making 43 percent of total taxation; indeed, the indirect taxes to GDP ratio of 17 percent lies above the long-term EU average of 14 percent.

On the other hand, direct taxes represent a much smaller share of total taxation, that is 23.4 percent against the 1996 EU average of 31.2 percent, and make up only 9 percent of GDP, well below the 1996 EU average of 13 percent. This fact can be explained through the relatively low level of tax payers' average income and the very low level of the corporate tax rate (18 percent).[6]

Social contributions' share in total revenue of 33.6 percent lies below the 1996 EU average of 36.3 percent. Social contributions are by law levied predominantly on employers (fraction 0.82), whereas the employees' share amounts to 0.16 of the total and self-employed persons contribute only 0.02 of the total.

The development of the system from the early to the late 1990s

The evolution over time of the tax structure during the transition period starting in 1991 has been characterized by important structural changes that have been achieved in order to bear up to the fiscal systems of EU countries. In the period from 1991 to 1996 the economic transition involved marked changes of both the level of total taxation and the relative weights of levies on the factors consumption, employed labor, capital and business, included self-employed labor (see section 9.4).

The level of aggregate taxation was decisively lowered from 47 percent of GDP to 41 percent between 1991 and 1996 and has remained around 39 percent. This reduction is explained by a substantial reduction in the direct taxes to GDP ratio, which passed from 12.9 to 9 percent, remaining roughly stable from then on, and also by a decrease in the social contributions to GDP ratio from 16.6 to 13.8 percent in 1996 and 13.0 percent in 1999. The indirect taxes share of GDP lowered to a smaller extent (17.2 percent of GDP in 1991 and 16.6 percent in 1999), showing an increasing contribution of VAT (6 percent of GDP in 1991 and 8.5 percent in 1999) in spite of the excise duties.

The apportionment of revenue among government layers

The splitting of the total revenue by receiving administrative levels as percentages of GDP shows that, in 1999, the central government received 22.4 percent and the local governments only 3.2 percent (the social contributions funds to GDP ratio was, as already said, 13 percent). The share of central government in 1999 was 58 percent of total revenue or 88 percent of taxes without social contributions; non-central government received 8.3 percent of total revenue or 12 percent of taxes without social contributions, composed of 40 percent of the personal income tax, of a local business tax, the taxes on land and buildings, one half of taxes on property transfer and more than one half of the motor vehicle taxes. The share of central government on total revenue did not change much during the 1990s, being 58.8 percent in 1991, while there has been a slight increase in the local governments' share, from 5.6 to 8.3 percent of total revenue (EU Commission 2000a).

In 1999, the share of total local governments' revenues on GDP, generally used as an indicator of the size of local governments, was 11.1 percent and the share in consolidated national government revenue amounted to 26.7 percent. As to the composition of total local governments' revenues, grants from the central budget accounted for 50 percent, tax revenues for 33 percent and non-tax revenues for the remaining 17 percent. Notice that since the system of local taxes (not compulsory) was implemented in 1991,[7] both the number of local governments collecting local taxes and their revenues have been steadily increasing: in 1999, 93 percent of local governments applied local taxes and these accounted for some 18 percent of all current revenues, to be compared with the mere 3.5 percent in 1990.[8] Among the local taxes, a major role is played by the local business tax, which accounts for some 85 percent of all local governments tax revenues.

Finally, looking at the revenue autonomy, local governments financing can be split into 33.3 percent of own revenues, 18.5 percent of general grants and tax sharing arrangements and 48.2 percent of specific grants. In 1999, tax revenues were almost equally divided between own taxes and tax sharing with the central government (OECD 2002c).

A comparison with other main New Members and the EU average[9]

In 1998, the level of aggregate taxation in Hungary (38.9 percent) was exactly equal to the selected New Members average and less than four percentage points below the EU 15 average (42.6 percent). The difference in total fiscal pressure was therefore not very large; moreover, almost the same proportion between tax revenues and social contributions held (two thirds and one third) in Hungary and in the EU. What changes is the distribution of tax revenues: as shown in Table 9.1, if in the EU direct taxes account for 13.7 percent of GDP and indirect ones for 13.9 percent, in Hungary direct taxes account for only an 8.7 percent of GDP against the 16.3 percent of indirect taxes. The same imbalance holds also in other New Members – to a major extent in Estonia and Slovenia where the direct taxes to GDP ratio is only 7.8 percent.

Looking at the levels of decentralized expenditure, Hungary's quota on GDP in 1999 is 10.4 percent, the second highest level after the Polish one (12.1 percent) among European and Baltic New Members (average 7.2 percent); however, compared with the EU countries' average value of 16.2 percent, this decentralization indicator appears rather low. The share of taxes on total local government revenues (33 percent) is lower than in all other New Members (56 percent on average), with the exception of Poland where tax revenues account for only 25 percent, and is lower than in EU countries (43 percent). On the other hand, the quota of local revenues financed by central government's grants is almost the highest (50 percent) among the New Members, a very high value if compared with the EU average of 46 percent. Finally notice that Hungary is characterized by the highest proportion of specific grants on total local financing (48.2 percent of total local revenues) among the New Members (OECD 2002c).

Table 9.1 Structure and development of fiscal revenue in Hungary, New Members and EU 15 as a percentage of GDP, 1992–98

	1992			1994			1996			1998		
	Hungary	New members	EU	Hungary	New members	EU	Hungary	New members	EU	Hungary	New members	EU
Direct taxes, of which	10.1	10.1	13.5	9.4	10.0	13.5	9.0	9.6	12.9	8.7	9.2	13.7
Personal income	7.5	6.4	9.6	7.4	7.0	9.3	7.1	7.1	9.3	6.5	6.7	9.3
Corporation income	2.2	3.6	2.3	1.9	2.9	2.4	1.8	2.5	2.4	2.2	2.5	3.0
Indirect taxes, of which	17.9	15.6	13.4	17.9	16.5	13.7	17.8	16.9	13.7	16.3	15.5	13.9
VAT	6.0	5.1	6.7	7.7	7.4	6.8	7.5	7.4	6.9	7.9	7.9	7.0
Excise duties	6.2	3.4	3.4	4.2	4.2	3.5	3.9	4.1	3.4	4.2	4.1	3.5
Others	5.8	9.3	3.3	6.0	5.0	3.4	6.4	4.9	3.4	4.2	3.6	3.5
Total tax revenue	28.0	25.7	26.9	27.3	26.4	26.6	26.8	26.5	27.1	25.0	24.7	27.6
Social contributions	18.0	16.1	14.5	17.2	15.7	14.9	13.8	14.3	15.3	13.9	14.2	15.0
Employers	14.0	10.0	8.1	13.5	9.0	7.9	11.4	8.0	8.3	11.6	7.9	8.2
Employees	3.3	5.3	4.8	3.1	5.1	5.2	2.1	4.8	5.1	2.1	4.8	5.0
Self employed	0.7	1.8	1.6	0.6	1.6	1.8	0.3	1.5	1.9	0.3	1.6	1.9
Total fiscal revenue	46.0	41.8	41.4	44.5	42.2	41.5	40.6	40.8	42.4	38.9	38.9	42.6
Administrative level												
Central government	24.9	25.9	22.8	24.8	25.8	22.4	23.8	25.4	22.4	21.5	23.9	22.9
Local government	3.1	3.0	3.0	2.4	3.5	3.2	3.0	3.4	4.0	3.5	3.7	4.0
Social Security	18.0	12.9	14.5	17.2	12.9	14.9	13.8	11.5	15.2	13.9	11.4	14.9

Sources: EU Commission (2000a) for Hungary and New Members (unweighted average); Eurostat (2000) for EU-15 (1997 unweighted average).

Notes
Czech data start in 1993 and Social security is only health.

9.3 Some quantitative and institutional features of main taxes[10]

Personal income tax – PIT (Személyi jövedelemadó)

The personal income tax in Hungary, envisaged by the Law n.117 of 1995, is payable by resident individuals and the tax revenue accrues to both central and local governments; the tax sharing arrangement is fixed by the annual budget law:[11] in 1999 the local governments' share amounted to 40 percent.[12]

The tax base is the worldwide income of any kind, but different rules with respect to deductions and rates apply to different classes of income. The aggregate income (which includes mainly income from dependent and independent personal services and private pensions) is taxed at a progressive rate, but various credits are deductible from the tax liability. From 1 January 2002, pensions, provided on the basis of statutory provisions, are fully exempt from income tax; payments received from a private pension fund are taxable, but a credit equal to 50 percent of the tax calculated by applying the higher progressive rate, up to the actual tax due, is granted; pensions from a mutual insurance fund are exempt if the recipient has contributed to the pension fund for at least three years. The most important tax credits, deductible from the tax due, are granted for wage income, income from intellectual activities, social security contributions (both mandatory and voluntary),[13] life insurance premiums, education fees, housing mortgage loans, family allowances, donations.

The taxing unit is the individual. As of 2004, there are three classes of taxable income: the minimum tax rate of 18 percent is due on the first HUF800,000 (about €3156); 26 percent is levied on the excess up to HUF1,500,000 (about €5917) and the top rate of 38 percent on the excess over HUF1,500,000.[14]

Incomes from capital and capital gains are taxed separately at a flat rate, but different rules apply. Interest income is generally exempt (technically taxed at a rate of 0 percent). Dividends are taxed by way of withholding at a rate of 20 percent for ordinary and 35 percent for 'excess dividends'.[15] Rental income derived from immovable property is subject to tax at a rate of 20 percent. Finally, capital gains from the disposal of property, whether movable or immovable, are taxed at a 20 percent rate, with the exception of gains on non-quoted derivative instruments which are included in the aggregate income and taxed at a progressive rate.

Corporate income tax – CIT (Társasági adó és osztalékadó)

Hungary has a partial integration system for the taxation of corporate profits. Corporate profits are subject to the corporate income tax, but dividends paid to natural persons are, as a general rule, taxed by way of the already mentioned flat rate withholding at 20 percent known as 'dividend tax', introduced in 1997. Dividends paid to resident corporate shareholders are, however, normally exempt.

The taxable entities for corporate income tax, which accrues to the central government only, are joint-stock companies, limited liabilities companies, cooperatives, state-owned companies, foundations, associations, public service companies, social organizations, churches, risk capital funds.

Resident companies are taxed on their worldwide income; the taxable base is computed from the accounting profits (including also financial profits), that is gross revenue minus all deductible expenses. From 1997 to 2003, the corporate income tax rate was 18 percent, but a special rate of 3 percent applied to the taxable profits of offshore companies.[16] Since January 2004 these two rates have been changed to 16 percent and 4 percent respectively.

Value added tax – VAT (Átalános forgalmiadó)

Hungary applies a VAT system under which tax is levied at all levels of the supply of goods and services. The beneficiary of the VAT revenue is the central government. VAT applies to all natural persons and legal entities supplying or importing goods or services on a regular basis for profits; business with an annual turnover below 2 million forint (about €7890) may opt to be exempt from accounting for VAT.

The taxable amount is given by the value of goods and services supplied or imported (excluding VAT but including customs duties). Important exemptions include transactions relating to financial services, health care services, lease of dwellings, insurance and education. Under reciprocity agreements, non-residents doing business in Hungary may reclaim the VAT paid on Hungarian supplies of goods and services including the importation of goods.

The standard rate is 25 percent. A reduced rate of 15 percent applies to certain basic foodstuffs, medicines, medical supplies, certain textile materials, coal and electrical energy. A 5 percent rate (joint with the deduction of the tax paid on inputs) applies to exports as well as to textbooks and specified medicines and medical equipment. The 5 percent rate also applies to the development of gas and electricity infrastructures and to construction works.[17]

Excise duties (Jövedéki adó)[18]

The main items subject to excise duties in Hungary are as follows.

a   *Alcoholic products.* The beneficiary is the central government and the taxpayer is the person producing or importing the excise good. Rates increase from sparkling wine to intermediate products, beer and spirits. As from 1 August 2000, the system of consumption taxes and excise duties has been amended; the major change concerned wine that, within the framework of EU harmonization, became an excise product (the tax rate on grape wine initially set was HUF5 per liter – about €0.02 – against the previously applied consumption tax rate of 11 percent; since 1 January 2004 the rate became HUF8 per liter – about €0.03).

b   *Tobacco products.* Again the excise duty's revenue accrues to the central government. The tax base is the retail price (including tax and value added tax) and thousand units. As of 2004, for cigarettes tax rates are HUF6450 (about €25) per thousand units and 23 percent of the retail price.

c   *Fuels.* The beneficiary is the central government and the tax is levied on any mineral oils produced or imported. Tax rates increase from diesel (HUF85 per liter – about €0.33), to unleaded petrol (HUF103.50 per liter – about €0.41), to leaded petrol.

Consumption taxes (Fogyasztási adók)

Consumption taxes accrue to the central government. The most important are levied on:

a   *coffee.* The applicable tax rate is 12 percent;
b   *passenger cars.* The tax rates vary from 10 percent applied to a car up to 1600cc equipped with a catalytic converter to 32 percent applied to a car over 1600cc without a catalytic converter;
c   *products made of precious metals (other than silver).* The relevant tax rate is 35 percent.

Local taxes

In Hungary, local governments benefit from tax revenues coming from both tax sharing arrangements with the central government and own taxes. The main taxes shared with the central government are the personal income tax (40 percent sharing), the tax on onerous property transfer (50 percent sharing), the taxes on inheritance and gifts (50 percent sharing), and the motor vehicle tax (the share of local governments has increased to 100 percent since 2003).

There also exist a number of taxes that local governments can impose autonomously. The most important of them are as follows.

a   *Local business tax (helyi iparú zési adó).* Since 1991, municipal authorities have been authorized to levy local business tax on corporate taxpayers who have their seat, or who are registered, within their jurisdiction. Some municipalities do not charge such tax (but the number of these municipalities is decreasing over time) and a number of municipalities grant tax incentives. The tax base for commercial activities is the net sales revenues of product sold or service provided less the purchasing costs of goods and subcontractors' fees. Manufactures may fully deduct the costs of materials. The maximum rate for local business tax was 1.7 percent in 1999 and 2 percent from then on.[19]

b *Land parcel tax (telekadó)*. Introduced in 1991, this tax is levied annually on the owner of a land parcel; the tax base can be or the actual area in square meters or the adjusted market value of the parcel.

c *Building tax (építményadó)*. As before, the tax, which is due by the owner of a building, is calculated on the floor space in square meters or on the adjusted market value of the building.

d *Communal tax (kommunális adója)*. This tax can be levied on private individuals or on entrepreneurs. If on individuals, the occupants of a household dwelling pay HUF12,000 (about €47) per dwelling as a maximum annual rate, regardless of the number of inhabitants. This tax is suited to localities that have many government-owned social flats and cannot rely on property taxes for revenue. If levied on entrepreneurs, the enterprise pays a maximum annual rate of HUF2000 (about €8) per employee.

Social security contributions (Társadalombiztosítási járulékok)

Hungary reformed its pension system in 1997, introducing a multi-pillar system combining a PAYG state pension pillar and a fully-funded mandatory second pillar consisting of privately-operated pension funds. A voluntary third pillar of supplementary private pension was also introduced. Employees may either participate in the first and second pillars or remain covered by the state pension system only.

Social contributions are levied at a rate of 29 percent as the employers' share[20] (pension security contribution at a rate of 18 percent and health security contribution at a rate of 11 percent) plus 11.5 percent as the employees' share (pension contribution at a rate of 8.5 percent, reduced to 1.5 percent for members of private pension funds,[21] and health insurance contribution at a rate of 3 percent).[22]

In addition to the social security contributions, employers are obliged to pay a fixed health care contribution, which amounts to HUF3450 (about €14) per employee per month since 2003,[23] and a sick-leave benefit contribution equal to 33 percent of the overall employee's sickness benefits.

Finally, contributions must be paid to the unemployment fund, with the employees' applicable rate equal to 1 percent and the employers' contribution equal to 3 percent (*payroll tax*).

Other minor taxes

Besides the personal income tax, the motor vehicle tax is a shared tax. This tax was introduced in 1992. Motor vehicles – except those owned by public institutions or non-profit organizations and used for public transportation or communal services – are taxed according to their weight. Local governments are the taxing authorities, but the central government can set up the minimum and maximum rates. The minimum rate is HUF400 (about €1.58) per 100 kg and the maximum rate is HUF800 (about €3.15) per 100 kg. Since 2003, as already noted, all motor vehicle tax revenues contribute to the local budgets.

Among the taxes accruing to the central government, in 1998 a tourism contribution (*Turisztikai hozzájárulás*) has been introduced: this tax is levied on enterprises involved in tourism, like hotels, car rentals, casinos, travel agencies etc, at a rate of 1 or 2 percent, depending on the type of activities carried out, of the net sale revenues. Another tax introduced in the 1990s to the benefit of the central government only is the gambling tax (*Játékadó*), payable by gambling organizers on draws, totalizer-type bets, gambling machines, bets based on casinos.

Finally, the Hungarian taxation system envisages a number of 'environmental' taxes to the benefit of both central and local governments: the environmental protection fee, the air pollution levy, the water pollution levy, the toxic waste levy, the noise abatement levy.

9.4 The fiscal burden

The distribution of tax charge: taxation by economic functions and implicit tax rates

The assignment of total revenue according to the economic function of the tax base allows the subsequent calculation of the relative tax load on different production factors and on consumption, which is part of the relative factor prices and hence has an impact on factor allocation. The implicit tax rate is calculated to serve as a macroeconomic indicator for the factor tax loads.

Table 9.2 shows the structure of Hungarian taxation according to economic function as a percentage of GDP (EU Commission 2000a). In 1998, the main source of tax revenues was employed labor, which accounted for 19.0 percent of GDP. The second highest contribution to tax revenues came from consumption, whose taxation amounted to 13.8 percent of GDP. On the contrary, the shares of self-employed labor and of capital and business were significantly lower, being respectively 1.2 and 5 percent. The main component of capital and business taxation was profits (2.7 percent of GDP), whereas taxation on financial activities was very low (0.3 percent of GDP). Finally, in 1998, environmental

Table 9.2 Structure and development of taxation by function and by implicit rates in Hungary, New Members and EU 15, 1992–98

	1992			1994			1996			1998		
	Hungary	New members	EU	Hungary	New members	EU	Hungary	New members	EU	Hungary	New members	EU
Economic functions												
Consumption	15.9	13.6	10.9	15.6	14.5	11.2	15.3	14.7	11.3	13.8	13.5	11.4
Labor employed	23.4	19.7	20.6	22.6	19.4	20.7	19.3	19.0	21.4	19.0	17.9	21.2
Labor self-employed	1.8	2.9	2.4	1.7	2.8	2.4	1.4	2.6	2.4	1.2	2.6	2.3
Capital and business	4.9	4.3	7.2	4.5	5.0	6.8	4.6	4.3	7.1	5.0	4.5	7.5
Implicit tax rates												
Consumption	18.8	16.3	16.2	18.5	17.4	16.5	20.6	17.8	16.7	18.9	16.6	16.8
Labor employed	42.9	37.1	39.0	44.6	38.3	40.2	42.3	37.4	42.0	41.9	38.0	41.9
Capital and business	–	–	32.2	–	–	30.3	–	–	30.5	–	–	31.1

Sources: EU Commission (2000a) for Hungary and New Members (unweighted average); Eurostat (2000) for EU 15 (1997 unweighted average).

Notes
Taxation according to economic function is as a percentage of GDP. Total may stay over total fiscal revenue in Table 9.1 because of some double counting.
Estonia's 1992 implicit rates and all Czech rates refer to 1993. Implicit rates for capital and business are available only for Estonia and Slovenia.

taxation accounted for 3.3 percent, of which 2 percent was covered by taxes on energy.

Looking at the evolution of the functional structure of taxation from 1991 to 1999, the decrease in the aggregate taxation from 46.7 to 38.6 percent of GDP can be explained mainly by the reduction in the levies on employed labor (−4.7 percent), through a lowering of social contributions, and the reduction of taxation in capital and business (−2.7 percent). Taxation of consumption has been kept relatively constant in the 1991 to 1996 period and then has been slightly reduced to 14 percent since 1997. Taxation of energy was, and is, relatively high in Hungary: it was reduced from 4 to 2 percent of GDP from 1991 to 1996, and increased again to nearly 3 percent in 1999.

Considering the factor taxation expressed as a fraction of total taxation (including social contributions), the fraction on consumption, after an increase in the first half of the 1990s, remained around 36 percent since 1997. The fraction on employed labor, which reached 51 percent in 1993 and 1994, decreased to 46.5 percent in 1999. Finally, the fraction jointly assignable to capital and business and self-employed labor was 17 percent in 1999, more than two points below the value at the beginning of the decade.

The implicit tax rates, shown in Table 9.2, confirm the overall picture: relatively high on consumption and not so high on employed labor. In 1998, the implicit tax rate on consumption was nearly 19 percent, whereas the implicit tax rate on employed labor more than 40 percent.[24] The evolution in the 1990s of the implicit tax rates for both consumption and employed labor shows an increasing trend in the first half of the decade, as a consequence of the economic transition, whereas since 1996 both figures have started to decrease. Indeed, the implicit tax rate on consumption decreased from 21.1 in 1995 to around 19 percent through the years 1997 to 1999 and the implicit tax rate on employed labor was reduced from 43 percent in 1997 to 40 percent in 1999.

The ability to attract foreign direct investment

Hungary attracted considerable inflows of foreign direct investment over the last decade, resulting in the creation of a competitive and dynamic economy. During the period from 1992 to 1995, Hungary was the main recipient of FDI flowing to the Central and Eastern European countries, both in absolute term and as a percentage of GDP (Mitra and Stern 2003). Out of a total of nearly US$21 billion in FDI received by the region, the Hungarian share was 45 percent; indeed, FDI reached 5.7 percent of GDP in that period against an average value for the whole region of only 0.5 percent. During the subsequent period, from 1996 to 1999, when FDI to the Central and Eastern European countries was more than US$50 billion, the relative position of Hungary changed, with Poland and the Czech

Republic being the major recipients. Nevertheless, Hungary continued to perform well, with a share of FDI in GDP of 3.8 percent compared with an average of 3.3 percent.

In the early 1990s, a skilled labor force available at internationally-competitive wages combined with numerous tax incentives in the form of tax credits and tax allowances was a major factor attracting foreign investments to Hungary. These tax incentives were phased out at the end of 1993, but foreign investors still continue to benefit from other incentive schemes: the offshore incentive regime, which entails a corporate income tax to be levied at a rate of 4 percent,[25] and a tax deferral for dividends in the case of reinvestment. However, in order to comply with the EU's requirements, new tax incentive regimes will replace the existing ones from the date of Hungary's accession to the European Union. In addition, other more general reforms need to be introduced for Hungary to continue in its economic growth and continue to attract investments (OECD 2002b), such as intensifying up-skilling efforts, reducing disincentives to labor force participation arising from the early retirement's system and disability benefits, and reducing the high burden of social security contributions.

A comparison with other New Members and EU 15 countries[26]

The structure of taxation according to economic function in Hungary shows some striking differences both with other New Members and EU 15 countries. Hungarian taxes on consumption have a much higher role than in the EU average and a higher role than in other New Members, with the exception of Slovenia: considering the factor taxation expressed as a fraction of total taxation, in 1999 the fraction on consumption was still higher than 36 percent, in marked contrast with the 1996 EU average of 27 percent. On the contrary, as in most of the New Members, the share of taxation on employed labor displays minor differences with respect to EU 15 countries (46.5 percent against a 1996 EU average of 51 percent). Finally, the fraction jointly assignable to capital and business and self-employed labor, equal to 17 percent, was still well below the long-term EU average of 21 percent and also below the corresponding figures of Estonia, Poland and the Czech Republic. The implicit tax rate confirms the overall picture: in 1999, the implicit tax rate on consumption was 19 percent, against a 1996 EU average of 14 percent, whereas the implicit tax rate on employed labor of 40 percent was slightly below the 1996 EU average of 43 percent.

9.5 Tax reforms and further steps to get closer to the EU

Macroeconomic and budget outlook

Hungary is one of the fastest growing OECD economies. Growth has averaged 4.5 percent in the late 1990s and the unemployment rate fell from 8.9 percent in 1997 to 5.8 percent in 2001. Despite rapid output growth, the pace of consumer inflation decelerated over the same time period from 19 to 7 percent and the current account deficit was reduced from almost 7 percent to below 6 percent of GDP. To a large extent, this macroeconomic performance reflects radical liberalization and microeconomic reforms achieved through the transition, substantial fiscal stabilization and the supportive exchange rate regime which helped preserve the international competitiveness of the economy while contributing to gradual disinflation. From the second half of 2001 on, the economy faced its first endogenous slowdown of the post-transition period, while a new exchange rate regime tightened monetary conditions in order to attain a more ambitious disinflation objective. Despite slowing, economic growth proved more resilient in 2001 than in many other OECD countries, with GDP being maintained at close to 4 percent: public infrastructure investment and private consumption offset the strong decline in exports and private business investment. Whereas, during the late 1990s, the government achieved significant progress in fiscal consolidation, reducing the general government deficit in 2000 to 3 percent of GDP, in 2001 a significant loosening of the fiscal stance of up to 2.5 percent of GDP took place. Fiscal policy was also highly expansionary in 2002: the deficit of the general government reached approximately 9.2 percent of GDP, due to both one-off expenditures and significant permanent expenditure increases, notably on wages and pensions as well as health-related spending (EU Commission 2003).

After the 2001–02 slowdown, economic expansion was slightly accelerating, with GDP rising by 3.7 percent in 2003 and by a forecast 4.1 percent in 2004. As in 2002, growth throughout 2003 has been primarily driven by domestic demand. New inflation targets were agreed between the Central bank and the government, at a maximum of 4.5 percent average in 2003 and 4 percent in 2004. Given the targets proposed in the government's medium-term pre-accession program to the European Union, a sharp fiscal tightening is required in the period 2003–04. The 2003 budget is based on optimistic growth assumptions on the revenue side and planned spending cuts across the entire public sector. Overall, a stabilization of the deficit at around 5 percent of GDP on an ESA basis is a preliminary result for 2003 and a further reduction to below 4 percent is expected in 2004.

Recent years' and planned tax reforms

Hungarian tax reforms in recent years appear to have been driven by the commitment gradually to harmonize with the EU and by the desire to improve further the environment for doing business. In contrast to the EU 15, however, tax revenues continue to depend much more on indirect taxes while the shares of revenue generated by income taxes on capital and labor as well as property taxes remain relatively low.

The EU targets for harmonization has informed the VAT regime and the 2000 excise duties reform, even if transitional arrangements have been requested to the EU. The VAT system applied is very close to that within the EU and the standard rate of 25 percent is the higher among the New Members; however, the reduced rates of 15 percent and 5 percent continue to be used as social policy instruments. As stated by the EU legislation, excise duties are levied on alcoholic beverages, tobacco and hydrocarbon fuels, but rates on alcohol and especially on tobacco are again to be adjusted to the higher EU levels.

Looking at social security contributions, the major change has been that the government has tried to compensate employers for massive increases in minimum wages and strong wage inflation by cutting the social security contributions, which fell between 2000 and 2002 from 33 to 29 percent of gross wages.

The Hungarian tax regime provides an advantageous environment for the business sector. The corporate income tax, at 16 percent, is significantly lower than those rates applied in most EU countries (the EU average rate is 29.3 percent) and generous incentives ensure that large corporations can achieve tax breaks by investing above minimum thresholds. In addition, offshore firms are subjected to a corporate tax of only 4 percent.[27] Finally, the dividend tax regime introduced in 1997 provides a dividend reinvestment incentive for foreign investors in the form of a tax deferral. In 2001, the government also helped reduce the tax burden on SMEs (i.e. medium-sized and small enterprises) by eliminating a special turnover tax on tourism transactions, speeding up the pace of VAT refunds and by providing an income tax credit.

The need for further steps

The tax system in Hungary seems relatively close to the EU 15 ones, so no major or structural changes in taxation have been decided for the near future (except perhaps for the elimination of the foreign companies tax regime), only gradual adjustments regarding rates and procedures.

On the grounds of efficiency considerations, it would be desirable to continue the process of reduction of social-security contributions (pension and health contributions) in order to reduce the tax burden on labor and further stimulate employment, especially for the low-skilled, and growth.

This is particularly important for small firms, which were hit hard by the increase of the minimum wage mentioned above: a timely first step would be abolishing the flat-rate health charge, financing the measure by cutting other subsidy programs (OECD 2002b). Furthermore, to enhance the nation's growth prospects, the authorities ought to reduce the use of multiple rates of VAT as social policy instruments[28] and, similarly, ought gradually to adjust excise duties on alcohol and tobacco products to higher EU levels. In addition, in the new context of relatively low inflation, it would be advisable to widen the tax base for personal income by including interest income: the extra revenues generated could be used to finance offsetting cuts in taxation of wages, further improving the incentive to employment. Looking at corporate taxation, as already noted, relatively high social-security contributions and payroll taxes coexist with a low taxation of profits and a wide range of tax incentives for firms: in view of the EU accession, the current incentive regime, especially for offshore companies, should be abolished in order to prevent a dangerous tax competition between EU members to attract FDI (Mitra and Stern 2003).

Further recommended actions involve the pension system. After the 1997 reform, which introduced a system combining a PAYG pillar and a fully-funded mandatory second pillar of privately-operated pension funds, planned adjustments have been postponed and key parameters modified: the mandatory nature of the second pillar has been abolished and the contribution rates to such accounts have not been increased from 6 to 8 percent, as originally planned, but only to 7 percent. At the same time, the government has announced that it intends to modernize the existing PAYG system, making it more attractive for all workers. These measures trade off a short run cash flow gain against long-term liabilities. Given the importance of the long run sustainability of the public pension system, these moves ought to be reconsidered by the authorities.

In general, the fulfillment of the short and medium-term fiscal objectives, as well as longer-term tax and expenditure reduction policies, require a thorough reform of public spending. Longer-term spending reduction is important in order to reduce the high tax pressure (39 percent of GDP in 2001), but it presents a real challenge: substantial new spending on infrastructure, public health, education and environment protection is implied by national priorities and EU accession rules, so that the room for such items has to be provided by curtailing spending in other parts of the budget (EU Commission 2000b; OECD 2002b).

Besides the cut back of the government budget directed to reduce the high tax pressure, a further reduction of central taxes is required to give a place to, and higher potential for, the development of local taxation. Although important steps were achieved during the 1990s, the share of local governments' revenues in GDP and the revenue autonomy are still too low. In the last few years, two main development lines have been mentioned by Hungarian and foreign experts: first, to move towards the Scandinavian system giving the potential for local personal income tax or surcharges on the national personal income tax; second, to improve the present local building tax by moving towards an Anglo-Saxon type value base property taxation.

Notes

1 Department of Public and Environmental Economics, University of Pavia, Italy; ref. Ricerche per l'economia e la finanza, Milano, Italy. E-mail: fsala@ref-online.it. I wish to thank Mihály Lados of the West Hungarian Research Institute, Centre for Regional Studies of the Hungarian Academy of Sciences, for his careful revision of a preliminary version of the chapter.
2 This is the average exchange rate (ECB) in 2003.
3 At the beginning of the transition, the rate of revenue autonomy was only one fifth. In ten years it doubled, reaching 39.1 percent in 2000. In 2000, for the first year, the rate of state grants (block grants and specific grants) within the local budget (38.9 percent) was less than the rate of own revenues. The total government transfers, including shared taxes (15 percent in 2000), are over 50 percent of the total local revenues, whereas they were 70.9 percent in 1992, thus resulting in a significant change in the revenue structure of local governments.
4 This rate has been reduced from 18 to 16 percent since 1 January 2004 (law adopted by the Hungarian parliament on 10 November 2003).
5 In addition, these VAT reduced rates have been recently modified, being equal to 12 percent and 0 percent respectively until December 2003 (law adopted by the Hungarian parliament on 10 November 2003).
6 See note 3.
7 The Law No. C on local taxes was adopted by the Hungarian parliament in 1990 and has been in force since 1 January 1991. The first year (1991) of the new local tax system was a transitional year in which local governments were able to choose to use the new system or keep the previous one.
8 Local taxes accounted for 12.9 percent of total current local governments' revenues in 1999, and 13.4 percent in 2001. In the first year of the new local tax system (1991), this ratio was 1.5 percent.
9 A detailed discussion may be found in Mitra and Stern (2003).
10 This section owes much to EU Commission (2000a) and IBFD (2002).
11 The local governments' share of the personal income tax has been changed several times over the 1990s. In 1990 it was 100 percent, but it has been reduced to 50 percent since 1991 because of the waste differences in per capita personal income tax among local governments. Since 1998, the share is 40 percent.
12 Taxes on private individuals' income from the rental of arable land are wholly payable to local governments.
13 The pension system is a three-pillar system consisting of a statutory state pension, a mandatory private pension and a supplementary private pension.
14 Until 2003 the rates applied on individual income were 20, 30 and 40 percent and also the income brackets were slightly different. Modifications were adopted by the Hungarian parliament on 10 November 2003.
15 Excess dividends are defined as dividends paid in excess of a specified rate of return on equity, which is equal to double the prime discount rate of the National Bank of Hungary.
16 In the early 1990s, the rate of the corporate income tax was 36 percent.
17 See note 4.

18 Before the date of accession (1 May 2004), the Hungarian parliament will adopt a new law on excise duties.
19 The maximum rate for local business tax was 0.3 in 1991. After several modifications – 0.8 percent in 1993; 1.2 percent in 1996; 1.4 percent in 1998; 1.7 percent in 1999 – it has been 2 percent since 2000. Besides the change occurring in 1996, all increases of the maximum rate are related to the increasing possibilities for deduction of costs from the tax base.
20 Some changes have been carried out over the 1990s. In the first period of the decade the employers' rate was 44 percent. Between 1998 and 2002 the rate was changed four times: in 1998 it was 39 percent (24 percent pension plus 15 percent health care); in 1999, 33 percent (22 percent pension plus 11 percent health care); in 2001, 31 percent (20 percent pension plus 11 percent health care); finally, a further reduction to 29 percent was implemented in 2002 (18 percent pension plus 11 percent health care).
21 The contributions to the second pillar were initially levied at a rate of 6 percent of gross income, which were to have been increased to 8 percent since 2000. The planned increased contribution to the second pillar however has been postponed. The new government has reduced the rate from 2.0 to 1.5 percent for the first pillar and has increased to 7 percent the second pillar's one since 2003.
22 Since 2004 the rate for health insurance contributions is 4 percent.
23 The present government is, however, planning to reject this form of social security contribution before the end of the government period (2006).
24 Owing to a lack of confirmed data on the net operating surplus, an implicit tax rate for capital and business (including self-employed labor) could not be computed and thus is not available.
25 The rate, as already noted, was 3 percent until December 2003.
26 A detailed discussion may be found in Mitra and Stern (2003).
27 This offshore regime is contrary to the EU Code of Conduct for business taxation and has been listed as 'potentially harmful' by the OECD.
28 The main difference with the EU 15 is the existence of three rates, which should be reduced to two with the lower rate set closer to 10 percent than the actual 5 percent and 15 percent.

References

EU Commission (2000a) *Structure of the Tax Systems in Estonia, Poland, Hungary, the Czech Republic and Slovenia*, Brussels: EU Commission.

EU Commission (2000b) 'Recent fiscal developments in the candidate countries', Enlargement Papers 2, Brussels: EU Commission, Directorate General for Economic and Financial Affairs.

EU Commission (2002a) *Towards the Enlarged Union. Strategy Paper on the Progress towards Accession by Each of the Candidate Countries*, Brussels: EU Commission.

EU Commission (2002b) *2002 Regular Report on Hungary's Progress towards Accession*, Brussels: EU Commission.

EU Commission (2003) 'Economic forecasts for the candidate countries. Spring 2003', Enlargement Papers 15, Brussels: EU Commission, Directorate General for Economic and Financial Affairs.

Eurostat (2000) *Structures of the Taxation Systems in the European Union, 1970–1997*, Brussels: EU Commission.

Eurostat (2002) *Statistical Yearbook on Candidate and South-east European Countries*, Brussels: EU Commission.

IBFD – International Bureau of Fiscal Documentation (2002) *European Tax Handbook 2002*, Amsterdam: IBDF.

Mitra, P. and Stern, N. (2003) 'Tax systems in transition', World Bank Working Paper 2947, Washington, DC: The World Bank.

OECD (2002a) *Revenue Statistics 1965–2001*, Paris: OECD.

OECD (2002b) *OECD Economic Surveys. Hungary 2002*, Paris: OECD.

OECD (2002c) *Fiscal Decentralization in EU Applicant States and Selected EU Member States*, Paris: OECD.

Tanzi, V. and Tsibouris, G. (2000) 'Fiscal reform over ten years of transition', IMF Working Paper 113, Washington, DC: IMF.

Websites

http://www.ksh.hu/pls/ksh/docs/index_eng.html – Hungarian Statistical Office.

http://www.kum.hu/euint/index.html – Ministry of Foreign Affairs of Hungary. Hungary's EU integration website.

10 Poland

Lucia Vergano and Francesca Zantomio[1]

10.1 Introduction and executive summary

Poland, with its 312,685 km^2 and 38,600,000 inhabitants, is the biggest economy among the EU New Members. At the end of the Second World War, Poland experienced a communist regime until the regime's collapse in 1989–90, when Poland became a democratic country. In 1997, the National Assembly approved its parliamentary Constitution.[2] As with other EU New Members, Poland entered into NATO in 1999 and also entered *de facto* into the EU in 2004, as established by the Nice Treaty (2001) and finally agreed during the Copenhagen Summit (2002) and signed in Athens (2003). The local currency is the zloty (the exchange rate in July 2003 was ZL1 = €0.2254).

During the 1990s, the Polish economy showed a GDP average growth rate (4.5 percent) definitely above the EU average level (2.8 percent); nevertheless, recently, the unemployment rate has been growing (18 percent in 2002). At the beginning of the 21st century, Poland experienced an economic slowdown: GDP growth fell to 1–1.4 percent in 2001–02. Recently, symptoms of recovery have been observed: GDP growth for 2003 was 3.6 percent and, according to forecasts, it will be even higher in 2004 (4.5–5.1 percent). At the end of the 1990s, the general government deficit was between 3 and 4 percent, but has grown in the last few years.

Owing to the main features of its tax system, during the 1990s, Poland – unlike other transition economies – has not experienced any kind of fiscal crisis. Altogether, the Polish tax system is not very diversified and the level of aggregate taxation is more stable than that of most other transition economies.

In 1998, the level of total Polish fiscal revenue was about 38 percent of GDP, a high value with respect to some OECD countries but below the EU average. As for direct taxes and social contributions, the revenue does not reach the EU average level: as a consequence, the Polish total fiscal pressure is close to the average of selected New Members, but is about 5 percent below the EU-15 average. Following the common trend of New Members, indirect taxes play a larger role than in the EU as a share of total taxation and the opposite happens in the case of direct taxes (Mitra and Stern 2003).

The Polish budget system, traditionally very centralized, has been progressively decentralized starting from the reform of local governments in 1991–93 and then of the public administration in 1998: even though the principal aim of this reform was to transfer policy functions to the level of government, where these policies could be implemented, local governments still maintain a little autonomous power in making tax policy decisions and strongly depend on central government subsidies. Therefore, the process of delegating tax policies to regions has still to be completed, and will be needed even more due to the demands of EU aid funds systems (see Table 10.1).

At present, the broad features of Polish main taxes, as reformed in the early 1990s, are not very different from the corresponding EU models, even though they show some distinctive peculiarities. The basis of assessment of the income tax, collected by the government and partially distributed to the local communities, includes all revenues from labor, capital, business, property, but there is a wide and generous set of allowed deductions and exemptions. The corporate income is taxed on the basis of the *classical system* but, to reduce the impact of double-taxation, dividends are taxed at only 15 percent.[3] The general VAT tax rate of 22 percent and the two reduced rates for certain categories of goods and services, 3 and 7 percent, result from the reform proposed since 1999 by national authorities, in order to harmonize VAT with EU requirements in view of accession. Excise duties are charged on consumer products, referred to as 'excisable products', with tax rates widely ranging from 25 to 1900 percent. The major

Table 10.1 Fifteen years of budget consolidation and tax reforms: an essential calendar

1988	Plans of tax reform
1989	Beginning of the transition, massive reforms. The same CIT obligation for state owned and private companies
1990	State budget regains its balance after the 1988–89 crisis
1991	Public finance split into the state and local government parts. New budget crisis
1992	Introduction of PIT
1993	Turnover tax substituted by VAT and excise taxes
1997	New constitution (60 percent public debt-to-GDP limit). Act on Rules for Taxation
1998	Act on Public Finance
1999	New reform of local governments system
2001	Beginning of new budget crisis, the budget is unbalanced until today
2002	Negotiations between Poland and EU are over. Final tax adjustments must be introduced until 2008
2004	Massive reforms of local government finance, CIT (19 percent), PIT, VAT and excise duty, in order to adjust the system to the EU regulations.

remaining state sources of revenue are the social security contributions, paid by the employers, the employees and the self-employed individuals and which are earmarked for large extra-budgetary social security funds. The picture is completed by the Agricultural Property Tax, the Forestry Property Tax, the Real Estate Property Tax and some other minor taxes.

As to the distribution of the fiscal burden, the main source of revenue arises from employed labor, followed by consumption. Implicit tax rates confirm for Poland that employed labor is the factor most heavily taxed, but it can be seen that in the recent years there has been a process of gradual substitution in taxation, from labor to consumption, which has also been a saving inducing incentive. Looking at the structure of revenue according to economic function, the peculiar features of Poland are the significant difference of taxes and contributions on employed labor from the EU average, being seven percentage points lower, and the higher share in total taxation of taxes on consumption.

Although Poland is actually seen as one of the most successful transition economies because of its efforts to start developing those structural reforms needed to get closer to the EU (Tanzi and Tsibouris 2000) – such as the stabilization of the economy, the reorganization of the public finances, the implementation of an effective monetary policy, liberalizations and privatizations – unemployment has risen and investment has fallen, as a result of the recent economic slowdown.

The general government deficit has widened in 2003 (6.4 percent): further structural expenditure reforms and a redefinition of budget priorities are necessary in order to make the public debt reach the constitutional and Maastricht limit of 60 percent. Entry into the EU could artificially decrease the deficit, due to the much more permissive methodology of public accounts' calculation used by the EU. The needed reforms of public finance expenditures are being prepared at the end of 2003. The main goal is to narrow the budget deficit.

The tax reform proposals launched in 1999 by the authorities have been only partially enacted in 2000. In particular, the proposed changes regarding the PIT, providing for a progressive reduction of the tax rates so as to create a tax regime inducing more job creation, have not been completely adopted: the current high tax rates and social security contributions involve a particularly high tax wedge that leads to high unemployment and to an oversized underground economy. Moreover, further measures need to be taken in order to reduce the amount of disability and sickness pensions and early-retirement pensions. A new tax reform is expected for 2004: its main outcome will be the reduction of the CIT from 27 to 19 percent, which could improve Polish enterprises' competitiveness and encourage FDI inflow. In addition, entrepreneurs paying the PIT will be charged with only one rate equal to the CIT rate (19 percent). In 2004, for the first time, incomes from the stock exchange will be taxed by a 20 percent tax.

Another recommended reform concerns the autonomy of a tax policy for local governments, which should be given the opportunity to manage their own tax base. This reform is needed due to the opportunity of profiting from EU structural funds. To meet these requirements, a new act for local government finance is being prepared for 2004.

A final relevant need is to unify different tax rates on capital incomes and, in order to get closer to EU requirements, to introduce charges on those products that are damaging the environment, such as coal, fertilizers and leaded gasoline.

10.2 The structure of the system at the end of the 1990s

A broad view at the current structure of taxes and social security contributions

At the end of the 1990s, one of the main features of the Polish tax system was its capacity to generate a sizeable revenue on a continuous basis, so as to finance government spending and lower the budget deficit. Because of this, unlike other transition economies, Poland has not experienced any kind of fiscal crisis (OECD 2002).

In 1998, the level of total fiscal revenue was about 38 percent of the GDP, which is high with respect to some OECD countries, but not compared with the EU average level (OECD 2001). This ratio of revenue to GDP is a legacy from the years of central planning, when high public spending was due, in particular, to the generous public pension schemes.[4]

The general government revenue can be split into the main three broad categories of direct taxes, indirect taxes and social security contributions, each of which respectively contributes approximately 30, 40 and again 30 percent of total revenue (Bartoszuk and Lenain 2000), but with a tendency of decreasing importance of direct taxes revenues.

Expressed as a ratio of GDP, direct taxes revenue (11 percent of GDP) is instead below the EU average (14 percent of the GDP): this is due to the low personal income tax revenue. Indirect taxes revenue amounts to 12 percent of GDP (very close to the EU average): the VAT and excise duties revenues are substantially in line with that of the EU countries (Eurostat 2002). As for the social contributions, the revenue does not reach the EU average level (11 percent instead of 15 percent of GDP[5]), but is quite high if compared with the average of the OECD countries: this feature is partially another legacy from the communist system and is also shared by Hungary, the Czech Republic and several other Eastern European countries.

The tax system is less diversified than in other countries: small taxes, such as property, inheritance or environmental fees, produce almost no revenue. Thus, Poland has a somewhat narrow range of tax instruments.

The development of the system from the early to the late 1990s

The taxation reforms in Poland were connected with political, economic and cultural changes at the beginning of the transition period. The only common tax was a tax imposed on salaries (20 percent), which was invisible for the workers, because it was paid directly by the employers. At the same time, as an acute budget deficit that emerged in 1991–92 showed, the new tax system was necessary in order to keep the budget deficit under control. The old system was not able to cope with new demands and the tax authorities were highly inefficient in terms of tax collection. It is common to refer to the scope and speed of the reforms taking part in the years 1991–93 as a 'tax revolution' (Owsiak 2002).

The Polish tax system has been distinguished from that of most other transition economies because of its stable – instead of decreasing – revenue-to-GDP ratio: at the end of 1990s, the total fiscal revenue was almost the same as that at the beginning of the transition period, in 1991.

Nevertheless, in the early years of the 1990s, the level of aggregate taxation experienced some fluctuations: from 37 percent of GDP in 1991, it grew to 42 percent in 1993, but then it went back again to slightly below 40 percent in 1995, reaching a minimum of 38.5 percent in 2002. In the coming years, this ratio is expected to grow, in most part due to the inflow of EU structural funds aid. Moreover, there were some great structural shifts within the categories of indirect taxes (the introduction of VAT and excise duties in 1993, the abolishment of previous turnover tax in 1994) and direct taxes (personal income tax revenue started in 1992 and corporate income tax was lowered from 1992 onwards) – see Table 10.2.

These structural changes resulted in the following developments.

1   The gradual reduction of the load, in terms of implicit tax rates, of taxes and social contributions levied on employed labor from nearly 16 percent in 1991 to about 14 percent in 1996.
2   The rise of the tax revenue from self-employed labor from about 3 percent of GDP in 1991 to 5 percent since 1993.
3   The fall of the revenue from capital and business (excluding self-employed labor) from nearly 9 percent of GDP in 1991 to about 4.5 percent in 1995 and after: this was mostly due to a reduction in the legal rates of corporate income tax.
4   An increasing amount of taxes on transfers, because state pensions were taxed like other personal income.
5   The appreciable contribution of the taxation of energy from 1994 onwards.

Table 10.2 Structure and development of fiscal revenue in Poland, New Members and EU 15 as a percentage of GDP, 1992–98

	1992			1994			1996			1998		
	Poland	New members	EU	Poland	New members	EU	Poland	New members	EU	Poland	New members	EU
Direct taxes, of which	12.2	10.1	13.5	12.5	10.0	12.9	11.7	9.6	12.9	11.2	9.2	13.7
Personal income	7.6	6.4	9.6	9.2	7.0	9.3	8.7	7.1	9.3	8.3	6.7	9.3
Corporation income	4.6	3.6	2.3	3.2	2.9	2.4	2.9	2.5	2.7	2.9	2.5	3.0
Indirect taxes, of which	14.6	15.6	13.4	16.1	16.5	13.7	15.6	16.9	13.7	14.4	15.5	13.9
VAT	0.0	5.1	6.7	6.7	7.4	6.8	7.3	7.4	6.9	7.9	7.9	7.0
Excise duties	0.0	3.4	3.4	4.0	4.2	3.5	4.0	4.1	3.4	3.9	4.1	3.5
Others	14.6	9.3	3.3	5.4	5.0	3.4	4.2	4.9	3.4	2.7	3.6	3.5
Total tax revenue	26.8	25.7	26.9	28.6	26.4	26.6	27.3	26.5	27.1	25.6	24.7	27.6
Social contributions	11.3	16.1	14.5	12.0	15.7	14.9	12.4	14.3	15.3	12.2	14.2	15.0
Employers	4.1	10.0	8.1	4.3	9.0	7.9	4.4	8.0	8.3	4.4	7.9	8.2
Employees	4.2	5.3	4.8	4.4	5.1	5.2	4.6	4.8	5.1	4.5	4.8	5.0
Self employed	3.1	1.8	1.6	3.3	1.6	1.8	3.3	1.5	1.9	3.3	1.6	1.9
Total fiscal revenue	38.1	41.8	41.4	40.6	42.2	41.5	39.7	40.8	42.4	37.8	38.9	42.6
Administrative level												
Central government	24.1	25.9	22.8	25.6	25.8	22.4	23.8	25.4	22.4	22.3	23.9	22.9
Local government	2.8	3.0	3.0	3.0	3.5	3.2	3.5	3.4	4.0	3.4	3.7	4.0
Social Security	11.3	12.9	14.5	12.0	12.9	14.9	12.4	11.5	15.2	12.2	11.4	14.9

Sources: EU Commission (2000a) for Poland and selected New Members (unweighted average); Eurostat (2000) for EU-15 (1997 unweighted average).

Notes
Czech data start in 1993 and Social security is only health.

The apportionment of revenue among government layers

In 1991, the public finance system was split into two parts: central and local governments. Local governments took over most of the revenues from minor taxes and also participated in CIT and to PIT (after its intro-duction) revenues.

Poland has inherited a very centralized budget system: still, in 2001, the greater part of revenues went to the state (19.1 percent of GDP) and the social security administrations (16 percent), but one third of the social security revenue goes through the central budget as appropriated alloca-tions, subsidies and additional funds.[6] Among non-central tax revenue, more than half is derived from individual income tax, of which the central government transfers a share of 0.276 percent to the municipality of resi-dence of the taxpayer; 5 percent of the CIT is paid by the companies regis-tered in the area where the enterprise is run (Denek *et al.* 2001). The remainder comes mostly from the real estate tax levied by non-central government and a few minor taxes (EU Commission 2000a).

This kind of splitting did not change much during the 1990s, but in 1998 the authorities introduced an important reform of Polish public adminis-tration, beginning with a process of gradual decentralization, in order to attribute to local governments (*Gminas, Poviats* and *Voivodships*)[7] a growing role in expenditure decisions. Following the principle of subsidiar-ity, the reform has actually brought policy functions closer to the people, transferring them to the level of government where these policies can be implemented.

Nevertheless, local governments maintain a little autonomous power in making tax policy decisions and a strong dependence on central govern-ment subsidies (grants and transfers). These subsidies (special purposes subsidies, education subsidy, general purpose subsidy, compensation grants) are based on the size of the population living in each region: while helping local governments to cover the expenditure they are responsible for, they do not succeed in closing the income gap between regions (EU Commission 2000b). Local governments have no power to change the level of main taxes (PIT, CIT, VAT, social taxes) and have limited possi-bilities to change the rate of a few less important taxes.

Moreover, this contrasts with the principle of attributing more powers to localities to implement their policy decisions and their development strategy. The process of decentralizing tax policies to regions is still far from being completed. The new reform prepared for 2004 is aiming to increase incomes of local governments mainly through higher participation in PIT and CIT revenues: *Gminas* will get 41.4 percent of their revenues from PIT, *Poviats* 10.6 percent from PIT and *Voivodships* 18.4 percent from CIT.

In 1991, local governments took over 8.9 percent of public finance rev-enues from taxes. In 1995, it was 11 percent, and in 2000 13.2 percent

(Misiag 2002). Their participation in revenues is rising and the tendency will continue after Polish accession into the EU.

A comparison with other main New Members and the EU average

It has already been shown that, in 1998, the Polish total fiscal pressure (about 37.8 percent of GDP) was close to the average of selected New Members (38.9 percent), but was about 5 percent below the EU 15 average (42.6 percent). This spread is explained firstly by the social contributions: the lower revenue from the social contributions levied on the employers (about half of that of the EU 15) is just partially compensated by the higher social contributions revenue levied on self-employed people (EU Commission 2000a). The same could also be said with respect to the New Members, but the average spread is not as large.

In addition, the level of total taxes helps explain the difference between the Polish and the EU 15 tax system revenue: even if the system is more advanced with respect to the average of the New Members, it maintains a gap between direct and indirect taxes revenue that is still larger than in EU 15 countries. This is due to the lower revenue from the personal income tax, which is only partially compensated for by the higher revenue from VAT and excise duties. The common trend of New Members is actually that indirect taxes as a share of total taxation play a larger role than in the EU and the opposite happens in the case of direct taxes.

Public finance deficit evolution in the transformation

One of the most important problems for Poland in the coming years is the growing budget deficit. In the period of so-called 'shock therapy' (1989–91), Poland underwent dramatic budgetary problems, which were worsened in 1992 after the 'Russian crisis' (export decline to the Eastern markets). The new budgetary law introduced at the beginning of 1991 allowed the deficit to lower, which in the best year reached 2 percent, but was not balanced even in the 'golden years' when GDP growth was 7 percent. The most important weakness of the public finance system was the reform of pension system negligence. Neglected public finance reforms resulted in budgetary problems since the end of the 1990s; some costly reforms (pension system, health care system, educational system and the new administrative division) worsened the situation. Structural reforms in the 'old economy' (heavy industry, coal mining, iron companies) were postponed, due to their social and political costs (Misiag 2002). The slowdown in the economy resulted in a lower increase in fiscal revenues, whereas most of the expenditures were 'fixed'. At the same time, revenues from privatization started to fall. New reforms are needed even more due to the fact that Poland in the coming years is facing external demands.

In 1990, the public debt was estimated at 95 percent, mostly as a consequence of the foreign debt inherited from the socialist period. The budget was never balanced, but owing to the faster GDP growth and the reduction of foreign debt (Paris and London Clubs) the government debt was reduced to 40 percent in 2000.

10.3 Some quantitative and institutional features of main taxes[8]

*Personal income tax – PIT (*Podatek dochodowy od osób fizycznych)

The personal income tax was introduced in the Polish tax system with the Tax Law of 26 July 1991 and came into force in 1992. The main beneficiary of the revenue is the central government, even though 27.6 percent of the yield is then distributed to communities where taxpayers have their place of residence.

Personal income tax has to be paid by Polish citizens, who are taxable on their income from national sources and, in the absence of bilateral taxation treaties, also from foreign sources, through specific rules. It has also to be paid by foreigners staying in Poland for a period longer than half a year.

The unit of taxation is optional in that it can be chosen by the individual taxpayer: generally each individual is taxed separately but it is also possible to apply for a joint taxation system based on the average income of a married couple (half of their joint income), taxed at the same rates.[9] Dependent children's income has then to be added to parents' income.

The basis of assessment includes all revenues from labor, capital, business, property and established incomes such as scholarships, pensions and benefits.

In particular, the law lists, as income to be taxed, the following categories:

a income from dependent services such as employment or pensions;
b income from independent services, such as professional, intellectual, artistic or sports activities;
c income from business;
d income from specialized branches of agriculture;
e rental income;
f income from monetary investment and property rights;
g income from the sale of real estate and of property rights;
h other incomes, such as social security benefits, grant scholarships or others, not belonging to the other categories, unless they are exempt.

Losses can be carried forward at one third each, against the income of the next three years, even though prior losses cannot increase current ones. One peculiar feature of the Polish tax system is the wide and generous set of allowed deductions, even though recently reduced. First of all, for each category of income, expenses sustained to produce this income are deductible: in some cases, they are deductible as a fixed percentage of earned income (20 percent for independent activities, 50 percent for license fees for inventions or copyright royalties) while the same rules regarding corporate income have to be applied to business income.

Then, from the aggregate net income, it is possible to deduce further:

a   social security contributions (unless they have already been deducted as expenses in some category of income);
b   donations to advocate science, education, culture, religion, sports, ecology and charity, up to 10 or 15 percent of income;[10]
c   costs for training and continuing education, in connection with tax-payer's income;[11]
d   cost of earning income, deducted automatically as a fixed percentage of 25 percent, unless the real cost of earning income can be proved to be higher (so that the entire real cost will be deductible);
e   expenditures on annuities, donations to corporate bodies[12] which pursue socially worthy causes (with the upper limit of 15 or 10 percent of income) and expenditures on rehabilitation;
f   interest on loans for housing purposes.[13]

The Polish law also provides for a large number of exemptions, the most important of which are:

a   income from non-specialized agricultural activities;
b   income from forestry;
c   gains from selling agricultural or forestry land for agricultural or forestry use;
d   social welfare benefits and benefits paid by social funds in case of accident, long illness or death;
e   income from selling of a flat or building, when proceeds are used within two years for the purchase of another flat or building;
f   most fringe benefits.

Income from interests on bank accounts, if unconnected to business activities, and income from sale of compensation certificates and from interest and discount of government securities and local government bodies, have been taxed at 20 percent since 2002.

Taxable income, net of income deductions, is then subject to a progressive schedule with three different brackets and three marginal tax rates: in 2002, 19 percent from 0 to ZL37,024 (corresponding to about €9600[14]) with a tax credit of ZL530.08 (about €135), 30 percent from ZL37,024 (about €9600) to ZL74,048 (about €19,200) and 40 percent above

ZL74,048 (about €19,200).[15] It is important to observe that, because of the narrow income distribution, the bulk of taxpayers falls into the first bracket: in 1999, 94.9 percent of PIT taxpayers were in the first bracket, 3.9 percent in the second and 1.2 in the third; in 1992 it was respectively 96.1 percent; 3.2 percent and 0.7 percent (Misiag 2002). The present tax rates are lower than the previous ones (in fact, in 1996, the three marginal rates were 21, 33 and 45 percent) and, moreover, the purpose of the future aforementioned reform of PIT will be to reduce further the three rates, going towards a flat rate income tax.[16] It must be stressed that, at the moment, farmers are excluded from PIT obligation, and pay Agricultural Property Tax, which is not connected with their real incomes. It creates complications for the health care system, revenues of rural minas (local governments) and social insurance system.

Finally, the law provides for particular regimes, based on the payment of lump-sum taxes, for particular categories of taxpayers, with the aim of simplifying their fiscal duties: they are the 'tax card' and the 'lump sum income tax' on registered revenues from small businesses.

With the tax card the taxpayer has to pay a lump sum tax that substitutes his personal income tax, so that he does not have to prove with documents all his revenues and costs, to keep the register, to declare income received and to pay the monthly advance tax payments. This scheme is designed for people having small-scale production, providing particular kinds of services and running production activities, such as retail trade in groceries, door-to-door sales of commodities, catering, transportation services, entertainment activities, home meal sales, veterinary services, free professional health services. The amount to be paid is a fixed amount, decided by the Tax Authority for each particular period;[17] then the tax rate can be increased or reduced according to the individual situation. Particular preferences are designed for people running their business in areas with high structural unemployment.

The lump sum income tax, based on turnover, is designed for people running own small businesses (small-scale entrepreneurs with turnover below €250,000 in the year before the current one) who do not meet the conditions to use the tax card. The taxpayer has to keep a simplified register of revenues and purchases and to hand in information about the amount of revenues in the first half of the year and after a year. People running some activities are excluded from this form of taxation: they are people running a pharmacy, legal services, an exchange office, pawnshop or services in accountancy. The particular tax rate depends on the activity the taxpayer runs: 3 percent on revenues from trade and catering, 5.5 percent on revenues from manufacturing, construction and cargo transport and 8.5 percent on revenues from services. Since 2002, there are two additional rates: 17 percent for some services and 20 percent for people running more sophisticated businesses (teachers, nurses, veterinary surgeons). In comparison to PIT, there are very limited possibilities for deductions – mainly the sum paid as social contributions.

There is also a special lump sum tax for clerics. The sum paid by them depends on the number of people living in the parish and the position of a cleric. In 2003 the minimum was ZL100 (approximately €23) and maximum ZL1100 (approximately €240).

Corporate income tax – CIT (Podatek dochodowy od osób prawnych)

The uniform income tax for legal entities – the corporate income tax (CIT) – was introduced in 1989, replacing two existing separate profit taxes for legal entities in the public and private sectors of the economy (Bartoszuk and Lenain 2000). This tax was first reformed in the early 1990s (Tax Law 15 February 1992), in order to achieve the standards in force in the European Union countries. From 1989 to 1996, the CIT rate was 40 percent, but in the following years it decreased: 38 percent in 1997, 36 percent in 1998, 34 percent in 1999, 30 percent in 2000, 28 percent in 2001 and 27 percent in 2003. A new reform of corporate income taxation was passed into law[18] and became effective in 2000: the main purposes were to lower the tax rate and to broaden the tax base at the same time. A new reform is being prepared for 2004. The rate will be reduced from 27 to 19 percent, but the number of deductions will be reduced as well.

All legal entities (joint-stock companies, limited liability companies, state enterprises and cooperatives) incorporated in Poland are subject to corporate income tax on their total incomes, including income from abroad (*unlimited tax obligation*). All legal entities incorporated abroad (with head office or managing board situated abroad) are instead subject to tax only on income gained on Polish territory (*limited tax obligation*). Partnerships are not treated as companies[19] and some institutions without legal personality – schools, educational associations, health service bodies – are not treated as corporations. The exemption from tax is provided for a list of institutions: State Treasury, National Bank of Poland, budgetary economic units, purposeful funds, international holdings, communities and units of communities. The number of bodies exempted from CIT will be limited from 2005.

The CIT is based on the *classical system*, i.e. corporate income is fully taxed and distributed profits (dividends) are taxed once again by way of withholding: to reduce the impact of double-taxation, however, under the personal income tax, dividends are taxed at only 15 percent, but the tax rate will be increased in 2004 to 19 percent. The tax may be credited against the receiving company's tax debt. Dividends may be distributed only from after-tax profits.

The tax basis is the worldwide income of the resident corporate entities, including the capital gains from the sale of business assets, after the deduction of the expenses sustained to obtain such income.

The incomes exempt from the corporate income tax are the following:

a income from non-specialized agricultural activities and from forestry;
b gains from the sale of agricultural and forestry land that remains used as such;
c indemnities received;
d income from foreign sources as far as provided in an international agreement;
e income allocated and transferred to legal entities for charitable purposes and for the furthering of science, education, health, culture, sports, infrastructure development and environmental protection.

Exemptions are also granted in 17 Special Economic Zones (SEZs): economic entities operating in SEZs are eligible for tax allowances, preferential treatment and other benefits (Easson 1998). The income of entities whose investments exceed a certain threshold, characteristic of each zone, or investors, which create a certain number of jobs, are totally exempted from CIT, through a period equal to half of the period for which the zone has been established. After that time, the exemption of taxation is granted up to 50 percent of the income. Preferential treatment and other benefits are granted to entities not eligible for tax exemption. As a consequence of the tax reform enacted in 2000, no new tax exemptions will be granted in SEZs starting in January 2000. This issue was a subject of hard negotiations between Poland and the EU for a long time: eventually, after Poland's entry into the EU, no preferences for companies starting their activity in the zones will be allowed.

After the last reform of the capital income tax, the number of depreciation rates has been reduced to ten and investment incentives (previously offered in the form of investment allowances to encourage investments in certain sectors of activity) have been eliminated in order to broaden the income tax base.

The 2003 corporate income tax rate is 27 percent, but according to the reform being prepared now, from 2004 it will decrease to 19 percent.[20] According to the new proposition, the same flat rate will be offered for enterprises now taxed under the personal income regime, but the number and scope of deductions available for such firms will be sharply limited.

Value added tax – VAT (Podatek od Towarow I Uslug)

The value added tax was introduced in the Polish tax system in 1993 after five years' preparations.[21] In 1993, the turnover tax, with more than 100 rates, was removed. Previously, the rates of turnover taxes varied, depending on the kind of purchased good (Owsiak 2002). The only beneficiary of the revenues is the central government. The tax is payable by natural persons, legal persons and organizational units (and, with agreement of the Treasury office, also branches of them) that sell or import taxable goods and services in Poland and that have an annual turnover which exceeds €10,000 (if they do not reach this sum, they are not obligated to register for VAT). But once they decide to be a VAT payer, that decision could not be changed for a period of three years.

The basis of assessment is the compensation received for goods supplied and services rendered, less the VAT; for imported goods, the tax base also includes excise duties and custom fees. The tax is levied at each stage of the production and distribution process; according to a tax-to-tax scheme, the input tax on purchases is deductible from the output tax.

In addition, are also subject to VAT:

a   the donation of commodities and providing of services for advertisement needs;
b   the donation of commodities and providing of services for personal needs of taxpayers, partners, shareholders, members of supervisory board and managing board, members of association, employed and former workers;
c   the exchange of commodities and services;
d   the donation of commodities;
e   the providing of services without payment;
f   the providing of commodities or provision of services in return for debts;
g   the provision of services or providing of commodities instead of payment.

On the contrary, the exemptions from VAT include

a   unprocessed agricultural products, unprocessed foodstuffs;
b   financial, insurance, educational, health, art, cultural and social services, communal services;
c   apartment rental;
d   the sale of the whole or part of a company;
e   activity in random-games;
f   illegal activity.

People paying income tax in tax card form were exempt from VAT until the end of the 1990s, but this is not a rule anymore. Moreover, VAT does not apply to some sales in duty free zones and also agricultural production is not subject to VAT. Currently, the general tax rate is 22 percent, while there are two reduced rates, 3 percent (milk and dairy products, raw meat, poultry, fish and some of their products and folk and artistic handicraft products) and 7 percent (most processed foodstuffs, most construction raw materials, some construction works, long distance passenger transport, medicines and pharmaceuticals, articles for children) for certain categories of goods and services. To exports, books, magazines, and basic agricultural inputs, a 0 percent rate applies.

Since 1999, national authorities have proposed tax reforms aimed at harmonizing VAT with EU requirements of the Sixth Council Directive, in view of accession, and some changes, accepted by the parliament, became effective from 2000. Looking at Poland, the standard rate of 22 percent and the reduced rate of 7 percent are well above EU requirements; moreover, the tax reform enacted in 2000 decrees that municipal services have also to be taxed with a 7 percent rate, and that construction materials and services have to be taxed with an increasing tax rate, set to 22 percent since 2003, while for other goods or services (articles for children, new residential constructions, legal services, newspapers) there will be transition periods towards EU requirements for social and political reasons. In 1993, there were three rates: standard 22 percent, reduced 7 percent and 0 percent. In 2000, the 3 percent rate was introduced for agricultural goods. For a period of time (1999) there were new 'transitional rates' of 2 percent, 4 percent and 12 percent; more and more goods were shifted from 0 percent to higher rates. In the future, only exports will be charged with 0 percent. At the moment there are four rates: 0 percent, 3 percent, 7 percent and 22 percent (standard). The new Act on VAT is being prepared for 2004 in order to adjust the law to the EU requirements: the most important changes will relate to demands of intra-community trade regulations. In particular, they will relate to territorial scope, categories of taxpayers, and the definition of the concept of tax duties. According to the draft law, the VAT rates' structure will not change much.

Excise duties (Podatek akcyzowy)

The excise tax was introduced in 1993, with the value added tax and excise duty Act. The taxpayers are manufacturers and importers; the duty is to be paid before introducing a commodity into the market (Bartoszuk and Lenain 2000). The excise tax applies to the sale and exchange of excisable goods, as well as to importations or donations; it is not levied on exports. Excise duties do not apply to some sales in duty-free zones.

If there is turnover of goods by manufacturers, the tax basis is the value of commodity increased by duty. For other goods, the tax basis is the quantity or the sales price diminished by the VAT due.

Excise duty is charged on consumer products, referred to as 'excisable products', including: alcoholic beverages, tobacco, fuel, passenger cars, luxury electronic equipment, gambling, salt, plastic packaging, furs, cosmetics, luxury boats, sailboats. The most revenue for the central budget comes from fuel, alcoholic beverages and tobacco excise taxes.

In 2002, the tax rates ranged from 25 percent to 1900 percent. At the moment, there are goods in which the share of excise duty reaches 90 percent (Ziolkowska 2002).[22] According to the Polish Ministry of Finance, up to 2003 the adjustment of the excise duty tax to the EU requirements has been almost completed. However, the most important adjustments are still to be made for tobacco products, for which the excise duty tax will be substantially increased until 2008.

Social security contributions (Skladki na ubezpieczenia spoleczne)

The contributions to the Social Insurance Office (*Zaklad Ubezpieczen Spolecznych – ZUS*) are paid by the employer (18.4 percent of gross wage), the employee (18.7 percent of gross wage) and self-employed individuals, who must pay both the employer and the employee contributions (Bartoszuk and Lenain 2000). These contributions finance the first and the second pillars[23] of the old-age pension system, the disability pension regime and other social benefits. While most direct and indirect taxes are collected by the state to finance the general budget, the social security contributions are earmarked for large extra-budgetary social security funds (Social Insurance Fund, Health Fund, Pension Funds). They are split into different accounts: old-age pension (19.52 percent), disability pension (13 percent), health and maternity insurance (2.45 percent) and work injury insurance (percent rates of wage differentiated, depending on the branch). The exemptions are limited to a few professions and activities.

The basis of the contributions is individual income as defined for income tax purposes, except for farmers, judges and prosecutors. For self-employed persons there is a maximum base of assessment for pension and disability insurance which amounts to 30 average salaries as projected for the respective year: with respect to health, maternity and injury insurance there is no such maximum.

Obligatory premiums are also due to the Labor Fund (2.45 percent of the payroll expenditures) to finance unemployment benefits and the active labor market.

A contribution equivalent to 7.5 percent of taxable income was introduced in 1999, as part of the health insurance reform, to provide financial resources to the newly created health funds. Employers and other providers of income must withhold insurance premiums and pay them directly to *ZUS* on a monthly basis: *ZUS* then channels these premiums to the National Health Fund.[24] Most income sources (salaries, self-employed income, farmers' income, pensions and other social benefits) are subject to the health insurance premium, while income from financial sources (interest, dividends and capital gains) is not. The health insurance premium is entirely deductible from personal income tax liability.

Finally, employers must also pay contributions, treated as business costs, to the Wage Guarantee Fund, in order to satisfy the claims of the employees in the case of bankruptcy proceedings against an insolvent employer, a business closing down or when an employer factually ceases the business and does not have the financial resources to pay off the wages due to his employees.

There is a special system of social insurance for farmers, called *KRUS* (Agriculture Social Insurance Fund). Farmers pay a much lower amount and the fund is highly subsidized by the state (more than €3 billion per year). The system is abused by people running other businesses, who keep small farms in the agricultural areas and avoid paying much higher standard social taxes from other economic activities.

Agricultural property tax (Podatek ronly)

This tax obligation was imposed with the Act of 15 November 1984 as a property tax: currently, local governments derive a benefit from the relative revenues. The taxpayers are the owners of agricultural property (those who are in possession of a farmland) apart from the fact of carrying out farming and gaining income from it.

The basis of assessment is the area of the farm in conversion hectares; that is, a conventional unit whose conversion rate is based on three objective criteria (land location, kind of land, soil quality).

The law provides for a number of exemptions from this tax: for example, land used for activities different from agriculture, land of historical interest, wasteland, land with drainage systems, land along the border, land under lakes, running water, dams and water containers, arable land where the production has been ceased for three years (up to 20 percent of total farm land). Some specific tax exemptions are allowed; the tax rate is constant and depends on the purchase price of rye: the tax corresponding to a single conversion hectare is equivalent to the gains from 2.5 quintals of rye.

Forest property tax (Podatek lesny)

This tax was introduced in 1991, with the Taw Law of 28 September: again, the beneficiary is local government. This tax is very similar to the Agriculture Property Tax: the taxpayer is the owner of the property, and the basis of assessment is the number of conversion hectares of the owned forest even though in this case the conversion rate depends on the three main species in the strand and on the classification of the strand for each species, as they result from the plan of arranging the forest on 1 January, every year.

The tax on a single conversion hectare is equivalent to the proceeds from the sale of $0.2\,\text{m}^3$ of coniferous sawmill timber (the price used is that for the timber acquired by forest superintendence).

Real estate property tax (**Podatek od nieruchomosci**)

This subject is regulated by the law of 12 January 1999; again, beneficiaries of the revenues are the local governments. The tax is due by natural persons, legal persons and other units that own property or building structures not connected with land, that own or manage real estate or building structures that are National Treasury's or Communes' property, that are perpetual lessees of the property.

The basis of assessment is the area covered, in square meters, of buildings or part of them, structures for economic activity (leaving out agriculture and forestry) and land not subject to agriculture or forestry tax and used for activities different from agriculture or forestry.

The law provides for numerous kinds of exemptions: for example, property used for public purposes, property in special economic zones, property of foreign states or International organizations, real estate exempted on the basis of separate legislation; the local council then has the power to introduce further exemptions.

Minimum and maximum rates are defined by the decree of the Ministry of Finance every year and, within these boundaries, local government councils determine the yearly rate.

Other minor taxes

To the central government are also due the customs duties and the gambling tax: different from the VAT revenues coming from gambling, the tax rate and the basis of assessment vary according to the kind of game.

Among taxes paid to the local government, natural persons gaining a donation or a legacy situated on Polish territory at no cost (inheritance or donation) are subject to inheritance and gift taxes: the basis of assessment is the net market value of all property received by the beneficiary (Bartoszuk and Lenain 2000). Natural and legal persons that are owner of a motor vehicle must also pay a tax on the means of transportation, dependent on the kind of motor vehicle.[25] Finally, the fiscal charge payable on transactions is collected by the central government, but it constitutes a source of income for the local government (see Table 10.3).

10.4 The fiscal burden

The distribution of tax charge: taxation by economic functions and implicit tax rates[26]

Generally speaking, the classification of revenues according to economic functions clearly shows how any factor contributes to the total amount of revenue: each value is given by the ratio of the total tax revenue attributed to that factor to a measure of total tax revenue or to GDP.

Table 10.3 Tax items in Poland by starting years

Tax items	Starting years	Revenues in 2000 (mn zl)	Apportionment of the revenues (%)	
			State	Local governments
Legacy and donation tax	1983	162.7	0.0	100.0
Agricultural property tax	1984	720.8	0.0	100.0
Personal income tax	1991	32,099.9	69.9	30.1
Real estate property tax	1991	6644.1	0.0	100.0
Forest property tax	1991	96.4	0.0	100.0
Transport Vehicles Tax	1991	386.8	0.0	100.0
Corporation income tax	1992	17,852.8	94.5	5.5
Value added tax	1992	51,749.8	100.0	0.0
Excise duty tax	1993	27,312.0	100.0	0.0
Tax card income tax	1993	315.0	0.0	100.0

Source: see text.

By looking at Poland, we can see that the main source of revenues arises from employed labor, which contributed up to 14 percent of GDP in 1998 (of which 4.7 was paid by employers and 9.3 percent was paid by the employees). This is not at all uncommon; in addition, an unusually high value characterizes consumption, which contributed up to 13 percent of GDP. Revenues from self-employed labor amounted to a comparatively high 5.1 percent of GDP, while revenues from capital and business, whose main components come from profits (2.9 percent) and real estate (1.1 percent), amounted just to 4.2 percent of GDP.

By looking at the same categories, but related to total revenue, and not to GDP as above, we can see that taxes and contributions on employed labor were 37.1 percent of total revenue, while taxes on consumption gave 34 percent of total revenue; taxes and contributions on the self-employed and non-employed labor covered 13.4 percent of total revenue and, in the end, taxes on capital and business covered 11.4 percent of total revenue. Finally, if we consider that in Poland state pensions are taxed as personal income, we note that taxes on social transfers amounted to 1.6 percent of GDP at the end of the 1990s.

By going now to the dynamics of revenue according to economic function, from the beginning to the end of the 1990s we observe that taxation of consumption increased from 9.7 percent of GDP in 1991 to about 14 percent in 1993 and has been almost constant since then. In an opposite trend, the load of taxes and social contributions attributed to employed labor has been slightly reduced from 15.6 percent of GDP in 1991 to 14 percent of GDP in 1998. Tax revenue from self-employed labor shows an increase from 3.2 percent of GDP in 1991 to 5.3 percent in 1993 and has remained constant since then; finally, revenue from capital and business (with the exclusion of self-employed labor) shows a gradual but noticeable decrease from 8.6 percent of GDP in 1991 to 4.2 percent in 1998, due to the reduction in legal tax rates of corporate income tax (see Table 10.4).

The implicit tax rate on an economic factor is the ratio of the total tax revenue attributed to that factor to the total income or cost of that factor, expressed as a percentage. Thus, for instance, the implicit tax rate for employed labor is given by the ratio of paid taxes and social contributions on employed labor to the compensations of employees; and so on for capital and final consumption.[27] These tax rates show the relative weight of fiscal burden, which falls on every factor, irrespective of the amount of the tax base considered.

The implicit tax rates for Poland confirm that employed labor is the most heavily taxed, at an implicit tax rate that was 32.2 percent in 1998, even though the dynamic of this rate shows a progressive decline from the early (37.3 percent in 1991) to the late 1990s. The implicit tax rate for consumption was 16.3 percent in 1998 and its dynamic in the 1990s shows a progressive increase from a value of 11.9 percent in 1991 to one of approximately 18 in 1995, followed by a very weak decrease during the subsequent years. Thus, it is possible plainly to observe a process of gradual substitution in taxation mix, from labor to consumption, that may also be a saving incentive.

Other indicators of fiscal burden

Labor tax wedge

Poland presents a particularly high labor tax wedge that contributes, together with a rigid labor market, to a low employment rate and an oversized underground economy. The joint impact of social security contributions and personal income taxes creates a large gap between labor costs and workers' disposable income. The gross average tax rate reached 42 percent of the labor cost for the average productive worker in 1999, while the marginal tax rate was 45 percent (Bartoszuk and Lenain 2000).

This is surely due to the generous pension schemes that characterize Polish public spending:[28] on the one hand this is very important for the social cohesion of the country but on the other hand, considering that Poland spends more on pensions than on education, research and development and public investments, it has become necessary to change this tradition. A new pension fund system was established in 1999: however, the reduction of the large tax wedge remains an important objective for Poland.

Gini coefficient

Historically, egalitarian countries, as the New Members were, have traditionally stood out for the lowest values of the Gini coefficient,

Table 10.4 Structure and development of taxation by function and by implicit rates in Poland, New Members and EU 15, 1992–98

	1992			1994			1996			1998		
	Poland	*New members*	*EU*	*Poland*	*New members*	*EU*	*Poland*	*New members*	*EU*	*Poland*	*New members*	*EU*
Economic functions												
Consumption	11.5	13.6	10.9	14.4	14.5	11.2	14.1	14.7	11.3	13.0	13.5	11.4
Labor employed	14.7	19.7	20.6	14.7	19.4	20.7	14.3	19.0	21.4	14.0	17.9	21.2
Labor self-employed	4.7	2.9	2.4	5.2	2.8	2.4	5.2	2.6	2.4	5.1	2.6	2.3
Capital and business	5.9	4.3	7.2	4.6	5.0	6.8	4.4	4.3	7.1	4.2	4.5	7.5
Implicit tax rates												
Consumption	13.8	16.3	16.2	17.9	17.4	16.5	17.6	17.8	16.7	16.3	16.6	16.8
Labor employed	31.2	37.1	39.0	35.2	38.3	40.2	33.0	37.4	42.0	32.2	38.0	41.9
Capital and business	–	–	32.2	–	–	30.3	–	–	30.5	–	–	31.1

Sources: EU Commission (2000a) for Poland and New Members (unweighted average); Eurostat (2000) for EU 15 (1997 unweighted average). Estonia's 1992 implicit rates and all Czech rates refer to 1993. Implicit rates for capital and business are available only for Estonia and Slovenia.

approximately 0.2, while the same coefficient reaches a higher value in less egalitarian countries, where powerful elites dominate the economy; in the USA, the value of the Gini coefficient has been approximately 0.4 in the 1990s (and it is still rising), while in most European countries it is around 0.3.

Generally, it is expected for a transition economy to experience a sizable increase in the Gini coefficient, during the transition period: this is due to the pre-tax distribution of income, which becomes more unequal because of the shift to a market economy. The transition, and the shift to a market economy, is believed to cause a change in the distribution of income because of the privatization of public assets (that is responsible for changes in ownership, wages and occupational choices); the development of new markets in privately-provided substitutes to public services (such as telephones, schools, health care); and changes in the returns associated with different skills that is responsible, with a more flexible labor market, for an increase in earnings inequality. Actually, transition economies reported some of the largest increases (around ten percentage points) in Gini coefficients between the early 1980s and the early 1990s.

Then, if conventional wisdom suggests that the pattern of sharply rising inequality has been nearly universal for transition economies, Poland's experience is in a striking contrast with this pattern: Poland's transition started with the 'big bang reform' of August 1989–January 1990 and, since then, Poland is one of the few transition economies that has experienced substantial growth with real GDP, which stayed 28 percent higher in 1999 than in 1989, when the transition began.

However, household level data (Polish Household Survey, Ministry of Finance) show that since then, income inequality fell slightly below a pre-transition level (that was approximately 0.25) during 1990–92, when the Gini coefficient registered a value of approximately 0.23. Since this time, the inequality started increasing only gradually, rising just slightly above pre-transition levels by 1997, when it reached about 0.275.

Poland experienced, as in other transition economies, a relevant increase in labor earnings inequality: the returns to education increased and, in particular for workers with college and high school degrees, wage premiums nearly doubled from 1989 to 1996. It has also been noticed (Sibley and Walsh 2002) that earnings inequality is higher in regions that are more advanced in restructuring (higher labor productivity/job realloca-tion rates): there is a positive relationship, at the regional level, between earnings inequality and the stage of transition, while at the national level rapid growth does not seem to be associated with earnings inequality.

A comparison with other New Members and EU 15 countries

When compared with the EU average, the structure of revenue according to the economic function of Poland, shows some remarkable differences, as we can see from Table 10.3. First of all, taxes on consumption have a higher share in total taxation than in the EU, and also with respect to New Members' average. Second, taxes and contributions on employed labor differ significantly from the EU average, being seven percentage points lower. This is a peculiar feature of Poland, and not a general characteristic of New Members. Their value for taxes and contributions on employed labor stays at an intermediate level between Poland and the EU average. As to taxes and contributions on self-employed labor, we can distinctly observe that the value for Poland is approximately three percentage points higher than the EU average and, again, this is a peculiar feature of Poland's tax system: contrarily, the value for the New Members is on average quite similar to that of EU countries. Finally, taxation on capital and business in Poland is close to the average of the other New Members: their value is three percentage points lower than the EU one.

The implicit tax rate on consumption is quite similar in Poland, in the New Members and in the EU, even if in Poland it is slightly lower and was much lower at the beginning of the 1990s (13.8 percent in Poland, 16.3 percent in the New Members and 16.2 in the EU in 1992). A more relevant difference is observable for employed labor: the Polish implicit tax rate is approximately ten percentage points lower than the EU one.

10.5 Tax reforms and further steps to get closer to the EU

Macroeconomic and budget outlook

Poland is actually one of the most successful transition economies: during the 1990s, it made relevant efforts to stabilize the economy, to improve the public finances, to run an effective monetary policy, to liberalize and privatize, and to start developing those structural reforms needed to get closer to the European Union (EU Commission 2000b).

During the decade, as inflation gradually fell, the output grew at strong annual rates of 6–7 percent, mostly as a consequence of the dynamism of the private sector – except at the end of the 1990s, when in 1998 the economy decelerated sharply in the wake of the Russian crisis. The objectives to be reached during the next decade have been envisaged as stable growth, inflation under control, adequate finance for the large current account deficit and, finally, strong efforts to consolidate public finances and implement structural reforms for improving public spending quality and reducing the excessive tax burden. In 2000, the general government deficit reached 3.5 percent of GDP (Eurostat 2002), primarily owing to deficits in social security funds, state enterprises' arrears on their social contributions and increased borrowing of local governments.

The first two years of the current decade have not been easy because of cyclical weaknesses of the Polish economy and, as a result of the economic slowdown, unemployment has risen and investment has fallen. Poland entered 2003 with the beginnings of a recovery supported by the growth of private consumption and exports (partly because of the effective depreciation of the zloty). Growth was about 3.6 percent in 2003, while, for the following years, due to the present large output gap, a strong recovery is forecast (5–5.5 percent for the middle of the decade). Price stability has been reached: inflation was below 2 percent at the end of 2003 (Ministry of Finance of Poland).

High unemployment, along with the rising budget deficit, are the two most important problems of the Polish economy when entering the EU. The general government deficit widened in 2003 (6.4 percent), chiefly due to the deficits of agricultural agencies and social security funds, and public debt increased to about 52 percent of GDP. Thus, the strong need for further structural expenditure reforms is pushing to scale down the budget deficit to the Maastricht limit of 3 percent, to avoid the chance that the public debt reaches the (also constitutional) level of 60 percent, and, finally to rearrange budget priorities (partly in view of co-financing EU-financed projects)[29] and to face a need to pay higher rates of foreign debt.

At the end of 2003, the government announced a new strategy of government debt stabilization: the main part of which is a rationalization of social expenditures and a reduction of state administration expenditures. According to many observers, it will be extremely hard to reach these goals, also because there is an election coming in 2005: there is a danger that inability to fulfill the Maastricht criteria would postpone Polish accession to the EMU. As for now the most probable date is 2009–10.

At the same time, Poland will have to cover the EU contributions and payments. Due to the relative centralization of the public finance, the government has to transfer important resources to the regions in order to make available their participation in the EU structural funds. In the coming years, Poland will face a need to pay higher rates of foreign debt.

Polish accession to the EU is going to bring changes in the structure of public finance: according to forecast for the years 2004–06, the EU will be a net payer to Poland. Poland will gain resources from many EU funds and from the special budgetary compensation negotiated on the Copenhagen Summit at the end of 2002; substantial support will be directed to agriculture and industry, also without state budget intermediation. According to the forecast of the Ministry of Finance, in 2004 Poland will get an appropriation of payments of €2.5 billion, paying at the same time €1.3 billion as a contribution: the net effect would be surplus of €1.2 billion. In 2005–06 the surplus is forecast to be €2.1 billion and €3.6 billion, but most of the resources will omit the central budget and will go directly to the regions, agriculture and industry. The public sector revenues/GDP ratio is expected to grow in the years 2004–06; this fact is mostly attributable to the growing value of aid funds coming from the EU. After a gradual decline from 41.9 percent in 1995 to 38.5 percent in 2002, total fiscal pressure is expected to grow to 41 percent in 2006 (Polish Ministry of Finance 2003).

Recent years' and planned tax reforms

Tax reforms have been remarkable during the last years in Poland, because the authorities are trying to continue replacing the old communist tax system, which rested on transfers from state-owned enterprises, with a new system suitable for a market economy: thus, in 1999, the authorities formulated tax reform proposals, partially enacted in 2000, designed to lower direct taxation and tax rates, to reduce tax allowances, to broaden the tax bases and to simplify the tax code.

While the proposed changes to CIT and VAT were adopted, those regarding PIT were vetoed by the President; with regard to CIT, the aim was to lower the tax rate (from 34 percent in 1999 to 22 percent in 2004) and at the same time to broaden the tax base, removing tax deductions for companies with high investment; with regard to VAT, the aim was the harmonization with EU requirements (EU Sixth Council Directive) with a view to future accession, introducing VAT rates for products so far untaxed (services, starting in 2002, and agricultural products, starting in July 2002).[30] In 2003, the CIT rate was 27 percent; at the end of 2003 new reform is being prepared. According to the act being prepared, CIT will be decreased to 19 percent from 2004 but almost all deductions and allowances will be removed. The same flat rate will be available for entrepreneurs paying taxes under the PIT regime. The main purpose of this reform is to improve the competitiveness of Polish enterprises and to encourage FDI flow to Poland; in the near future it is planned to raise the tax rate on dividends from 15 percent to 19 percent.

New Polish VAT Law is being prepared in order to harmonize completely Polish regulation with the EU standards. Among new regulations, the most important are those adjusting Polish law to the intra-community trade. These regulations are directly involved with the abolition of customs borders and they relate to the territorial scope, categories of taxpayers, definitions of the concept of tax duty and tax eligibility in transactions between EU-member states, specifying the persons obliged to pay VAT in intra-community transactions. According to the plans, the standard rate will stay unchanged (22 percent) as will the reduced rate (7 percent). Until 2008, a new rate of 3 percent for unprocessed agricultural products should be maintained. The same rate should be applicable for delivery of goods and services for agricultural production (except from machinery). Until 2007, the rate of 7 percent will be applicable on provision on construction, renovation and repair services. At the same time, certain books and magazines will be provisionally charged at 0 percent.

It is probable that after entering the EU the standard rate will be lowered and the reduced one increased.

The planned reform for PIT was not enacted, and a progressive reduction of the tax rates from the current three brackets (19, 30, 40 percent) to only two brackets of 18 and 28 percent in 2002 was abandoned. This plan was not enacted until 2003 and, according to the new act being prepared at the end of 2003, the 19–30–40 percent brackets will be unchanged in coming years. Most of the deductions and allowances will be systematically removed from the system, so that the tax base will be enlarged. At the same time, however, plans for the PIT rates' decrease are present in the political debate. Furthermore, some significant changes have been introduced (IBDF 2002b) under the amendments to the Individual Income Tax Law, applying from January 2001. The withholding tax rate on dividends paid to residents and non-resident taxpayers was reduced from 20 to 15 percent and will be increased again in 2004 to 19 percent, whereas individual income tax rates have remained unchanged, and the same will also be the case for 2002, 2003 and further. From January 2002, the level of tax exemption has been increased from ZL493.32 (about €128) to ZL530.08 (about €135); in addition, since March 2002, a 20 percent withholding tax applies to interests derived from bank accounts, securities issued by the state, bonds issued by local authorities and income from participation to investment funds; a lot of tax deductions and tax credits for expenditures borne for purchasing land to construct, for constructing dwelling houses or expanding for housing purposes have been reversed.

The amendments also provide for a deduction for interests on loans secured by a mortgage and taken up after January 2002, up to ZL189,000 (about €48,000) and for a 2 percent rate transfer tax, levied on capital transfers abroad, applying until December 2003.

As regards VAT, from July 2001 a decree of the Ministry of Finance provides for a repayment, in observance of particular conditions, in favor of foreign enterprises, for VAT incurred in the purchase of goods and services in Poland; from July 2001, amendments to the VAT and Excise Duty Law provides for a 7 percent VAT rate applying to Internet access services (with an exemption in favor of schools and educational facilities).

During 2001, new rules regarding income taxation of leasing for corporate and individual taxpayers, the new law on stamp duty and the law on tax on civil law transactions (replacing the law of 1989) also came into force. When it comes to excise tax, the main change will be the reduction in the number of goods charged with this tax. Most of the rates of tax will be removed or decreased. But the most important rise is expected in the case of tobacco products. In 2004 it will be increased by 9.1 percent, in 2005 by 10.4 percent and 18.9 percent in 2006 as a consequence of adjustments demanded from the EU (Polish Ministry of Finance 2003). The full harmonization is expected for the year 2008.

In 2004, Poland will join the European custom union: 75 percent of revenues collected on the borders with not-EU members will be redirected to the EU budget. As a result of Community Customs Tariff adoption, the effective custom duty rate is going to decrease (Pre-accession Economic Program 2003, Ministry of Finance, Warsaw). A new law for local government financing is planned for 2004. Among new regulations, the most important is further decentralization of tasks and public funds, which should also result in wider participation of local governments in the public funds. There is also a need to link the local governments' standings with the macroeconomic situation. The system will be more flexible in order to enable local government participation in EU funds. It is also planned that most of the local government tasks should be financed from their own resources and transfers from the state budget should play an additional role, what is not the case at the moment.

In recent years, a number of actions were adopted in order to improve the effectiveness of the tax collection system. A modern IT system was implemented in 2001. This system will improve co-operations among tax offices. In 2003, provisions of the Tax Code entered into force.

The new regulations aim at narrowing the scope of the 'hidden economy' and enforcing tax collection.

The need for further steps

Polish tax reform certainly represents a fundamental step towards the modernization of the tax system, which is thus becoming more equitable and incentive-inducing. Nevertheless, other relevant reforms are still needed. First of all, a reform of personal income tax is required, in order to lower tax rates and thus create a tax regime more favorable to job creation. The combined effect of current high tax rates and social security contributions involves a particularly high tax wedge that contributes to high unemployment and an oversized underground economy. An important step has been taken through the introduction, in 1999, of a comprehensive reform of the pension system, which is expected to make pension contributions more similar to saving, rather than a further tax, so as to stimulate the labor supply and the shifting of workers out from the underground economy (Bartoszuk and Lenain 2000); however, further actions need to be taken in order to reduce the amount of disability and sickness pensions and early-retirement pensions still applying to those born before January 1949.

Another recommended intervention regards the autonomy of the tax policy for local governments, which still rely on large financial transfers from central government. Local governments should be given the opportunity to manage their own tax bases. As to this point, an option could be that of a property tax based on the value (and not on the size, as currently arranged) of properties. However, careful supervision of local governments and monitoring of possible borrowing is strongly recommended in order to avoid a financial crisis and the worsening of budget imbalance at the central level.

Further, in order to get closer to EU requirements, Poland should introduce charges on those products that are damaging to the environment, such as coal, fertilizers, and leaded gasoline. Moreover, there is the necessity to reform property market taxation, by bringing residential construction into the tax net (applying the standard rate is required by the Sixth Directive, while, as permitted under Annex H, a reduced rate could be applied to social housing).

Another relevant need is to unify different tax rates on capital incomes, in order to reduce possible distortion in savings allocation and investments financing: at present, Poland has different effective tax rates on corporate income (according to the source of financing, the legal form of the investor, and the residence status of the lender) that should be aligned.

Finally, a fundamental step is that of improving and simplifying tax administration, partly in view of the EU accession, making the system more transparent and taxpayer friendly, for example by removing the need to fill in a tax return for most individual taxpayers, whose taxes are withheld (Bartoszuk and Lenain 2000). Similar measures could help keep a voluntary tax discipline in the future.

Notes

1 A preliminary version of this chapter has been carefully revised by R. Morawczynski of Krakow University of Economics, to whom we express our warmest thanks. L. Vergano is responsible for section 10.2 and for section 10.3 on the corporate income tax, the excise duties, the social security contributions and the other minor taxes. F. Zantomio is responsible for sections 10.4 and 10.5 and for section 10.3 on the personal income tax, the VAT, the agricultural property tax, the forestry property tax and the real estate property tax.
2 In 1997, tax issues were regulated in the new constitution. In the same year, The Act on Rules for Taxation came into force: it regulates tax liabilities, tax information, tax proceedings, tax audits, and fiscal confidentiality.
3 From 2004 it will be 19 percent.
4 A new pension fund system was introduced in 1999: labor taxes have been substituted with contributions to individual pension accounts, which are a form of compulsory savings.
5 The system is highly subsidized from the central budget: another 5 percent comes from the budget.
6 Calculated on the basis of data from the Central Statistical Office.
7 *Powiats* are basic levels of the state administration, *Gmina* is a basic level of local government, whereas *Voivoidship* is a mixture of both at the middle level.
8 This section owes much to EU Commission (2000a) and IBDF (2002a).
9 There are some typologies of income which cannot be subject to joint taxation between married couples: incomes from given loans, dividends on shares and other shares in net profits of corporations, incomes which are paid to help police, organs of state protection and treasury control, incomes from undisclosed sources of revenues and from winnings in games and competitions.

10 In 2004 changes are expected: the percentage limit will be liquidated and instead of it there will be the limit of ZL350.

11 In 2004 it will be probably liquidated.

12 In 2004 the number of such bodies will be reduced: entities will be expected to be officially recognized for their social role.

13 Not valid since 2002.

14 The exchange rate used (2002) is ZL3.85742 for €1; in 2003 it is ZL4.5 for €1, due to rapid depreciation. At the end of October it is ZL4.7.

15 Expressed in Polish currency, brackets are the same for 2003. Due to the depreciation of the Zloty, in euros it would be (€1 approximately ZL4.5) €8200, €16,500; tax credit €115.

16 Owing to the huge deficit, PIT reduction in the coming years is not to be expected, in particular the flat rate system is not probable. Nevertheless, this issue is still discussed in the political arena.

17 The tax authority decides every time, but in general the decision is based on the official tables. The amount is based on three aspects: number of employees, number of people living in the place, where the enterprise is run and on the kind of activity.

18 In accordance with the 1997 Constitution of the Republic of Poland, taxes and other public contributions cannot be levied unless the appropriate statutory law has been passed.

19 Partners are subject to individual taxation on their share of income.

20 In the previous years, the CIT rates have been the following: 34 percent in 1999; 30 percent in 2000; 28 percent in 2001 and 2002.

21 Actually the preparation started in 1988; one of the most important obstacles was fear of inflation.

22 In general, the scope of goods charged with excise duty tax is much wider compared with that of other accession or EU member countries. Thus, the number of goods charged with excise tax will soon be decreased in order to adjust to EU regulation and to prepare for competition with neighboring countries (especially for alcoholic beverages). On the other hand, excise tax on cigarettes will be increased in a stepwise manner until 2008 (Ziolkowska 2002).

23 The pension insurance is a 'three pillar system'. Pillar I: obligatory public system financed through the Social Security Fund (ZUS); Pillar II: obligatory private pillar based on private pension funds; Pillar III: all voluntary private pension plans, life insurance, etc. Persons born before 1949 are obliged to stay in Pillar I only. Persons born after 1969 should participate in Pillars I and II, while Pillar III is voluntary for them. Persons born between 1949 and 1969 have the opportunity to choose one of the two systems presented above: once the decision is made, there is no possibility to change it (Denek *et al.* 2001).

24 Since sickness Funds were liquidated, there is only one centralized institution: the National Health Fund.

25 Among the more interesting taxes there is a tax charged on the owners of dogs, equal to ZL37 (€8) per year (Denek *et al.* 2001).

26 This section is mainly due to EU Commission (2000a).

27 Because of the unavailability of data, it is impossible, at present, to calculate implicit tax rates for capital and business.

28 The Polish population age distribution, quite similar to that of the other New Members, is characterized by a small share of people in retirement age: the dependence ratio, quite reassuringly, is about 0.18 (calculated according to Eurostat data for 2000 on the population structure): it means there are about 5.4 men of working age to provide for any one old man.

29 It is to be noticed that there is a huge difference in the calculation of the public finance deficit while using Polish and ESA'95 methodologies. According to ESA'95 methodology, the Agricultural Market Agency and research development units do not belong to the government sector. The second important difference is the second pillar of pension system (*OFE*), which according to ESA'95 belongs to the public system. At the moment, according to the Polish methodology, *OFE* represents the private sector and the government has to transfer almost ZL12 billion (€3 billion). Furthermore, the ESA system is based on the accrual basis, whereas Polish methodology uses the cash basis, which results in different attitudes to several operations. For example, the ESA system does not include projected payments (Pre-accession Economic Program, 2003, Ministry of Finance, Warsaw). As the result, according to the ESA'95, Polish public debt is much lower. According to Polish methodology, the public debt amounted to 47.2 percent in 2002; 51.5 percent in 2003, is forecast to be 54.8 percent in 2004 and will almost reach the constitutional limit of 60 percent in 2005. Using ESA methodology it will be 41.6 percent in 2002, 44.8 percent in 2003 and 51.4 percent in 2005.
30 For a more detailed description of the reform, see subsection in section 10.3 on VAT.

References

Bartoszuk, L. and Lenain, P. (2000) 'The Polish tax reform', Economics Department Working Paper, Paris: OECD.

Denek, E., Sobiech, J. and Wolniak, J. (2001) *Finanse publiczne*, Wydawnictwo naukowe Warszawa: PWN.

Easson, A. (1998) 'Tax competition heats up in Central Europe', *Bulletin of International Bureau of Fiscal Documentation*, May, pp. 192–97.

EU Commission (2000a) *Structure of the Tax Systems in Estonia, Poland, Hungary, the Czech Republic and Slovenia*, Brussels: EU Commission.

EU Commission (2000b) 'Recent fiscal developments in the candidate countries', Enlargement Papers 2, Brussels, EU Commission, Directorate General for Economic and Financial Affairs.

Eurostat (2000) *Structures of the Taxation Systems in the European Union, 1970–1997*, Brussels: EU Commission.

Eurostat (2002) *Statistical Yearbook on Candidate and South-east European Countries*, Brussels: EU Commission.

IBFD – International Bureau of Fiscal Documentation (2002a) *European Tax Handbook 2002*, Amsterdam: IBDF.

IBFD – International Bureau of Fiscal Documentation (2002b) *Annual Report, 2001–2002*, Amsterdam: IBDF.

Misiag, W. (ed.) (2002) *Public Finance in Poland 1989–2001. Case Study of Transformation*, Warsaw.

Mitra, P. and Stern, N. (2003) 'Tax systems in transition', WB Working Paper 2947, Washington, DC: The World Bank.

OECD (2001) *Revenue Statistics 1965–2000*, Paris: OECD.

OECD (2002) *Fiscal Decentralization in EU Applicant States and Selected EU Member States*, Paris: OECD.

Owsiak, S. (2002) *Finanse publiczne. Teoria i praktyka*, Warszawa: PWN.

Polish Ministry of Finance (2003) *Pre-accession Economic Program*, Warszawa.

Sibley, C. W. and Walsh, P. P. (2002) 'Earnings inequality and transition: a regional analysis of Poland', IZA Discussion Paper 441.

Tanzi, V. and Tsibouris, G. (2000) 'Fiscal reform over ten years of transition', IMF Working Paper 113, Washington, DC: IMF.

Ziolkowska, W. (2002) *Finanse publiczne. Teoria i zastosowanie*, Poznan: Wydawnictwo Wyzszej Szkoly Bankowej.

Websites

http://www.stat.gov.pl/english/ – Statistical Office of Poland.

http://www.mf.gov.pl – Ministry of Finance of Poland.

11 Slovenia

Matteo Maria Galizzi and Simona Scabrosetti[1]

11.1 Introduction and executive summary

This chapter is devoted to the description of the Slovenian fiscal system. Among all the East European countries, Slovenia not only presents a social and economic structure most similar to the current EU members, but it has also been often considered by international comparative surveys, so that many data are available.

Slovenia is a small country, covering an area of 20,273 km² (approximately half the size of Switzerland) and is populated by two million inhabitants. Since its foundation in 1918, Slovenia was part of the Kingdom of Serbs, Croats and Slovenes, which later evolved into the Federal People's Republic of Yugoslavia in 1945. In April 1990 there were the first democratic elections, followed in December 1990 by a referendum in which 88.5 percent voted in favor of an independent state. Slovenia officially declared its independence on 25 June 1991, and on January 1992 was officially recognized by the EU. On 1 February 1999 there came into effect the association agreement with the EU: Slovenia entered the EU on 1 May 2004.

The local currency is the Slovene Tolar, SIT, whose exchange rate in November 2003 was SIT236 = €1. Slovenian GDP in 2003 was about €24,580 million, nearly €12,208 per capita, about 60 percent of the EU average (unweighted PPP values). Real GDP has grown by 3 percent in the last two years, sustained by robust export expansion, both to the EU – mainly Germany, Italy, France, Austria and Croatia – and to non-EU markets. In 2004 there is expected to be a strong domestic demand to push GDP growth up to 3.7 percent.

The unemployment rate in 2002 remained stable at 6.4 percent, while inflation continued to stay at relatively high levels, despite the fact it was expected to fall from 7.5 percent in 2002 to 4.5 percent in 2004 – according to the latest government estimation – and it is now a priority target by the Bank of Slovenia.

Monetary policy in 2002 was tightened to some extent, leading to a slower growth in monetary aggregates M3. However, as a result of high capital inflows, an overall large monetary expansion has put downward pressure on the interest rate.

A consolidated general government deficit was reduced to 1.8 percent of GDP in 2002 and it is expected to reach just 1.2 percent in 2004, thus – together with the stock of public debt constant at 40 percent of GDP – contributing to fulfilling the Maastricht criteria (EU Commission 2003).

The overall fiscal burden in Slovenia amounted to 40.5 percent of GDP in 1998 – a level that lies between the average for EU-15 and the one for New Members – and comprised nearly two-thirds of tax revenues and the remaining one-third by social contributions. The latest available indicator for the fiscal burden, referred to 2002, is slightly lower, amounting to 39.5 percent of GDP. Tax revenue comprised mostly indirect taxes (18.9 percent of GDP): in particular, VAT represented the largest source of government financing, contributing more than 22 percent to the total fiscal burden. As a consequence, indirect taxes and social contributions seem to be too high compared with the other EU countries. The dominant role of these two sources of fiscal revenue is in sharp contrast with the suggestions by Mitra and Stern (2003), who indicate a recommended level for both indirect taxes and social contributions at about 10 percent of GDP each.

In conclusion, economic efficiency could be improved by raising rates of direct taxes, especially corporate and business, and in particular on self-employed income and on financial activities. Analysis of total taxation by functions, in fact, confirms that consumption and labor are by far the most heavily charged, while taxes on capital and business play a really marginal role. The same figure emerges from the analysis by Čok (2003) of average tax rates on active households, whose total burden from indirect taxes and social contributions amounted, on average, to 37.3 percent of gross income over a total burden of 45.8 percent. In addition, the recent proposal by the Slovenian government to prepare, among the others, a new law on corporate income tax seems to confirm the need to reform the fiscal system in the above direction.

11.2 The structure of the system at the end of the 1990s

A broad view at the current structure of taxes and social security contributions

In 1998, the overall fiscal burden in Slovenia amounted to 40.5 percent of GDP, an intermediate value as compared to European averages referring to EU-15 and New Members. Total tax revenue accounted for 26.7, whereas social security contributions made up the remaining 13.8 percent.

The structure of taxation system depicted in Table 11.1 shows that indirect taxes at the end of the 1990s were the most important component of total tax revenue, reaching 18.9 percent of GDP. Within this largest source

Table 11.1 Structure and development of fiscal revenue in Slovenia, New Members and EU 15 as a percentage of GDP, 1992–98

	1992			1994			1996			1998		
	Slovenia	*New members*	*EU*	*Slovenia*	*New members*	*EU*	*Slovenia*	*New members*	*EU*	*Slovenia*	*New members*	*EU*
Direct taxes, of which	7.4	10.1	13.5	7.8	10.0	13.4	7.7	9.6	13.7	7.8	9.2	13.7
Personal income	6.8	6.4	9.6	6.9	7.0	9.6	6.8	7.1	9.3	6.6	6.7	9.3
Corporation income	0.6	3.6	2.3	0.8	2.9	2.3	0.9	2.5	2.4	1.2	2.5	3.0
Indirect taxes, of which	14.5	15.6	13.4	17.4	16.5	13.7	18.2	16.9	13.7	18.9	15.5	13.9
VAT	6.8	5.1	6.7	7.8	7.4	6.8	8.4	7.4	6.9	9.1	7.9	7.0
Excise duties	3.6	3.4	3.4	4.5	4.2	3.5	4.6	4.1	3.4	4.4	4.1	3.5
Others	4.1	9.3	3.3	5.2	5.0	3.4	5.2	4.9	3.4	5.5	3.6	3.5
Total tax revenue	21.9	25.7	26.9	25.2	26.4	26.6	25.9	26.5	27.1	26.7	24.7	27.6
Social contributions	18.6	16.1	14.5	17.1	15.7	14.9	14.7	14.3	15.3	13.8	14.2	15.0
Employers	7.6	10.0	8.1	7.4	9.0	7.9	5.2	8.0	8.3	4.4	7.9	8.2
Employees	10.1	5.3	4.8	8.9	5.11	5.2	8.7	4.8	5.1	8.5	4.8	5.0
Self employed	0.9	1.8	1.6	0.7	1.6	1.8	0.8	1.5	1.9	0.9	1.6	1.9
Total fiscal revenue	40.5	41.8	41.4	42.3	42.2	41.5	40.6	40.8	42.4	40.5	38.9	42.6
Administrative level												
Central government	18.6	25.9	22.8	21.6	25.8	22.4	22.9	25.4	22.4	23.6	23.9	22.9
Local government	3.3	3.0	3.0	3.6	3.5	3.2	3.0	3.4	4.0	3.1	3.7	4.0
Social Security	18.6	12.9	14.5	17.1	12.9	14.9	14.7	11.5	15.2	13.8	11.4	14.9

Sources: EU Commission (2000a) for Slovenia and selected New Members (unweighted average); Eurostat (2000) for EU 15 (1997 unweighted average).

Notes
Czech data start in 1993 and Social security is only health.

of government financing, VAT played the dominant role: it contributed more than 22 percent to total taxation and its revenue as a percentage of GDP was larger than that of direct taxes.

More specifically, direct taxes accounted for about 19 percent of total fiscal revenue. Thus, the share of taxation on personal income was in line with all selected New Members, but lower compared to the EU average. However, the most relevant feature concerns corporation tax whose revenue, in terms of percentage of GDP, exceeded 1 percent from 1997, being slightly higher in the following years.

Social security contributions represented more than 34 percent of total taxation at the end of the 1990s. As in other EU New Members, the highest share is formally (or by law) charged to employees.

As regards the splitting of total fiscal revenue by receiving administrative levels, local government obtained only 3.1 percent of GDP, that is 7.8 percent of total taxation. Central government collected instead 23.6 percent of GDP, about 10 points more than social security institutions (pensions and health).

Comparing all these figures to the benchmark case proposed by Mitra and Stern (2003) it may be concluded that, in Slovenia, indirect taxes and social security contributions are actually too high. Cutting these two headings and increasing the share of direct taxes, especially on self-employed income, could possibly improve the economy efficiency.

The development of the system from the early to the late 1900s

According to theoretical literature suggestions, Slovenia started to cut social security contributions from 1994: the reduction was gradual but continuous and, in 1998, this source of fiscal revenue reached 13.8 percent of GDP, the lowest value, which also characterized the following year (Table 11.1). Among the chargeable persons, employers are the most advantaged: their share of social security contributions as a percentage of GDP fell from 7.6 percent in 1992 to 4.4 percent in 1998, whereas in the same period, the cut in the share charged to employees was only 1.6 percentage points.

On the other hand, from the early to the late 1990s, there was a significant increase in the revenue from indirect taxes. In 1992, such taxes accounted for 14.5 percent of GDP against 18.9 percent in 1998. VAT realized the most important rise, exceeding 9 percent of GDP, that is 22 percent of total taxation at the end of the period. Excise duties showed their highest value in 1996 and then started to slightly decline. Direct taxes alternately rose and fell, but their changes were not too significant. In particular, corporate income revenue as a percentage of GDP doubled from 1992 to 1998, reaching only 3 percent of total taxation. Personal income tax was instead always around 6.7 percent of GDP.

As a consequence of all these changes, total tax revenue rose by

4.8 percentage points, whereas total fiscal revenue was stable at about 40.5 percent of GDP.

The apportionment of revenue among government layers

The gradual but continuous reduction of social security contributions from 1994 and the related increase of indirect taxes also affected the distribution of fiscal revenue by levels of government. As shown in Table 11.1, during the 1990s there was a rise of five percentage points in central government resources and a symmetric fall in the social security institutions (pensions and health) revenue. As a consequence, in 1998 tax receipts belonging to central government were more or less a quarter of GDP, whereas the share going to social security bodies stayed below 14 percent. The apportionment of fiscal revenue to local government remained almost stable at around 3 percent of GDP.

According to OECD (2002), in 2000 the total sub-national revenue accounted for 5.3 percent of GDP, and 12.4 percent of total government revenue. It was composed of about 59 percent by tax revenue, especially taxes on incomes and on property, 18 percent by non-tax revenue, such as surpluses of trading enterprises, property income, administrative fees and charges, and of over 23 percent by general or specific grants from central government. The sub-national budget being balanced guaranteed that the total current sub-national government expenditure amounted in the same year to 5.3 percent of GDP, mainly represented by expenses in education, housing, general public services, transports and recreational activities, while the consolidated government expenditure reached a share equal to the 44.1 percent of GDP.

A comparison with other main New Members and the EU average[2]

According to the available data summarized in Table 11.1, in 1998 Slovenia's total fiscal pressure was at an intermediate value compared with European averages, whereas in the previous years, except for 1992, it was nearer the lower figure of selected New Members (Poland, Hungary, the Czech Republic, Slovenia and Estonia). The same can be said as concerns total tax revenue as a percentage of GDP.

At the beginning of the 1990s, social security contributions were higher than in the other New Members and European countries, but thanks to the important reduction which started in 1994, the levels became closer to the averages of reference.

On the other hand, the share of direct and indirect taxes in Slovenia, as a percentage of GDP, showed a very different tax structure both with respect to New Members and to EU-15 countries. In particular, Slovenian direct and indirect taxes are, respectively, the lowest and the highest compared both with those of selected New Members and with EU countries. This is in contrast with the suggestions of part of the economic literature (among the others, Mitra and Stern 2003) about a necessary reduction of indirect taxes financed by an increase in direct taxes.

Slovenia total government spending in relation to GDP was around 44 percent in 2000, a value in line with that of the existing EU-15 countries (45 percent) and of other New Members (40 percent). However, the decentralization of this expenditure was very different: in Slovenia the share of total sub-national spending in GDP, in 2000, was 5.3 percent, about two percentage points lower than the New Members' average and only a third compared with the EU countries' level, which stayed at 16.2 percent. However, this is not an uncommon feature of economies in transition, such as Slovenia.

Moreover, as concerns the composition of sub-national receipts, tax revenue was 15 percentage points higher, while central government grants were a little more than half compared with EU members' mean value. Sub-national authorities are given some freedom to determine their non-tax revenue, and in Slovenia that reached 18.1 percent of total receipts, one of the highest level among New Members (OECD 2002).

11.3 Some quantitative and institutional features of main taxes

Personal income tax – PIT (Dohodnina)

Individuals are subject to national income tax, property tax and inheritance and gift tax.

Individuals who have their permanent residence or usual domicile in Slovenia (that is who stay there at least 183 consecutive days in a calendar year) are residents for tax purposes. They are generally taxed on their worldwide income.

Each individual is treated as a separate taxpayer: there is no taxation of an household as a whole. The taxable base of each source of income is computed separately. The net results are aggregated at the end of the year.

The main sources of income are the *personal income*, which includes employment income, pensions, remuneration received under temporary contracts and state prizes and awards, the *income from agriculture*, given by the cadastral income from farmlands and woodlands, the *income from property*, as generated from profit-sharing and dividends (whose taxable base is the gross amount received reduced by 40 percent, as a way to mitigate double taxation), and from interest on loans (with the important exemption of interests on bank accounts and securities), the *income from property rights*, derived from copyrights, inventions, trade marks and technical innovations, irrespective of whether they are protected by law, the *capital gains*, derived from the sale of real estate, shares or other securities if realized within three years after the date of subscription, and, finally, the *profits from business and professional activities*, which is computed in the same way as profits derived by legal entities (see the next subsection). Regarding the latter, note that individuals who perform independent professional services and who have no employees may request that, instead of computing their profit on the basis used by private business, they determine their taxable base by making a lump-sum deduction of 40 percent from their gross income.

Exempt income includes retirement bonuses and severance payments, part of unemployment benefits and student grants, while incentives and benefits provided to employees are subject to personal income tax.

The final liability is computed after the deduction, up to a maximum 3 percent of the tax base, of certain personal expenses – such as the ones for the acquisition of long-term securities issued by the Republic of Slovenia or by funds that are earmarked for investments in research and development, for the acquisition and maintenance of residential buildings, for the purchase of medical aid, medicines, textbooks and tuition fees, for donations to non-profit organizations – and of personal allowances. Concerning the latter, notice that, besides allowances given to individuals with family responsibilities (10 percent of average annual salary allowance for the first child, five more percentage points for each additional child, and 10 percent for each adult family member without income), all taxpayers are entitled to a deduction from their income tax base of an amount equaling 11 percent of the average annual salary in Slovenia. Taxpayers above 65 years are entitled to an additional 8 percent allowance of average annual salary.

The final tax liability is computed by applying the tax rates (Table 11.2) to the aggregate taxable income. Marginal tax rates show a sharp progressivity, going from 17 percent of income below €5420 up to 50 percent for income above €32,520.

Corporate income tax – CIT (Dovek Od Dobicka Pravnih Oseb)

Slovenia adopts a classical corporate income tax system: corporate profits are subject to taxation on profits at the company level, and then subject

Table 11.2 Slovenian Personal Income Tax 2002

Taxable income (€)	Rate (%)
0 to 5420	17
from 5420 to 10,840	35
from 10,840 to 16,260	37
from 16,260 to 21,680	40
from 21,680 to 32,520	45
over 32,520	50

Source: EU Commission (2000a).

again at the shareholder level. Dividends received by resident individuals, however, are only taxable on 60 percent of the gross dividends received, while inter-company dividends are not subject to tax, provided profit tax has been paid by the paying company on its taxable profits.

All legal persons, except public enterprises, non-profit organizations and few other exemptions (see also section 11.4) are subject to the tax. Resident companies are taxed on worldwide income.

The starting point for the computation of the taxable base is the income reported in the profit and loss accounts, with the further qualification that only the expenses directly incurred on the performance of the activities are allowable. Several specific tax incentives aimed at encouraging investments and employment opportunities are available (see also section 11.4).

Profit tax is levied at the rate of 25 percent. Notice that the rate has been recently reduced from a previous 30 percent. A business loss may be carried forward for five years.

In addition to profit tax, all registered legal and natural persons who pay wages and salaries to individuals are obliged to pay a payroll tax on the gross amount of such remuneration, with a tax rate between 0 and 14.8 percent. A special withholding tax is levied on remuneration paid to persons employed under temporary contracts at a rate of 25 percent.

Value added tax – VAT (Davek Na Dodano Vrednost)

A VAT system, based on the Sixth EC Directive, replaced the sales tax on 1 July 1999. Taxable persons are entrepreneurs – individuals, partnerships and companies – whose annual turnover exceeds SIT5 million, approximately €21,000. The taxable amount is determined according to the Sixth EC Directive, and it coincides with the total consideration agreed upon and charged to the person receiving the goods or services.

The standard rate is 20 percent, while a reduced rate of 8.5 percent applies, among other items, to basic foodstuff, medicines, hotel accommodation and books.

Environment tax and excise duty on petrol and mineral oils

The Environment Protection Act of 1996 and the Decree on CO_2 Tax of 1996–98 established that any person who buys fossil fuels (motor or heating fuels) and who incinerates organic wastes has to pay €0.013 (SIT3) on each kilogram of emitted CO_2 gas. Exemptions are connected with the use of mineral oils. Table 11.3 summarizes the rates of the excise duty on petrol and mineral oils whose revenue belongs to the central government budget.

Table 11.3 Excise duty on petrol and mineral oils in Slovenia

Product designation	According to the law (1998)	Government Decree (1999)
	€/1000 liters	€/1000 liters
Leaded petrol	483,06	333,92
Unleaded petrol	406,78	282,61
Gas oil used as motor fuel	355,94	288,56
Gas oil used as heating fuel	25,42	25,42
Kerosene used as motor fuel	355,94	318,31
Kerosene used as heating fuel	25,42	25,42
	€/1000 kilograms	€/1000 kilograms
Heavy fuel oil	25,42	15,25
Liquid petroleum gas used as motor fuel	193,22	163,73
Liquid petroleum gas used as heating fuel	0	0
Methane	0	0
	€/one cubic meter	€/one cubic meter
Natural gas	0	0

Source: EU Commission (2000a).

Taxes on property (Davek Od Premoženja)

Individuals, owners or users, who possess or use buildings, parts of buildings, apartments, garages and owners of ships with size of at least 8 m (not used for attending activities) must pay taxes on property, whose revenue goes to local government.

As regards buildings or second homes, their values depend on specific 'points' determined yearly by municipalities and every year multiplied by the cost of living index. Unity tax rates are decided by the state and they vary from 0.15 to 1.5 percent. There are some exemptions concerning, for example, buildings of less than 160 m² (but not second homes), buildings used for agricultural purposes and cultural or historical monuments. For the tax payer with more than three family members living with him or her, the tax is decreased by 10 percent for the fourth and every additional member.

An annual lump-sum tax of €110 is established for a ship with a length between 8–9 m: this fixed amount is increased for each additional meter and decreased for every additional year of age of the ship.

Social security contributions (Prispevki Za Socialno Varnost)

Within this category there are contributions for pension and disabled insurance that are paid to the pension fund, contributions for medical care and sickness leave that go to the health fund and, finally, contributions for unemployment insurance and maternity leave that increase the central government budget. These contributions are withheld by the employer and they are calculated with respect to the amount of gross wages and other remunerations, including benefits in kind or the profit for self-employed persons. The rates charged to employers and employees are given in Table 11.4. It can immediately be seen that even if relatively high on employees, the rates for social security contributions are still much lower than the ones for EU members.

11.4 The fiscal burden

The distribution of tax charge: taxation by economic functions and implicit tax rates

Fiscal data for Slovenia, available only since independence in 1992, show that the total fiscal revenue as a percentage of GDP has not radically changed through the years, remaining at around 40 percent. On the contrary, it is the structure by economic function that varied rather drastically. Indeed, recent economic literature showed an increasing interest in classifying the fiscal receipts in terms of economic function, in particular according to consumption and production factors, in order to evaluate their impact on the economic incentives and choices.

Even if a consensus methodology is still under investigation, we refer to a classification based on two main categories: taxes on consumption and taxes and contributions on the production factors, in turn divided in employed labor and capital and business.

As regards consumption, taxes – namely VAT (sales tax before 1999) and excise duties – were raised from 14 percent of GDP in 1992 to over 16 percent from 1994 onwards, about 40 percent of total taxation.

On the other hand, taxation on employed labor decreased by 3.6 percent of GDP since 1992, still ensuring half of the overall fiscal revenue and accounting for 20 percent of GDP.

As for the other production factors, the total share of taxation on capital and business showed a significant increase during the 1990s, even if it represented in 1998 only 4.4 percent of GDP and less than 8 percent of

Table 11.4 Social security contributions' rates in Slovenia

Contributions for:	Employer (%)	Employee (%)
Pension insurance	8.85	15.50
Health insurance	7.09	6.36
Unemployment	0.06	0.14
Maternity	0.10	0.10
Total	16.10	22.10

Source: Ministry of Finance (2003).

total taxation. In particular, while the shares of taxes on self-employed labor and on financial activities (shares and savings) remained stable at about 1.3 and 0.4 percent of GDP respectively, taxes on entrepreneurial activities, rents and profits almost doubled in terms of percentage of GDP, reaching 2.5 percent in 1998.

About environmental taxes, their size with respect to GDP significantly increased, especially for energy and resources taxation, now contributing about 3 percent of GDP.

The sharp increase in the importance of indirect taxation and the related decrease in the share of labor taxes are also confirmed by the analysis of the implicit tax rates.

First, we refer to implicit tax rate (ITR) on consumption as the ratio of taxes on consumption and aggregate private and government consumption (net of government salaries). This rate increased in the 1990s as a consequence of the rise in indirect taxes: in 1995 it reached the highest value and then it stabilized at around 21 percent (Table 11.5).

Furthermore, the implicit tax rate on employed labor, defined as the ratio among taxes on employed labor and compensation of employees, shows that labor was the most heavily taxed factor with a rate of 38.4 percent in 1998, although the latter was still below the highest levels reached in 1993 and 1994.

Finally, it is possible to consider the ITR on capital and business, defined as the ratio between taxes on self-employed persons plus taxes on capital incomes at the numerator, and net operating surplus plus government interest payments at the denominator, only since 1995: it slightly increased up to 31.2 percent.

The overall tax burden on Slovenian households

Up to now we have described the structures and the rates of single tax in isolation. However, it may be argued that what is probably more relevant from an individual point of view is the overall effect of the tax system on effective purchasing power, rather than the average or marginal tax rates of a single type of tax.

Hence, it seems interesting to report the main results found by Čok (2003) whose analysis examines marginal and average tax rates for the comprehensive range of direct taxes and indirect taxes paid by Slovenian households. The analysis in particular, considered a sample, based on the Household Budget Survey, of 1860 households with at least one working member, employed or self-employed. Čok (2003) estimated direct taxes – income taxes, social security contributions and payroll taxes – for individual tax payers and added them together on a household level, and computed indirect taxes – VAT, excise duties and taxes on cars – on the basis of Engel curves on a household level.

Figure 11.1 represents the results found for the average tax rates, as a

Table 11.5 Structure and development of taxation by function and by implicit rates in Slovenia, New Members and EU 15, 1992–98

	1992			1994			1996			1998		
	Slovenia	New members	EU	Slovenia	New members	EU	Slovenia	New members	EU	Slovenia	New members	EU
Economic functions												
Consumption	13.9	13.6	10.9	16.1	14.5	11.2	16.4	14.7	11.3	16.0	13.5	11.4
Labor employed	23.7	19.7	20.6	22.7	19.4	20.7	20.6	19.0	21.4	20.0	17.9	21.2
Capital and business	2.9	7.2	9.6	3.5	7.8	9.2	3.6	6.9	9.5	4.4	7.1	9.8
Implicit tax rates												
Consumption	18.4	16.3	16.2	20.9	17.4	16.5	21.2	17.8	16.7	21.0	16.6	16.8
Labor employed	36.9	37.1	39.0	39.2	38.3	40.2	37.6	37.4	42.0	38.4	38.0	41.9
Capital and business	–	–	32.2	–	–	30.3	30.1	–	30.5	31.2	31.1	31.1

Sources: EU Commission (2000a) for Slovenia and New Members (unweighted average); Eurostat (2000) for EU 15 (1997 unweighted average).

Notes
Taxation according to economic function is as a percentage of GDP. Total may stay over total fiscal revenue in Table 11.1 because of some double counting. Estonia's 1992 implicit rates and all Czech rates refer to 1993. Implicit rates for capital and business are available only for Estonia and Slovenia.

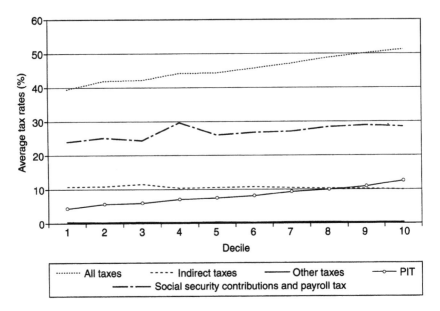

Figure 11.1 Average tax rates (% of gross income) for Slovenian active households
(source: Čok (2003)).

percentage of the gross income, reported by active households, ranked in
deciles according to the non-durable consumption per equivalent adult as
the best measure of life-time permanent income.

It may be noted that the average tax rate for a representative household is about 46 percent of the gross income, reaching the boundaries of
about 40 and 51 percent respectively at the bottom and at the top of the
ranking.

It is interesting to observe that proper personal income tax constitutes a
rate of only 8.2 percent of the gross income, indirect taxes amount for 10.6
percent, while the overall effect of all the social security contributions represents by far the larger fiscal burden on the households, on average 25
percent of the gross income. The large share of indirect taxes and social
contributions in the total fiscal burden on Slovenian households seems also
to be confirmed by the analysis of the marginal, direct and indirect, tax
rates (Figure 11.2).

The ability to attract foreign direct investments

The Slovenian tax system presents many incentives aimed at encouraging
investments. For instance, all the investment funds which distribute at
least 90 percent of profits from the preceding year by 30 November of the
current year are completely exempt from payment of the corporate

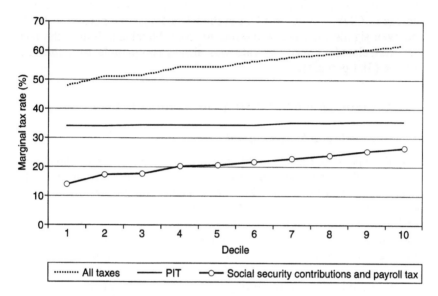

Figure 11.2 Marginal direct tax rates (% of gross income subject to tax) for Slovenian active households (source: Čok (2003)).

income tax, a regime that seems to be particularly attractive for foreign venture capital companies.

Moreover, specific tax incentives are available within the corporate tax structure. For instance, 40 percent of the amount invested by a company in equipment and intangible long-term assets can be deducted from the tax base, while up to 10 percent of the taxable income can be allocated to an investment reserve and deducted for tax purposes.

Furthermore, in order to promote employment opportunities by incoming firms, companies that employ a trainee or a previously unemployed person may decrease their taxable profit by 30 percent of his or her gross wages for the first year of employment.

A comparison with other New Members and EU 15 countries[3]

Table 11.5 clearly shows that, in the period 1992–98, both the share of taxation on consumption and the relative implicit tax rate were well above the EU and the New Members' averages.

As regards the taxation of employed labor, during the 1990s Slovenia always remained above the New Members' level, while approaching the EU average. At the same time, the Slovenian implicit rate on employed labor lay between the New Members and the EU average (41.9 percent in 1998).

Finally, the peculiar feature of tax composition for Slovenia emerges considering the taxation on capital and business, whose share, as a percentage of GDP, was at most half of the EU average (9.8 percent in 1998) and even significantly below the one for New Members, despite the fact that the related implicit tax rate was always comparable with the EU average (31.1 percent).

11.5 Tax reforms and further steps to get closer to the EU

Macroeconomic and budget outlook

Slovenia experienced a real GDP growth of 3 percent in 2001, a level that was lower than the one achieved in 2000, and which was significantly explained by export dynamics. In 2002, despite export growth continuing to be relevant, especially to non-EU markets, it was domestic demand, in particular investments, that retained GDP growth at 3 percent. Both domestic and external demand instead pushed growth to 3.4 percent in 2003 and available forecasts say that this increase should reach 3.7 percent in 2004.

Domestic demand was mostly constituted by investments, which – stimulated by industrial restructuring, approaching EU membership and export growth – increased by over 4 percent in 2003. This trend should continue for 2004 and determine an investments growth of 5.5 percent. On the contrary, private consumption, constrained by moderate rises in both real wages and employment rate, increased by only 2.5 percent in 2003. Available forecasts talk about a more optimistic 3.5 percent for 2004.

High net export growth in recent years contributed to a further sharp reduction in the trade deficit, from 3.3 percent of GDP in 2001 to 1 percent in 2002. At the same time, the services account increased as well, which led to a boost in the current account surplus of up to 1.8 percent of GDP in 2002.

Capital inflows, already strong in 2001, reached the record level of €1.5 billion in 2002 and were constituted mainly of foreign direct investment (FDI), driven by privatization in the banking sector (especially in the case of Nova Lubljanska Banka) and in the pharmaceutical sector.

Because of modest production growth, industrial restructuring and the elimination of the government program to subsidize labor training, employment growth in 2003 was stagnant, while in the same year the unemployment rate remained stable at 6.4 percent, both being expected to not vary too drastically in 2004.

Inflation, still at high levels, continued to decrease slowly from 7.5 percent in 2002 to 6.2 percent at the beginning of 2003. In 2003, the Slovenian government stated that the reduction of inflation to at least 4 percent by June 2004 is a priority target, as it announced its intention to enter ERM II by 1 January 2005. However, in 2003 inflation was at 6 percent and for 2004 it is expected to fall only to 5.5 percent – rates that are closer to, but still well above, the EU averages.

The overall government budget deficit, according to EU Commission (2003), was sharply reduced from 2.5 percent in 2001 to 1.8 percent in 2002, and it is expected to reach 1.2 percent in 2004.

Recent years' and planned tax reforms

The most significant set of fiscal reforms in Slovenia started in the 1990s. However, unlike in other countries with a comparable economic situation characterized by a fall in GDP and raised unemployment and retirement rates, this transitional period in Slovenia was not too dramatic, for instance the general government budget was always kept in balance.

The most relevant reforms in the fiscal system after 1991 concerned the introduction of Value Added Tax in place of retail sales tax in 1999, its modifications in the following years, and the change in the retirement system in 1999.

In particular, VAT was introduced according to the Sixth EC Directive with the original standard rate of 19 percent and reduced rate of 8 percent. However, from 1 January 2002, the Budget Law increased the standard rate up to 20 percent and the reduced rate up to 8.5 percent. Meanwhile, VAT administration also was modified. From 1 July 2001, three categories of liabilities have been identified for taxpayers according to their annual turnover. In addition, a new definition of foreign taxable person applied for the purposes of the VAT Law.

In 2003, the Slovenian government announced a proposal to launch new laws in three major areas.

First, the new law on personal income tax has almost completed the parliamentary debate. The main features regarding the introduction of taxation of personal income on a worldwide base, and of interests from bank deposits and securities, which are at present exempt. Furthermore, on one hand it abolishes some generous allowances for income from property rights, while on the other hand it raises the threshold for exempt income and gives higher tax allowances for children and students.

As regards the second proposal, the new law on corporate income tax is expected to reduce some investment tax allowances in order to enable the government to collect higher revenues from corporate profits, by still keeping the tax rate at 25 percent. However, as far as we know, no modification has yet been proposed for the fiscal treatment of self-employed income and financial activities, which at the moment seem to play a marginal role in the overall fiscal burden.

Finally, a comprehensive reform for health care, focusing especially on its financing, has been proposed, with the main objectives of inducing better accessibility, quality and efficiency of the services.

Notes

1 We are grateful to Mitja Čok of Lubljana University for his helpful comments on a previous version of this chapter. The chapter is a joint product of the authors. However, M. M. Galizzi is particularly responsible for sections 11.3.1, 11.3.2, 11.3.3, 11.4 and 11.5.2 and S. Scabrosetti for sections 11.1, 11.2, 11.3.4, 11.3.5, 11.3.6 and 11.5.1.
2 A detailed discussion may be found in Mitra and Stern (2003).
3 A detailed discussion may be found in Mitra and Stern (2003).

References

Čok, M. (2003) *Average and Marginal Tax Rates in Slovenia*, Slovenia: Economics Kardeljeva, Ljubljana.
EU Commission (2000a) *Structure of the Tax Systems in Estonia, Poland, Hungary, The Czech Republic and Slovenia*, Brussels: EU Commission.
EU Commission (2000b) 'Recent fiscal developments in the candidate countries', Enlargement Papers 2, Brussels: EU Commission, Directorate General for Economic and Financial Affairs.
EU Commission (2002) *European Economy*, 3, Brussels: EU Commission. Directorate General for Economic and Financial Affairs.
EU Commission (2003) 'Economic forecasts for the candidate countries. Spring 2003', Enlargement Papers 15, Brussels: EU Commission, Directorate General for Economic and Financial Affairs.
Eurostat (2000) *Structures of the Taxation Systems in the European Union, 1970–1997*, Brussels: EU Commission.
Eurostat (2002) *Statistical Yearbook on Candidate and South-east European Countries*, Brussels: EU Commission.
Ministry of Finance (2003) Taxation in Slovenia. www.sigov.si/mf/angl/taxation.pdf.
Mitra, P. and Stern, N. (2003) 'Tax systems in transition', WB Working Paper 2947, Washington, DC: The World Bank.
OECD (2002) *Fiscal Decentralization in EU Applicant States and Selected EU Member States*, Paris: OECD.

Websites

http://www.bsi.si – Official website of Bank of Slovenia.
http://www.gov.si – Official website by the Slovenian government.
http://www.sigov.si/mf/angl/taxation – Documents by Slovenian government on taxation.
http://www.sta.si – Website by the Slovenian press agency.

Index